THE
WORLD'S BEST
FISHING HOLES

E. L. "Buck" Rogers has spent the past twenty-five years roaming the globe with a fishing rod in hand. He is a former *Field & Stream* staffer, editor of *Outdoors* magazine, outdoor columnist, and contributor to major outdoor and travel publications. Formerly a travel professional, safari operator, and consultant to several airlines, he is also an elected member of the Fishing Hall of Fame and a past president of the Outdoor Writers Association of America.

THE
WORLD'S
BEST
Fishing
Holes

E. L. "Buck" Rogers

PRENTICE HALL PRESS • NEW YORK

to Margie

Published by Prentice Hall Press
A Division of Simon & Schuster, Inc.
Gulf + Western Building
One Gulf + Western Plaza
New York, NY   10023

PRENTICE HALL PRESS is a trademark of Simon & Schuster, Inc.

Library of Congress Cataloging-in-Publication Data

Rogers, E. L.
    The world's best fishing holes.

    Includes index.
    1. Fishing.   2. Fishing—Guide-books.   I. Title.
SH441.R654   1986   799   86-3266
ISBN 0-13-968892-7

Manufactured in the United States of America

1   2   3   4   5   6   7   8   9   10

First Edition

Contents

Introduction

This selection of fishing holes represents a lot of travel, a multitude of experiences, and more decisions than I want to make again in a long time. The decisions, incidentally, were the toughest part.

A well-known lake in Central America is one example. This venerable bass lake has quite a reputation, but it failed to impress me on the two occasions I fished it. The fish are small, and there is too much traffic to suit my taste.

Speaking of our better-known American bass haunts, I purposefully left out most of them because they're already well publicized by the outdoor media. You don't need my help to fish lakes like Powell, Dale Hollow, Clark Hill, and Kerr, so I decided to concentrate on "fishin' holes" farther afield.

If I had written this book ten years ago I would have included Lake Mead as a striper hot spot. Now, although still a great fishery, it isn't quite as good as it used to be.

I wanted to include more saltwater spots featuring inshore fishing for snook, tarpon, and bonefish, but because of space limitations I had to restrict the selection to just a few of the better destinations.

A spot that is worthy of further investigation is the Rio Atrato, which spills into the Caribbean near the Panama–Colombia border. Rumors indicate that this river is frequented by sabalo (tarpon) as long as dugout canoes. I don't believe them, because dugouts average thirty feet in this part of the world. Still, the matter bears looking into.

I omitted some areas because the gamefish are small, the fishing is unpredictable, and the prices are high. Some places were omitted because I simply couldn't get the facts needed to do a responsible reporting job. Ontario's Georgian Bay is one example. Washington and Oregon are others. And some destinations will have to wait until another volume.

Fishing regulations and prices quickly become dated, but I deemed information on the latter sufficiently important to be included. The former was not. Fishing fees are rarely of any consequence. Current regulations are obtainable from operators or state and provincial fish and game departments.

This book was obviously written for the angler who owns a passport and has both the time and means to use it. Far-off places and exotic gamefish are the stuff this book is made of, and my hope is that it will inspire some of you to explore the places described.

But this book was written for the rest of you, also. A person doesn't have to journey to Scotland to be interested in the Loch Ness monster. Perhaps the same situation applies to saltwater pike, 500-pound catfish, piranha, and saber-toothed payara.

If you like to fish and have a hint of an adventurous glint in your eye, this book is for you, too, even though you may never venture beyond your favorite neighborhood pond or stream.

THE
WORLD'S BEST
FISHING HOLES

Florida bass fishing features lots of surface action.

The United States: The Lower Forty-Eight

1

There are many good fishing holes scattered throughout this country. California, for example, has some super bass fishing. Trinity Lake is worthy of mention, and Lake Casitas too. A few years ago, Lake Casitas produced a 21-pound, 3-ounce bass that came close to setting a world record.

Arizona's Lake Powell is a good bass-fishing lake. So are Greers Ferry in Arkansas, Truman Lake in Missouri, and Watts Bar in Tennessee. Farther east, the historic St. Lawrence River and South Carolina's Clark Hill Reservoir also provide good bass fishing.

Virginia's Smith Mountain Lake is one of the best striped-bass lakes in the country. The venerable Santee Cooper must be rated in this category, too, and similar recognition should also be given to Kerr Reservoir in North Carolina, Oklahoma's Lake Texoma, and sprawling Lake Mead, located almost in sight of glittering Las Vegas.

Dale Hollow Lake, on the Kentucky–Tennessee border, has long been recognized as an outstanding smallmouth fishery, but it's also one of the best walleye lakes in the country. The stretch of the Mississippi River that snakes through Minnesota is a super walleye habitat, too, and so is the western basin of Lake Erie. Despite the tremendous fishing pressure that this body of water is subjected to, Lake Erie still is one of the outstanding walleye fisheries in North America.

Trout-fishing hot spots are Pennsylvania's Elk Creek, the Salmon River in New York, the lower White River in Arkansas, Utah's Flaming Gorge, and renowned streams like the Beaverkill, the Penobscot, the Madison, and the Henry's Fork of the Snake. Wisconsin streams like the Brule and the Kewaunee are also notable trout fisheries.

Although a little too crowded for my taste, Detroit's Lake St. Claire produces more muskies than any body of water that I know of. The St. Lawrence River is also a good place to catch one of these trophy fish, and so are any one of a dozen lakes in northern Wisconsin and northern Minnesota.

Fishing is good in this country of ours, but because it must be shared with

1

60 million other anglers, some of our better fishing holes occasionally look like a bargain-basement sale at Macy's. This is true of west coast fishing streams when the salmon are running. Lake Erie is a busy place all summer long. The relatively remote Current River, located deep in the Missouri Ozarks region, was termed a "wild river" a few years ago and now plays host to a thousand canoes on an average summer weekend.

Fishing pressure: It's a fact of life in the "lower forty-eight," and it's one of the reasons that this book doesn't contain more stateside selections. I could have filled these pages with descriptions of good U.S. fishing holes, but I couldn't guarantee that you wouldn't have a lot of company when you got there to fish.

THE BIGHORN RIVER ● Montana

The Bighorn River rises in Wyoming's Bighorn Mountains and flows north into Montana, where it eventually empties into the Yellowstone River.

Before 1965, when Bighorn Lake was finished, the Bighorn was a warm-water river with no particular appeal to the angler. Construction of the Yellowtail Dam changed all of this, creating a classic tailwater trout fishery that could be the best in our lower forty-eight states.

Water flowing from the base of the tall dam is cooler during the summer months, and warm enough in the winter to remain ice free. The result is a large river with many of the same characteristics of a spring creek. For those of you unfamiliar with spring creeks, the reference usually means a limestone geology, outstanding water clarity, constant temperature and flow, lots of nutrients, abundant aquatic growth, and water swarming with insect life. Such conditions usually add up to highly productive trout water, and that is exactly the case with the Bighorn.

Considered the most productive trout stream in Montana, the Bighorn is known to contain an average of 2,700 brown trout per mile, with 380 of this population exceeding 3 pounds in weight. Fish in the seven- to ten-pound category are taken with regularity, and the record brown trout weighed thirteen-and-a-half pounds. The largest rainbow taken to date weighed slightly more than 16 pounds. Although the Bighorn contains rainbow trout, it primarily is a brown-trout fishery.

The Bighorn flows through the Crow Indian reservation and was closed to outside anglers for a number of years while the courts tried to decide who had jurisdiction over its waters. The state of Montana won, but access is limited, and floating remains the primary method of fishing this river. Two different day floats are available. The first is from Afterbay Dam, twelve miles downstream to Bighorn Fishing Access. The second is from this state-owned access twenty-five miles on downstream to another access site near Hardin. Because all of the land on either side of the river is privately owned, and no camping is

Because access points are few and far between, floating is the way to fish the Bighorn.

permitted, a motor is required to make this trip in one day. No motors, incidentally, are allowed on the upper stretch of river.

Bighorn trout are cruisers, frequently feeding in schools with backs and dorsal fins showing. Hatches are intense, and the key to catching these fish is to select the largest, make an accurate cast, and drift your fly right over the feeding trout's nose. For this type of dry-fly fishing 5- or 6-weight rods work well. Tippets should range from 3 to 5 times, depending on circumstances. But big trout prefer something a little larger, so most Bighorn fly fishers tote heavier rods and throw large streamers tied to the end of fast-sinking lines. In this case, the object is to get the fly down deep as quickly as possible. Reels should be loaded with a hundred yards of backing because it is not unusual for a large trout to strip off seventy yards of backing in a sizzling first run.

This stretch of the Bighorn remains open during the winter, but the water cools sufficiently to slow the action. The best fishing periods, according to guide George Anderson, are April and May, and July through September. During July the river is frequently full of algae, but Anderson assured me that this nuisance does not keep anglers from catching fish.

The first stretch of water below Yellowtail Dam is restricted to artificial flies and lures. There is a daily bag limit of five trout, with only one rainbow included. In addition, there are "slot limit" regulations in force; these are designed to maintain a large population of trophy fish. These regulations, of course, are subject to change.

A number of guides operate on this stretch of the Bighorn and currently are charging $175 per party of two anglers for a day's float. Nearby Fort Smith is the place to stay; it has several good motels. Your guide will be happy to make recommendations and will make reservations for you. The closest commercial airport is at Billings, which is eighty-five miles from Fort Smith.

For general information on Montana, write to Travel Promotion Unit, Department of Highways, Helena MT 59601, Tel: (406) 444–2654. For details on angling regulations, write to Montana Department of Fish, Wildlife, and Parks, 1420 E. 6th Ave., Helena, MT 59620.

Three competent guide services operating on the Bighorn are George Anderson, Yellowstone Angler, 124 N. Main St., Livingstone, MT 59047, Tel: (406) 222–7130; The Sportsman's Lure, 1144 Grand Ave., Billings, MT 59102, Tel: (406) 245–6616, and Bighorn Outfitters, 85 Chestnut Road, Bozeman, MT 59715, Tel: (406) 222–7130.

CANYON CREEK RANCH • Montana

There are lots of dude ranches in our west, and most of them feature a swimming pool, hay rides, bingo, and hordes of squealing kids. Now, these kind of guest ranches have their place, and for a man who wants to put on a pair of cowboy boots and learn how to square dance, I can recommend them.

Canyon Creek is a different kind of guest ranch. It's located in the south-west corner of the state, about fifty miles from Butte. It's tucked away in a secluded mountain valley, at the end of the road, seventeen miles from the nearest highway. Incidentally, there is no other guest ranch within thirty miles. Canyon Creek is small (fourteen guests only), and the accent here is on trout fishing, horseback riding, and western-style outdoor living.

This facility features a rustic main lodge for dining and lounging. Guests are housed in individual two-room log cottages nestled in the trees on the bank of Canyon Creek. These facilities feature carpeted floors, indoor plumbing, a wood-burning fireplace, and comfortable furnishings. There is electricity, of course. Everything is first class.

Home-cooked meals are served family style in the main lodge, but cookouts are also featured, and the ranch's cowboy guides are all skilled at campfire cookery. To provide this type of personalized service, the ranch provides one staff member for each two guests.

Canyon Creek Ranch is located in the heart of Montana's finest trout-fishing area. Several "blue ribbon" trout streams are located within a brief ride or drive from the ranch, and a few of them are the Big Hole, the Beaverhead, the Jefferson, and the Ruby. Canyon Creek runs right through the ranch and provides guests with angling action when they're not fishing one of the nearby larger rivers.

As a part of its weekly package, the ranch offers each guest a two-day float trip on the famed Big Hole River. On this trip guests fish two to a boat (operated by a seasoned guide) and experience outstanding angling action for wild brown trout, rainbows, cutthroat, and brookies. Big Hole trout average twelve to sixteen inches, but according to the Montana fisheries people, brown trout up to seventeen pounds are known to exist in this stream. For the overnight, a tent camp is set up on a gravel bar, and angling guests can fish the early and late bites that occur on the Big Hole throughout the summer.

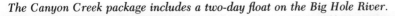

The Canyon Creek package includes a two-day float on the Big Hole River.

Six beautiful Alpine lakes are located in the vicinity of the ranch, and for a change of pace guests are invited to straddle a trail-wise saddle horse and ride up to one of them. On these trips, guests are accompanied by a cowboy guide who will set up an overnight camp if they desire. In these clear, seldom-fished lakes, the best fishing occurs early and late, so the overnight option is a popular one.

In the tackle line, bring a light flyrod for dry-fly fishing, and a heavier 8- or 9-weight rod to fish larger streams, like the Big Hole. Make sure that reels have at least one hundred yards of twenty-pound test backing. If you have a pack rod, bring it for your trail ride up into the mountains. Include flies, a pair of felt-soled waders, a fishing vest, and other angling paraphernalia. If you're a spin fisherman, bring a light outfit for the Big Hole, and ultralight equipment for other streams. Be sure to include sunglasses, insect repellent, and rain gear. On request, the ranch will send you a list of clothing and equipment to bring, as well as a recommended selection of flies and lures.

Canyon Creek operates from late June through September, and the price for an all-inclusive week there is $595 per person. There is no extra charge for the two-day Big Hole float or the overnight at a mountain lake. Butte's is the nearest commercial airport. If you plan on driving, you'll be sent instructions on how to get there.

For details on Canyon Creek Ranch, write to Grande Domain Retreats, 801 P Street, Lincoln, NE 68508, Tel: (402) 477–9249. For information on fishing fees and regulations, write to Montana Fish, Wildlife, and Parks, 1420 E. 6th Ave., Helena, MT 59620.

FLATHEAD FLOAT • Montana

The South Fork of the Flathead River rises in the 950,000-acre Bob Marshall Wilderness, which can be entered only by foot or on horseback. This is truly pristine wilderness, highlighted by a huge escarpment known as the Chinese Wall. The wall averages about 1,000 feet in height and extends for a distance of twenty miles along the Continental Divide. This is the domain of the mountain goat, the elk, and the grizzly. Eagles wheel high above lush spruce forests, jagged granite peaks, and flowering mountain meadows. Springs gush from rocky glens and tumble downward to spawn wild rivers like the South Fork.

In addition to being a beautiful stream, the South Fork is probably the best fishing river in North America for native cutthroat trout. On this float trip it is not uncommon for anglers to catch and release thirty to fifty cutthroat per day on flies. These are wild mountain trout averaging a pound or so, with trophy

The Flathead rises in the Bob Marshall Wilderness, which is restricted to travel by foot or horseback.

fish exceeding three pounds. Dolly Varden also abound in this river and, like the cutthroat, are found only in "west slope" streams, with the Flathead system possibly being the most productive in the lower forty-eight. Dollys run to ten pounds in these waters, but they average less than two pounds. Whitefish are also native to these waters and provide excellent table fare as well as fine sport on light tackle.

Because there are no roads in the Bob Marshall Wilderness, and aircraft are not allowed either, horses are used to backpack in for a leisurely three-day float back down the South Fork.

Spotted Bear Ranch is headquarters for this package trip, which begins with the guest's arrival in Kalispell, Montana, on Friday and ends the following Thursday. Saturday and Sunday are days to pack into the "Bob," with each day's time in the saddle limited to five hours. The next day is spent fishing the upper South Fork, a tributary stream, and two lakes in the vicinity. Tuesday through Thursday are spent floating and fishing, with frequent stops made to thoroughly fish certain spots or to allow guests to stretch their legs. Trips operate from early July to the first of September on a Saturday-through-Thursday basis.

The price of this six-day package is $895 per person and includes all meals, five nights' camp accommodations, one guide per each two anglers, horses, pack equipment, tents and other camping gear (except sleeping bags), and round-trip transportation between Kalispell and the ranch. Not included are expenses in Kalispell, a fishing license, and other items of a personal nature. If you don't have a sleeping bag, or you're flying commercial air and can't bring yours, the management will probably loan you one.

Because this is a camping trip, you are urged to travel as light as possible. Do bring plenty of warm clothing, though, and a rain suit. Lightweight chest waders will keep you dry when wade fishing and are comfortable to wear in the float craft. Otherwise, bring an extra pair of sneakers and trousers to wade in. Include insect repellent, sunglasses, suntan lotion, a flashlight and extra batteries, and a waterproof container for your camera.

Bring two flyrods—a light rod for dry-fly fishing and a heavier stick for underwater work. Fifty yards of backing for the larger reel is a good idea. If you are a spin fisherman, bring one light rig and one ultralight outfit.

For details on this trip and other similar outings, write to Grand Domain Retreats, 801 P St., Lincoln, NE 68508.

SAN JUAN RIVER ● New Mexico

"You've got to include it," Jack Sampson told me.

"What's the name again?" I asked.

"The San Juan," he replied. "It could be the best western trout stream in North America."

Jack is probably prejudiced, because he lives in New Mexico these days. But since he was the editor of *Field & Stream* for a number of years, his opinion has to be taken seriously.

The river we are referring to boils out of the concrete face of Navajo Dam in the Four Corners region of New Mexico, Utah, Colorado, and Arizona. It then flows westward for a distance of some 200 miles to spill into sprawling Lake Powell on the Arizona border. In its lower reaches, this river is a muddy irrigation ditch, but the headwaters of the San Juan are prime trout water. Here, in a twenty-mile stretch of river, anglers frequently catch a dozen four- or five-pound trout in a day's fishing, and catches in the seven- and eight-pound category are not uncommon. Primarily a rainbow fishery, the upper San Juan is also stocked with browns and Snake River cutthroat.

The half-mile stretch of river immediately below the dam is managed as a catch-and-release fishery restricted to artificial flies and spinning lures with barbless hooks. All fish taken in this part of the river are released. The next three-and-a-quarter-mile section of river is designated as "trophy water" and is also restricted to artificial lures and barbless hooks. One fish per day per fisherman may be taken from this fishery, but it must measure at least twenty inches in length. From this stretch of river, downstream to the town of Aztec, the San Juan may be fished by any legal hook-and-line method. Most anglers use artificials, but braggin'-sized trout are still taken by towheaded youngsters using worms or chunks of marshmallow for bait. From what I have been able to ascertain, six- and seven-pound trout are not uncommon in this stretch of river either.

In its upper reaches the San Juan is crystal clear and bone-chilling cold. Its average temperature is 44 degrees, and it doesn't vary from winter to summer. Local anglers fish it in the wintertime with good success, but the best fishing period appears to be from April through November. The only time the San Juan gets much fishing pressure is on summer weekends, but compared with streams like the Madison and Yellowstone, it is uncrowded even then. According to experts like Sampson and Jesse Williams, the best time to fish this trout stream is in late summer or fall, when there is little demand for irrigation water and the river flow is constant.

Getting up before dawn is not a prerequisite for successfully fishing this stream. Because of the constant cold temperature of the water, the trout do not usually rise until mid-morning. The "hatch," if you can call it that, usually lasts until dusk.

Jesse Williams, public affairs officer for the New Mexico Department of Game and Fish, told me that the growth rate of trout in the San Juan is enormous. These fish, according to Williams, feed primarily on the bountiful supply of aquatic insects but augment their diet with snails and minnows. "Average size," he told me, "is around nineteen inches."

"How much will a nineteen-inch trout weigh?" I asked.

"Four or five pounds," he replied.

Catches average four or five pounds in the San Juan River, and eight-pounders are not uncommon.

While I mulled that over, he added that the New Mexico record, an 11-pound, 10-ounce fish, was caught in the San Juan, and that a thirteen-pound trout had been taken by biologists and released back into the river.

The San Juan is a big river, fifty to sixty yards wide in many places, and fordable in only a few spots. Felt-soled chest waders are recommended if you are to fish this stream, and because the water is so cold they should be insulated or worn over long underwear.

Fishing tackle, either fly or spinning gear, should be capable of handling trout in the five- to seven-pound category. Fly reels should be loaded with at least fifty yards of backing. Open-face spinning reels are preferred over spin-cast models. Some fish are taken on dry flies, but the majority are caught on streamers and nymphs fished close to the bottom. A variety of small spoons and spinning lures are effective in these waters, as are small, minnow-like lures. All artificials, flies included, should have barbless hooks.

The best place to stay is at Abe Chavez's motel, located right on the river and priced at less than $40 per night. Even if you don't stay there, Abe's is the place to purchase a fishing license and obtain first-hand information on river conditions and on fishing the San Juan. It also is the place to inquire about the services of a fishing guide. Two of the best are Chuck Rizutto and Larry Federici. These men and other guides in the area charge $150 per day and can take care of two fishermen. Motel accommodations and angling services are also available at Aztec, eighteen miles downstream.

For more information on fishing the San Juan, write to Abe Chavez, P.O Box 6428, Navajo Dam, NM 87503, Tel: (505) 632–2194. Chuck Rizutto may be reached at 200 Sunset Place, Farmington, NM 87401, Tel: (505) 334–6143. An additional source of information on fishing the San Juan is Jesse Williams, Public Affairs Officer, New Mexico Department of Game and Fish, State Capitol, Santa Fe, NM 87503, Tel: (505) 827–7882.

TOLEDO BEND • Texas

Toledo Bend is the largest man-made impoundment in the South. It sprawls along the Texas–Louisiana border for a distance of sixty-five miles and inundates 185,000 acres of land. Unlike most east Texas lakes, Toledo Bend is unusually clear, with deep flooded creek bottoms, immense stands of dead timber, and a seasonal abundance of aquatic vegetation.

Impounded and stocked in 1966, Toledo Bend peaked as a bass fishery in the 1970s. In those days it seemed that there was a largemouth bass lurking in the shadow of every stick-up and log in the lake. On a good day it was not unusual for an angler to catch his limit of fifteen bass in an hour's time and release three times this number of fish before the angling day was done. Those days are gone, but Toledo Bend is still one of the best bass fisheries in the country. The lake has stabilized now, and with its abundant structure, it is a classic lake for worm fishermen.

But Toledo Bend has something else going for it, too. Striped bass were stocked in this lake a number of years ago, and the species has thrived here. In fact, there is reason to believe that Toledo Bend may just be coming into its own as a striped-bass fishery. It presently holds both the Louisiana and Texas records with a thirty-seven-and-a-half-pound fish taken in 1983, and there is reason to believe that this record will be broken again. Unlike those at other well-known striper lakes, the average catch on Toledo Bend is getting larger and larger.

Striped bass are taking over as the predominant gamefish in this large Texas impoundment.

The key to catching striped bass is finding them. Unlike largemouth bass, which usually hold to varied forms of bottom structure, the striper is an open-water predator that follows roaming schools of shad, much in the same manner that wolves followed buffalo herds in the past. Stripers generally keep on the move, and in huge Toledo Bend they have a lot of elbow room. Generally they prefer deeper water than the largemouth, but they also have a propensity for surface feeding. When either traveling around the lake or fishing, keep a sharp eye open for surface-feeding stripers. Stripers are also light sensitive, and for this reason they feed most voraciously early in the morning or late in the evening. If you can locate a school of these silvery fish at such a time, you'll almost certainly see some fast-paced action.

Both striped bass and largemouth are taken at all seasons on Toledo Bend. In the spring, the bass move into the shallows to spawn, and the stripers gather in large schools, presumably for the same purpose. To date, however, it is not known if Toledo Bend stripers spawn naturally or not. At any rate, both species of fish are relatively easy to find in the spring, and the fishing can be good if the weather cooperates.

Summer is the time when bass fishermen probe Toledo's structure with plastic worms, and when striper fishermen cruise the open waters of the lake looking for surface action or with eyes glued to their flasher screens. Much of the best action occurs early and late. Some anglers do most of their fishing at night.

Fall is the best time to fish Toledo Bend, in the opinion of many. When the water begins to cool, both stripers and largemouths feed more voraciously, and they're easy to locate. There is also little wind during this season. The weather is usually delightful, and because a number of fishermen are now following their gun dogs around, there is a minimum of angling pressure.

When planning a trip, it will pay you to determine what kind of fishing you want to do and hire a guide who can provide the type of services desired. Striper fishing, for example, is specialized to the extent that it requires different tackle and equipment, specific know-how, and different fishing techniques. Some guides specialize in striper fishing; others are bass experts. Regardless, even if you have your own boat, it might pay you to hire a guide for the first day to pick up a few tips.

Anyone serious about fishing for thirty-pound striped bass should have the tackle capable of handling fish of these dimensions. Recommended is a two-handed six- or seven-foot spinning or casting rod equipped with a reel spooled with at least 200 yards of sixteen-pound test line. Spincast reels are not recommended.

Toledo Bend bass come in good-sized packages but do not require any special equipment. It should be noted, however, that this lake is one huge submerged brush pile. It doesn't normally require a twenty-four pound line to haul a wriggling three- or five-pound largemouth up out of the depths, but when you have to wrestle a few tree limbs in the process, the heavier line comes in handy.

There is an abundance of facilities on this lake, both on the Texas and Louisiana side. All of the marinas have launching ramps, and most of them also have restaurants, motel rooms, and fishing guides. The guides are, for the most part, private operators, charging an average of $125 per day for their services. This price is for one or two persons. Some of the marinas have mobile-home units for rent, some housekeeping cottages, and some motel rooms. Average price for the mobile-home units (with cooking facilities) is $45 per night. A few of the more notable ones are Carmichael's Marina, Box 84, Hemphill, TX 75948, Tel: (409) 579–3075; Huxley Bay Marina, Box 666, Shelbyville, TX 75973, Tel: (409) 368–2995; Pendleton Bridge Marina, Box 321, Many, LA 71449, Tel: (318) 256–2958. A fairly nice resort catering to fishermen is the Fin and Feather Lodge, Box 810, Hemphill, TX, Tel: (409) 579–3368. For more general information on Toledo Bend, write to the Sabine River Authority, Box 270, Burkeville, TX 75932. For facts on the fish and the fishing in Toledo Bend, write to: Fisheries Division, Texas Parks & Wildlife Department, 4200 Smith School Rd., Austin, TX 78744.

LAKE TANYCOMO ● Missouri

Statistics tell the story. Tanycomo, a 21,000-acre impoundment tucked away in the Ozark hills of southern Missouri, produced more than a million trout for the anglers who fished it in 1984.

Some of these are nice fish, too. In March 1984, young Matt Beard dropped his line into the water at the mouth of Turkey Creek and shortly thereafter walked away with a nine-pound rainbow. This was a nice catch, but it's not an isolated incident. According to Gordon Proctor, a fisheries biologist, Tanycomo is producing 8,000 or more trophy-sized trout each year.

"What's a trophy-sized trout?" I asked him.

"A sixteen- to twenty-inch fish," he replied, " a trout which will put a bend in a man's rod and let him know he's been in a fight before he reaches for his landing net."

Lake Tanycomo was created in the early 1900s to provide hydroelectric power for residents of this isolated Ozarks region, and it was turned into a trout fishery in 1958 when the White River was impounded upstream. The discharge from the bottom of Table Rock Dam was too cold to support anything but trout, so a hatchery was constructed on Tanycomo and the Missouri Conservation Department began stocking rainbows a year later.

The next major development occured when biologists introduced a small freshwater crustacean called a gammarus, which provided Tanycomo with a new source of food. This little crustacean virtually exploded in its new environment, and so did Tanycomo's trout population. Today, on this rich diet, these trout grow three quarters of an inch per month, or almost nine inches per year.

This means that a twelve-inch Tanycomo trout will grow to sixteen-inches in a period of six months, or into a burly twenty-inch, three-pound fish in a year.

To increase the number of trophy trout in the lake, anglers have been asked to release any fish between twelve and sixteen inches long. This voluntary program is working, and the number of trophy trout in the lake is increasing with each passing day.

Lake Tanycomo is a long, narrow impoundment that more closely resembles a river in its upper stretches than it does a lake. There is a current here, and depending on the amount of water being released, it can be substantial.

Lake Tanycomo produced more than a million trout for the anglers who fished it last year.

Although all of the lake is trout water, trout tend to congregate in the upper third of the lake, where the current is. This is where most anglers fish, and where most Tanycomo trout are caught.

Bank fishing can be effective. I caught and released several nice trout while fishing just below the dam, and I consider this prime wading water when there's not much current. Downstream in the city of Branson, anglers can be observed fishing from park benches on the lakeshore, and they appeared to be catching fish, too.

Fishing from a boat is usually more productive, because anglers are more mobile and can adapt their fishing methods to changing conditions. In this respect, Tanycomo is no different from other tailwater fisheries. When the turbines open, the fish begin to disperse and perhaps go on a feeding spree. When the water is slack, fish act differently. In this respect, tailwater trout are not unlike saltwater fish, who live with and utilize tidal movements to their advantage.

Fishing is good in Tanycomo throughout the year because the water is relatively uniform in temperature. Autumn is beautiful in the Ozarks, however, and at this season the trout run upstream to escape lowered oxygen levels in the lake. Fishing is also good in the summer, though. The same situation is applicable in the spring, but at this season high water is a possibility.

Branson is a little storybook town that has lots of experience in catering to tourists. A few miles to the west is Table Rock Lake, and in between is a solid mass of restaurants, motels, country music emporiums, gift shops, and other tourist attractions. Branson doesn't appear to be a tourist trap, however. I found the people courteous and the prices reasonable.

For instance, you can rent a fishing boat and motor for less than $30 per day. For $75 you can retain the services of a boat, motor, and guide for a day. A McDonald's hamburger costs the same as it does elsewhere in the state. So does a gallon of gas and a motel room. A fishing trip here is a bargain.

For more information about fishing Lake Tanycomo, write David Aller, Fall Creek Campground and Trout Dock, Star Rt. 1722, Branson, MO 65616. Another source of information is the Branson Chamber of Commerce, P.O. Box 220, Branson, MO 65616, Tel: (417) 334–4136.

GREAT LAKES FISHING

When I lived on the shore of Lake Michigan in the late 1950s, it was a dead sea. A few anglers were catching yellow perch from the piers, but not many. The lake trout were gone, their ranks thinned by pollution, commercial fishing, and the lamprey eel.

Mathons in Waukegan was the closest you could get to a fish in those days, but the owner of this famous seafood restaurant, Mathon Kyritsis, was having to import everything he served. Incidentally, Mathon was also a commercial fisherman in those days, but his boats never left the harbor. Lake Michigan was a dead sea.

Fewer than ten years later, Michigan fisheries biologists introduced the coho salmon into Lake Michigan waters and started a chain of events that transformed this lake into one of the world's greatest sports fisheries. Chinook stockings followed, and they proved to be equally successful. Today, these salmon are well established in all of the Great Lakes, and their numbers and size rival those of their parent species in the Pacific Northwest.

Coho and chinook salmon are relatively short lived in the Great Lakes.

Both are stocked in larger tributaries as fingerlings and shortly thereafter migrate into the open water. Some early-maturing chinook males return to their home streams after two years. Other males, and most females, delay this process several more years. Unlike chinook, coho all return to their streams to spawn in one and a half or two years. Coho average under ten pounds in most of the lakes and are somewhat larger in Lake Ontario. Chinook vary by their age but average fifteen to twenty pounds and go to more than forty pounds. Especially in Lake Ontario, experts are predicting that someone will soon boat a 50-pounder. Like all West Coast salmon, coho and chinooks die after spawning.

Several hundred thousand Atlantic salmon fingerlings have been stocked in

Now stocked with Skamania steelhead, Michigan streams are producing fishing superior to west coast streams.

the Great Lakes, and a few of this species are now beginning to show up in anglers' bags. Atlantic salmon do not die after spawning, and therefore they are much longer lived than their Pacific cousins. The Atlantic salmon goes to eighty pounds—larger in its ocean habitat—and biologists expect it to eventually reach fifty pounds in the Great Lakes.

Lake trout, native to the Great Lakes, have been restocked and are doing well. Unlike salmon, they are not anadromous. They never leave their lake environment and are extremely long lived. Lakers prefer cooler temperatures than salmon and stay in deeper water as a result. Today, lake trout average slightly more than ten pounds but originally grew to sixty pounds or more in these waters.

Rainbow and brown trout have prospered in the Great Lakes too and now can make up a substantial portion of anglers' catches. Both species spend some time in the tributaries and do not die after spawning. Steelhead, which are rainbow trout that have gone to sea (in this case a large lake), lose most of their coloration and become more streamlined. Anglers who have caught both fish consider the steelhead a much stronger fighter. This is particularly true in southern Lake Michigan waters, habitat of the Skamania steelhead. Relatively new to the Great Lakes, this anadromous rainbow can go to twenty-five pounds and is a brute of a fish.

Although overshadowed by salmon and trout, other species of fish are also found in the Great Lakes, and now that these lakes have been cleaned up they are thriving. Lake Erie and a part of Lake Ontario contain excellent walleye fishing, and Lake Superior and Lake Huron's Georgian Bay are renowed for their northern pike and muskellunge fishing. Yellow perch, the pier fisherman's staple, are found throughout the Great Lakes.

Pollution, the lamprey eel, and commercial fishing endangered the original fish population of the Great Lakes, but today these lakes are proof that wise management of a body of water can bring its population back. Right now, the Great Lakes are great again.

SOUTHERN LAKE MICHIGAN ● Indiana

I never thought I'd be including the Chicago skyline and the industrial stench of Gary, Indiana, in a select list like this, but I've got to.

Why?

A special breed of steelhead, that's why. Clear water that's literally teeming with a variety of trout and two species of salmon. A fishery that produces fine fishing eight months out of the year and is getting better all the time.

Shallow southern Lake Michigan warms first as the ice goes out in mid-March, attracting hordes of alewives and other baitfish. Coho, chinook salmon, steelhead, browns, and lake trout follow, turning the southern end of the lake into a fishbowl. The northern end of the lake, in the meantime, is still clogged with ice or is too cold and forbidding to fish.

Captain Jack Parry with his thirty-eight-pound Chinook salmon, which is the Indiana state record.

In March and April, coho in the four-pound range supply most of the action. When taken on light tackle they leap wildly and put up a strong fight. In May the chinook salmon begin to become more aggressive. This heavy-weight of the salmon family averages five to twenty-five pounds, depending on the age of the specific fish. Coho are still around and are growing larger as they feed voraciously. By the time July rolls around, the water temperature is ideal for all species of Lake Michigan fish. They're on the move, slashing through schools of baitfish, feeding savagely. Limits of all species are common.

Now, let me tell you about the Skamania.

In the mid-1970s, the fishing always slowed at this end of the lake in July, when native Michigan and Wisconsin fish headed north for their own pastures. Needed was a fish that would stick around during the summer, and in their search for such a fish Indiana biologists discovered a strain of steelhead native to the Skamania River in Washington. The fish was a summer spawner, it averaged twelve to twenty pounds when grown, and was reputed to be a great gamester. So the Hoosier fisheries people got a few thousand partially hatched Skamania eggs, tenderly raised them into fry, and made an initial stocking of the species. This process was repeated throughout the late 1970s and early 1980s and now, I'm told, more than a million of these special steelhead have been stocked in Indiana waters.

Mania for Skamania soon spread into Michigan waters, and now a number of Michigan streams are being stocked with this fish. Illinois and Wisconsin also got into the act, and experimental stockings are being made in these states as well. The St. Joseph River is one example. This stream, which empties into Lake Michigan at Benton Harbor, is being turned into a Skamania fishery during its entire course through Michigan and Indiana. Fish ladders were constructed at the dams, and new hatchery was built at Mishawaka. Soon the St. Joe, never much of a fishing stream in the past, may be one of the première steelhead rivers in the country.

How good a gamefish is the Skamania steelhead?

"Fantastic," Al Spiers told me. Al is a resident of Michigan City, owns his own cruiser, and has been fishing these waters for more than twenty years. Because he usually doesn't use many superlatives, I sat up and took notice at the use of the word.

"Give me an example," I said.

"How about stripping all the line off of an Ambassadeur 6500," he said.

"That's hard to do," I agreed.

"Jumps more times than a coho or a regular steelhead."

I whistled softly.

"You won't land one out of three," he warned.

I frowned.

"They're big," he added. "We've caught 'em up to twenty-four pounds, and they're getting larger every year."

Jack Parry concurs with these observations. Jack runs a charter operation out of Portage and currently holds the Indiana chinook record with a 38-pounder he landed a year ago. He rates Lake Michigan fishing on a par with the saltwater angling in British Columbia and Alaska and is quick to point out that it costs a lot less.

Parry's boat, *The Tight Line*, is a seaworthy twenty-eight-foot cabin cruiser equipped with a dinette, toilet facilities, space-age electronic safety equipment, and fish-finding gear. He fishes up to four clients and stresses the use of light tackle for optimum fishing pleasure. Guests can bring their own if they desire; otherwise it is furnished, along with lures that are most likely to take the species of fish being fished for at the time. Charters are for six hours and are priced at $240. The tour operates from mid-March through July (when the

Skamania run is over), and from the middle of August through October. This fall season is when some of the largest salmon are caught, with many of them taken in water as shallow as only eight feet deep.

These waters are particularly handy for anglers wishing to fly into Chicago's O'Hare Airport, fish a day or so and then return home with a cooler full of frozen fillets or smoked salmon. At Burns Harbor, where Parry docks his boat, there are facilities to smoke fish, and people skilled in this art.

Accommodations are available at a pair of quality motels located less than a mile away. If transportation is needed from O'Hare, the Tri-State Coach Line offers an economical limousine service that operates on a regular basis throughout the day and takes less than two hours for the trip from airport to motel. In these cases, where the client does not have his or her own car, Parry provides ground transportation to and from the boat dock.

If you want to bring your own tackle, bring either casting or spinning gear, but make sure that your rods have long two-hand handles, and that reels are loaded with at least 200 yards of fifteen- or twenty-pound test line. Spincast reels are not recommended because they do not have a drag system capable of handling Lake Michigan gamefish. As a rule, it is advisable to let the charter operator furnish leaders and lures.

For more information on fishing these waters, get in touch with Captain Jack Parry, 1624 Graham Drive, Chesterton, IN 46304, Tel: (219) 926–2467. For information on fishing farther to the east, write to Mike McKee, 201 Lawndale Place, Michigan City, IN 46360. For general information on fishing this section of Lake Michigan, write to the Indiana Department of Natural Resources, Fisheries Section, 607 State Office Bldg., Indianapolis, IN 46204, Tel: (317) 232–4002.

MANISTEE RIVER ● Michigan

Two starboard lines tore out of their downrigger snaps, and from above Captain Emil Dean yelled, "Fish on!"

Ed Hanson and I bumped into each other in our eagerness to respond, managed to grab the two rods, and set the hooks. A hundred feet back in the boat's wake, a pair of glistening fish came somersaulting out of the mist-shrouded water, and the battle was on.

My fish, a sleek silvery thing, continued the aerial circus, while Ed's submerged like a submarine and headed for the other side of the lake. Five minutes later, my 8-pound steelhead was in the net. Ed's fish took another ten minutes to subdue and turned out to be a broad-shouldered brown trout that tipped the scale at fourteen pounds.

We limited out that morning and caught five species of fish in the process. The only Great Lakes salmon or trout that we didn't catch was the Atlantic salmon, and this was not surprising. Although this gamefish was first stocked

Modern fishing machines prowl Lake Michigan waters and rarely fail to bring limits for anglers aboard.

in Lake Michigan more than ten years ago, the species didn't really thrive until a special Swedish strain of salmon was stocked some years later. Atlantics are present in this part of Lake Michigan, but they are not as plentiful as the other species of salmonoids.

Fishing gets started in this part of the lake around the first of May, and most of it takes place in the Manistee River itself. Chinook salmon and brown trout are the primary species, with the former averaging less than twenty pounds, and the browns half this weight. As the shallow water begins to warm, the fish move out into deeper water and the boats follow. Mixed bags are the rule throughout the summer, with the major run of cohos occurring in late August and September. Summer fishing will get still another boost in 1986–87 when the Manistee's planting of Skamania steelhead come back to spawn in large numbers. These fish are superb fighters and go to twenty-five pounds or more.

Captain Emil Dean fishes out of Manistee and is considered one of the better charter boat captains on the Great Lakes. This veteran charter boat captain has eighteen years of experience fishing these waters, and there is literally nothing he doesn't know about the subject. As a result, the average angler fishing with Dean is fairly well assured of seeing lots of action.

Emil's boat is a sleek 32-footer with a twelve-foot beam, and it is loaded with electronic fish-finding and navigation equipment. With a skilled mate aboard, this spacious cruiser can troll ten or twelve lines astern and frequently does so.

From the first of October through April, Emil fishes the Manistee River for steelhead, which average five to fifteen pounds and are good fighters. For this type of fishing he uses a special twenty-two-foot shallow draft boat that will fish up to four persons. Artificial lures are used, and techniques vary depending on the water fished. In a typical day's fishing, Dean told me, he fishes seven or eight miles of river.

Current bag limit is five steelhead. A similar limit is applicable for Lake Michigan and can include both salmon and trout.

The charter rate for lake fishing is $320 per day, which may be shared by up to six persons. The season, as mentioned previously, is from the first of May through September.

Manistee is located on the eastern shore of Lake Michigan between Ludington and Traverse City, both of which are served by airports. Restaurants and motels in the area provide adaquate meals and accommodations.

For details on fishing this part of Lake Michigan, write to Emil Dean, Box 21, Bear Lake, MI 49614, Tel: (616) 362-3760. If he is booked, I am certain that he will recommend one of several other charter boats operating out of Manistee. For information on fishing regulations in Michigan waters get in touch with the Department of Natural Resources, Fisheries Division, Box 300028, Lansing, MI 48909, Tel: (517) 373-0908. For other general information on fishing in Michigan contact Travel Bureau, Michigan Department of Commerce, Lansing, MI 48909, Tel: (800) 248-5700.

NIAGARA GORGE ● New York

The Niagara River, draining one of the largest lake systems in the world, comes swirling out of Lake Erie, flows northward for a distance of seventeen miles, and then plunges 182 feet downward into the gorge below. This spectacular falls is one of the wonders of the world, a place of awe and beauty, and has long been recognized as a mecca for vacationers and honeymooners.

Now Niagara Falls, particularly the eighteen-mile stretch of river below the falls, is rapidly becoming known as a fishing hotspot. The outdoor scribe Bill Hilts claims that it's the best fishing hole in the east, and he's in a good position to know.

It all started with the Great Lakes salmonoid program and substantial Lake Ontario stockings of lake trout, brown trout, rainbows, coho salmon, and chinook salmon. These fish found the lower Niagara on their own, liked what they found, and thrived there. More recently the New York Department of Environmental Conservation has been stocking the river itself in order to further improve this fishery.

Chinook salmon go to forty pounds in the Niagara River below the Falls.

The stretch of river below Niagara Falls is a tumultuous torrent of white-water rapids for a distance of some six miles. Thereafter the river becomes more placid before it empties into Lake Ontario a few miles farther downstream. The gorge is inaccessible by boat and hence sees little angling pressure. To work this stretch of river, anglers have to hike in on trails and fish from the bank.

Brown trout, ranging up to ten pounds, abound in the spring and are most abundant in the lower stretch of the river. Steelhead (rainbow trout) have been caught at up to twenty pounds and are in the river from November through January. Coho and chinook salmon are caught throughout the summer but virtually jam the river in September and October. Both species of salmon come in man-sized packages—coho to fifteen pounds, and chinooks in the forty-pound category. Walleye are taken occasionally, and the smallmouth bass is prevalent in these waters. These tough river bass average less than three pounds but can range up to six pounds.

There's a big difference between fighting a fifteen-pound steelhead in open water and tangling with the same fish in a raging river. As a result, long, relatively limber rods are recommended. Match them with large-capacity reels loaded with ten- or twelve-pound test line. When it comes to lures, keep an open mind and use whatever your guide suggests. In the clothing line, bring togs suitable for the season, regardless of whether you intend to fish by boat or from the bank. If you intend to fish the upper gorge, remember that you'll have to tote everything in with you, so go light. Telescope rods will come in handy. So will light stocking-foot waders you can wear with sneakers or hiking shoes. Make your lure selections in advance, and carry them in a fishing vest or in plastic boxes tucked away in a jacket pocket. Include rain gear, insect repellent, and suntan lotion.

Boats can be chartered to fish the lower river for $250 per day, or less, and local fishermen can be retained to take you into the upper gorge. You'll stay at Niagara Falls, which has an abundance of restaurants and motels, but bear in mind that this resort area can become quite crowded during the summer vacation season. During spring and fall, when the fishing is best, motel rooms will be available at discount rates.

For fishing information and the name of a good guide or charter boat captain, write to Mark Daul, 2201 Whirlpool St., Niagara Falls, NY 14304, Tel: (716) 285/-7255. Daul operates a tackle shop on the river bank and makes it a point to know what is going on. For additional information about the area write to the Niagara Falls Chamber of Commerce, 300 4th St., Niagara Falls, NY 13141, Tel: (716) 278–8010.

LAKE SEMINOLE • Georgia

Big Jack Wingate lobbed a battered Zara Spook back into a pocket in the weedbeds and gave it a couple of twitches. "There's a bass in there," he grunted.

"How do you know?" I asked.

"'Cause," he replied. "In this lake there's a bass in every hole like that."

Wingate should know. He grew up fishing the Flint and Chattahoochee Rivers before they were impounded in 1957 to create Lake Seminole, and in the intervening years he has become the authority on fishing the lake as well.

Seminole is a 37,500-acre impoundment tucked away in the southwestern corner of the state. The shoreline is 257 miles long and includes thousands of acres of flooded timber, miles of grassy bays and flats, several hundred islands, and numerous spring-fed tributaries.

The largemouth bass is the prime gamefish in these waters, and it comes in

Lake Seminole offers quality top-water bass fishing at a bargain price.

man-size packages. The lake record topped seventeen pounds, and trophy fish in the ten- to twelve-pound category are taken each year. Other species of gamefish in these waters include striped bass up to fifty pounds, hybrids to sixteen pounds, roaming schools of white bass, and a bountiful supply of crappie.

Because Seminole averages less than nine feet in depth, it is a top-water fisherman's paradise. The action begins in February, when the bass move into the shallows to spawn, and continues well into June. At this season, anglers toss surface lures and buzz baits into indentations in the shoreline and rarely come away empty-handed. For a change of pace, there is also fast-paced action for whites and hybrids up the Flint River.

During the summer months, the best top-water fishing occurs from dawn to mid-morning, and in the evening. At this season, whites and hybrids, with some largemouth mixed in, can also be found in large schools in the main lake. When the water cools in the fall, top-water fishermen again have a picnic fishing inshore cover.

Because of Seminole's stick-ups and thick aquatic growth, recommended fishing tackle is on the heavy side. Casting rods, equipped with revolving spool reels, are ideal and should be loaded with fifteen- to twenty-pound test line. Recommended lures are spinner baits, weedless spoons garnished with pork rind, and a wide variety of surface plugs. Plastic worms are also effective.

When you're fishing this lake, the place to stay is at Jack Wingate's Lunker Lodge. This camp is located on the lake a few miles south of Bainbridge and can accommodate thirty-two guests in motel rooms and cabins. Additional accommodations are available for sixteen men in the Stag Hangout, which is ideal for bass clubs and other small groups. The Wingate dining room is also the place to eat. Jack's barbecue skills are legendary in this part of the south, and his fried chicken and catfish are also reputed to leave diners licking their fingers.

For campers, nearby Bass Island Campground offers forty-eight tree-shaded sites, all with electricity and water connections. Other facilities include a launching ramp, a central shower and restroom building, dumping station, and other camping conveniences.

Prices are reasonable in this part of the south. A room at Lunker Lodge costs $25 per night, and a campsite (with hookups) costs only $7. Guides, fishing out of Lunker Lodge, charge $100 for a day's fishing and can fish two persons.

For more information on fishing Lake Seminole, write to Jack Wingate, Lunker Lodge, P.O. Box 1571, Bainbridge, GA 31717, Tel: (912) 246–0658.

OCALA NATIONAL FOREST • Florida

Want to catch a trophy largemouth for your den wall?

Cuba is a possibility. So is southern California or Mexico. But in my opinion, the best place to realize this objective is in central Florida, specifically in and around the Ocala National Forest.

This 366,000-acre chunk of Florida real estate lies between Silver Springs and Lake George and is dotted with several hundred lakes. Some of the most popular are Oklawaha (better known as Rodman Reservoir), Lake Kerr, Lake Bryant, Dexter, Half Moon, Skimmerhorn, Farles Prairie, and Lake Sellers. Most of these lakes are in wilderness settings, and the best ones do not have launching ramps or are even accessible by road.

Sellers is one example. The only way to reach this 4,000-acre prairie lake is use a trailer to take to a boat to it with a four-wheel-drive vehicle. Roughly 1,000 acres of this lake are open water, and the remainder is flooded prairie. Bait fish thrive in this environment and provide a bountiful food supply for the lake's bass population. This lake is deep by Florida standards, and because it is fed by underground springs it is incredibly clear and cold.

This latter element is necessary when it comes to raising big bass. For

Central Florida is the place to go to tangle with a bass large enough for your den wall.

example, it is unusual for a Florida bass to live much more than seven or eight years, and an average ten-pound female bass will be about this old. Unless this fish is caught by some fisherman, she soon will die of old age. Bass in colder water, however, have a longer life span and can probably live the eighteen years necessary to reach a record-breaking size of twenty-three pounds.

In addition to cool water, the National Forest lakes have other things going for them as well. Biologists report that these lakes harbor fewer parasites than other southern waters. Abundant plant growth gives shade and life-giving oxygen. An incredible variety of baitfish provides sufficient food to assure a rapid growth rate for their bass population.

But the proof is in the catching. I know a man who caught twenty bass over ten pounds in one week of fishing these lakes. I caught a 12½-pounder here a few years ago, and in this part of the country it didn't raise a single eyebrow. A number of bass in the sixteen-pound class have been taken from these lakes in recent years, and I'm of the opinion that even larger bass reside there.

Rodman is one of the largest and most accessible lakes in the region and as a result receives considerably more angling pressure. Despite this fact, it has a well-deserved reputation as a big bass lake, annually producing large numbers of trophy-sized fish.

The heavy weed growth in this lake is frequently cursed by anglers, but it could be one of the reasons this lake is so productive. Difficult to fish with artificials, Rodman is best suited to fishing with live wild shiners that can be free-spooled back beneath carpets of floating vegetation.

Incidentally, fishing with large wild shiners is a favorite angling method in this part of Florida because it is so effective in producing trophy-sized bass. Local guides tout this fishing method and usually recommend it to their clients.

During the February-through-April spawning season, fishing with shiners is extremely productive and should be considered. Later on, plastic worms, weedless spoons, and spinner baits can be effective when fished in the weeds. A second rod should be rigged with a surface lure to plug inviting pockets in the pad or rushes. Because forest lakes remain cool and oxygen rich throughout the summer, the fishing in these lakes does not fall off as it does on other southern waters.

The combination of large fish and thick cover make heavy tackle almost mandatory. Rods should have plenty of backbone. Revolving spool reels are recommended and should be loaded with twenty- or thirty-pound test line. Guides usually furnish the specialized gear required for shiner fishing, if this angling method is to be used.

Guides are essential if you are to fish the more inaccessible lakes and are recommended even for lakes like George and Rodman. They're available, and most are highly skilled and provide expert services for a moderate cost. The ones who regularly fish the back-country potholes and lakes own four-wheel-drive vehicles and special boat and trailer rigs suitable for off-the-road operations.

A variety of restaurants and motels is available in Silver Springs, which frequently is used as a headquarters for fishing this region. Should you want to get a little closer to the action, less luxurious facilities are available at Salt Springs or other locations within the National Park. Hire a guide, who will be happy to recommend the best places to eat and stay locally.

If you fly to Florida, I recommend that you rent a car for this fishing trip. Bear in mind that the area is remote and that fishing spots and places to eat and stay may be located some distance from one another. A rental car will come in handy and is obtainable in both Ocala and Orlando.

Even if you use a guide, eat at restaurants, stay in a motel, and hire a rental car, I still rate this trip as "modestly priced."

A first-class guide operation, known as Bass Champions, is located in Fort McCoy. Dave Doub is frequently the spokesman for this association of fishing professionals, and John Doub handles most of the bookings. For bookings and more information write to John Doub, Bass Champions, Rt., 3, Box 32637, Fort McCoy, FL 32637. For additional information on the area write to the National Forest Service, 227 N. Bronough Street., Suite 4061, Tallahassee, FL 32301, Tel: (904) 622–6577.

LAKE OKEECHOBEE ● Florida

This sprawling 750-square-mile lake is located in south Florida and could be one of the most productive largemouth-bass lakes in the country today.

Lake Okeechobee, first of all, is an extremely fertile lake with an abundant supply of forage fish. Because it is located so far south, the bass in it feed year round and do not experience an annual period of dormancy as they would farther north. With a twelve-month growing season, these largemouth have an extremely fast growth rate.

The lake also has plenty of cover. Reeds and bulrushes grow in the shallows and are laced with boat trails and islands of pepper grass. The latter type of vegetation is attractive to bass because it harbors food fish, provides shade, and gives off an abundant supply of oxygen.

Lake Okeechobee is a shallow lake, averaging only twelve feet in depth throughout. Most of the best fishing occurs in water six or eight feet deep, which means that bass will strike surface lures and are inclined to jump when hooked. This is bass fishing at its best. It is one thing to hook a largemouth in thirty feet of water and crank him unceremoniusly to the surface, and another to coax the fish into striking a surface lure. For this reason, fishing in Lake Okeechobee is more exciting than it is in deeper impoundments, where the most productive fishing method is dangling a plastic worm in deep water structure.

Finding elbow room to fish is no problem on this lake because virtually all of its 450,000 acres of water contains fish. This huge lake, the second-largest one in the country, is also located some distance from major centers of population. As a result, fishing pressure is light. Here, it's easy to find a bay that hasn't been fished recently, as well as fish eager to strike most of the lures thrown at them.

Okeechobee doesn't have the reputation of producing bass as large as that found in some other Florida lakes, but it should be noted that ten-pound bass are caught with regularity and that twelve- and fourteen-pound fish are a possibility. Currently the lake is experiencing an increase in its bass population, caused by a drought in the early 1980s that exposed much of the lake bottom. The result is the type of fishing that newly filled reservoirs usually provide.

This lake is fishable during all seasons of the year but is probably most productive during the February-through-April period. At this time,

Lake Okeechobee is possibly the most productive bass lake in the country.

largemouth move into the shallows along the shore, with newly emerging beds of pepper grass being particularly productive. Although this lake normally is best fished with a boat, wade fishing can also be effective when the bass are in the shallows. During the summer, bass move out into deep water and are best located with electronic flashers or by trolling.

The bass in this lake are usually found in or near aquatic vegetation, so medium to heavy tackle is recommended. Reels should be loaded with fifteen- to twenty-pound monofilament line. Best lures are plastic worms, weedless spoons, spinner baits, and surface lures that can be worked over or through the weedbeds. The best live bait is a golden shiner, fished with a float, or free-lined back beneath a mass of aquatic weed growth.

Because Lake Okeechobee is so large, and most of it looks the same, the use of a guide is highly recommended. Guides are available at most of the two dozen fishing camps scattered around the lake, but the better ones can be booked far in advance. This is particularly true during the February-through-May period. In addition to lakeside fishing camps, motels and restaurants are available in and near the towns of Okeechobee, Belle Glade, Clewiston, and Moore Haven. Rooms in the area average $25 to $35 per night. Most guides charge $150 per day and can fish two anglers.

For additional information on Lake Okeechobee, write to the following: Calusa Lodge Rt. 2, Hwy. 78, Moore Haven, FL 33471. Tel: 813 946–0544; Big Bass Lodge, Rt. 2, Box 120, Moore Haven, FL 33471. Tel: 813 946–1707; Clewiston Chamber of Commerce, PO Box 275, Clewiston, FL 33440, Tel: 813 983–7979, and Okeechobee Chamber of Commerce, 55 S. Parrott Ave., Okeechobee, FL 33472, Tel: 813 763-6464.

THE KEYS ● Florida

The Florida Keys are a string of highway-connected islands that stretch 130 miles in a southwesterly direction from the Florida mainland to Key West. Only twenty-five islands are involved, however. An additional 500 secluded and mostly uninhabited islands are scattered throughout a 4,000-square-mile segment of the Gulf of Mexico known as the Florida Bay. These low-slung, mangrove-studded atolls are situated amidst a morass of glistening marl flats, grass-covered banks, and jade-green basins, all laced together by a network of blue-water channels through which the tides ebb and flow.

A variety of gamefish inhabit these shallows. Vast schools of silvery tarpon begin to arrive in March and are present until late in July. Bonefish are permanent residents of the Keys' flats, but the best fishing occurs from March through October. Winter bonefishing is a possibility, but, depending on the weather, it can be good or awful. These bonefish are not as easy to catch as the Bahamas or Yucatan variety, but they grow a lot larger.

This is also the place to try to catch a permit, that elusive flats denizen that

Keys bonefish are not as easy to catch as Yucatan or Bahamas bones, but they grow larger and are still plentiful.

goes to fify-pounds in these waters. Note that I wrote "try to" catch. This powerful cousin of the pompano is not only hard to hook, it's even more difficult to land.

Tailing redfish offers an interesting change of pace for Keys fishermen, and so does the spotted weakfish, or seatrout. Florida Bay, particularly that portion in the shadow of Everglades National Park, may be the best seatrout fishery in the state. This is especially true during the fall and winter months, when large schools of trout concentrate in these waters.

Headquarters for fishing in the Keys is the town of Islamorada, which is a wide spot in the road sixty miles south of Miami. Formerly a retreat for oversized mosquitoes, rum runners, and derelicts of every description, Islamorada was discovered by the novelist Zane Grey and later popularized as a fishing mecca by such men as Joe Brooks and Ted Williams. Today, several dozen fishing guides operate out of Islamorada, and during the better fishing months most of them are busy.

Although only a twenty-minute drive from the Miami airport, Biscayne Bay offers surprisingly good fishing for bonefish during the spring and fall months, and excellent fishing for permit during March and April. Biscayne bones are bragging size, averaging six pounds and occasionally topping ten. A half-dozen good guides operate out of Key Biscayne, a little community which offers a variety of accommodations and restaurants.

Marathon is a community of some 4,500 inhabitants and is located halfway between Islamorada and Key West. This section of the Keys has less angling pressure than the Islamorada area and can offer excellent fishing for tarpon, bonefish, and permit. A dozen or more guides operate here, and most of them are prepared to take their boats north or south to get closer to the fishing action. Marathon has a number of lodges and motels to choose from, and an equal number of good restaurants.

Unlike other Keys communities, Key West is a real town with a population of 24,000 residents and a historic charm that never fails to fascinate a first-time visitor. There are lots of bars here, places to eat and stay, campgrounds, a flourishing gay community, tourists, drug traffickers, little old ladies in white tennis shoes, and a certain number of anglers. Despite the carnival-like atmosphere of Key West, its flats are relatively uncrowded and offer excellent fishing for tarpon, bones, and permit in season.

Islamorada is my favorite, though. Strategically located to allow anglers to explore to explore the Keys' "back country," this little community of 1,500 exists primarily for sports fishing. Guides stay relatively busy during the winter months poling tourists and casual fisherment around the flats, but when schools of tarpon begin to flood the area in March, fishing becomes a serious matter. Until late July, when the big silver kings mysteriously depart for unknown destinations, Islamorada lives, breathes, and talks tarpon fishing.

And why not? This fascinating gamefish frequently exceeds one hundred pounds in weight and is a challenge to hook and land. But, to catch a tarpon you first have to find one, and this means exploring banks and basins beneath a tropical sun, peering into green depths through polarized glasses, and poling across miles of shimmering flats. Finally a school of tarpon are within casting range, the line swishes out, and a fish takes the fly. Strike, a shower of spray as the twisting, silver-scaled body hurtles skyward, the scream of the reel as the fish steams across the flat in a long run. Perspiration, straining arm muscles, the flow of adrenaline, calming words of advice from your guide—all are a part of this scene. And it's the ride that counts. If you win the battle, the fish will be nursed back to fit form and released. If you lose, a smile from the guide will be apt reward. That's tarpon fishing . . . an angling experience that perhaps has no equal in thrills and excitement.

Tarpon are caught on both casting and spinning equipment, but more and more of these gamefish are now taken on the fly. If you choose this method, use a long #12 weight rod and a reel loaded with 200 yards of thirty-pound backing. Purchase flies locally, in accordance with your guide's recommendations.

Keys fishing isn't as costly as angling in Alaska, but it is still relatively expensive. Guides are true professionals and charge accordingly. The price of motel and lodge rooms is also relatively high during the busy seasons, and during that time availability is limited. From a practical standpoint, it will pay you to book both accommodations and a fishing guide as far in advance as possible.

The Holiday Isle Resort in Islamorada offers a modestly priced four-day package that includes two days' fishing with a boat, motor, guide, and bait, and three nights' accommodations. The address is Box 588, Islamorada, FL 33036, and the telephone number is 1–800–432–2875. Other sources of information include the Chambers of Commerce in Islamorada (305) 664–5403; Marathon, (305) 743–5417; and Key West, (305) 294–2587. All three can provide you with a list of available guides and motels in their respective areas. More knowledgeable on this subject is George Hommel, World Wide Sportsman, Box 787, Islamorada, FL 33036, Tel: (305) 664–4615.

Alaska 2

Five species of salmon spawn in Alaskan rivers, and two of these are highly sought after by sports fishermen. All of these species are silvery and have spotted or speckled backs and fins. When they enter fresh water, these fish develop hooked jaws, and the silver color changes to varying shades of red, depending on the species. All Pacific salmon die after spawning.

The largest and longest lived of Alaskan salmon is the king, or chinook, salmon. The average weight of the species is around twenty pounds, with catches three times this size not unusual. King salmon are the first on the scene, congregating at the mouths of their home streams in the spring and making their spawning runs in June and early July. These concentrations of salmon vary from river to river, however.

Silver salmon, also called coho, are the sportiest of the Pacific salmon and average around ten pounds. Current Alaskan rod and reel record is a 26-pounder taken in 1976, but silver salmon exceeding thirty pounds are known to exist. Basically a fall-run fish, the silver salmon returns to its home stream in late July and is most active in August and September.

Occupying Alaskan rivers in between the king and silver salmon are the sockeye (red salmon), pink salmon, and chum salmon. Of these fish, the sockeye is the best gamester when it can be induced to strike. Pinks are rather small, averaging around four pounds. Although larger, the chum salmon is of least interest to the sports fisherman.

Rainbow trout inhabit most of Alaskan streams and grow large in this habitat. Five-pound rainbows are relatively common, and trophies in the ten-pound category are taken frequently. Anadromous rainbow trout (called steelhead) are usually larger and are more powerful. They're most plentiful in Alaskan streams in late fall. Spawning runs of salmon have an effect on rainbow trout. At the height of these runs, the trout get crowded out of their

King salmon go to fifty pounds or more in most Alaskan streams, but average twenty or more.

37

normal habitat but get plenty to eat in the way of salmon eggs. This abundant supply of food is probably why Alaskan rainbows are so large and healthy. Southcentral Alaska and the Bristol Bay area are the best areas for this species of gamefish. The best fishing is in the spring, before the rivers are jammed with salmon, and in the fall. September is a delightful time to fish for rainbows. The rivers are low and clear, and the trout are particularly voracious.

Cutthroat trout abound in the streams and lakes of southeastern Alaska and are available in both freshwater and sea-run varieties. The latter, after spending three years in salt water, may weigh four pounds or more. The state record is an 8-pounder taken from Wilson Lake in 1977. Inland, cutthroat are found in both lakes and streams. In the ocean, they rarely stray far from the mouths of these spawning streams. Like steelhead, cutthroat spawn in the fall and winter in fresh water.

The Dolly Varden has the widest distribution of any trout or char in Alaska and is found along the coast from southeastern Alaska, including the Alaska Peninsula, through Bristol Bay and up around the coastline to Canada. The species may weigh twenty pounds or more, and in Alaska is primarily a saltwater fish. Dolly Varden follow spawning salmon upstream in the summer, where they feed on eggs and fingerlings, but the best fishing is later in September, when they make their own spawning runs. At this season, these fish are fresh from the sea and in good fighting condition.

Lake trout are found in Alaskan lakes from the Alaska Peninsula northward. Best fishing for this species is shortly after ice-out, when these fish are in shallow water. During summer and fall, good fishing may be found at stream mouths, where they pour into a lake, or at depths of up to fifty feet or more. Alaska's current record is a 47-pounder.

The Arctic grayling is abundant throughout central and northern Alaska, where it is found in both streams and lakes. Grayling in these waters average less than three pounds, with a 4-pound, 11-ounce fish being the state record. These beautiful little gamefish feed mostly on aquatic insects and are a favorite quarry of fly fishermen. Some of the largest specimens come from the Ugashik Lakes on the Alaska Peninsula, and from several Bristol Bay river systems. In most waters, grayling fishing is uniformly good throughout the summer.

The sheefish is found in the Kobuk, Kuskowim, and Selawik drainages, as well as many tributaries of the Yukon. Little is known about this fine gamefish, which is known to reach sixty pounds or more and is an outstanding fighter. Like many other Alaskan fish, the sheefish ascends certain streams each summer to spawn, returning in late fall to the ocean.

Northern pike are found from the Alaska Peninsula northward to the Arctic coast and throughout the interior of the state. Except for the Minto Flats, which is relatively close to Fairbanks, there is little fishing pressure for this species. As a result, one would think that monster pike would be waiting for the pike fishermen, but I no longer think this is the case. Pike in the twenty-pound category have been taken in Alaskan waters, but the state has yet to produce a thirty-pound fish of this species.

Alaskan waters contain more species of desirable gamefish than any other state, province, or country that I know of. This is fishing country, from the British Columbia border in the south clear around to the frozen Arctic Ocean.

Bugs and Bears

Alaska is also one of North America's last strongholds for the grizzly and the exclusive domain of the monstrous brown bear and black bear as well. Alaska is bear country.

The Alaska brown bear, the largest flesh-eating animal in the world today, will average more than eight feet in length and weigh up to 1,600 pounds. Its range is restricted to a narrow coastal strip of land and shore islands stretching from the tip of the Alaska Peninsula south into British Columbia.

Grizzly and black bears inhabit the rest of Alaska, occasionally straying into brown bear territory when the salmon are running. The grizzly is not as large as the Alaskan brown, but it is a powerful bear. Males reach a length of six to eight feet and weigh 500 to 750 pounds. Black bears, onto the other hand, rarely reach 500 pounds.

During the salmon runs, these bears become proficient anglers, gaining much of their sustenance from the wriggling salmon they scoop up onto the shore. In this process, these large carnivores become very possessive of their fishing holes and represent a hazard to humans fishing the same waters.

Bear attacks are well documented, and a study of these incidents reveals that bears are unpredictable. In most cases they will give ground or flee when encountering a human, but occasionally they will attack. Female bears with cubs are known to be particularly aggressive. So are males with a strong territorial instinct. Provocation isn't necessary, however. Records indicate that some people have been attacked from the rear, or from ambush. Others have been attacked in their tents, or pulled from sleeping bags. Grizzly bears are involved in a large number of these incidents, but black bears are also guilty. Fewer brown bears have been involved, but this fact does not make these large carnivores any less formidible. Don't believe in Gentle Ben or Smokey the Bear; bears are dangerous animals and should be treated with caution and respect.

How about firearms? If you employ a guide you can be assured that he'll be armed with a heavy rifle (30.06 caliber or larger), and if you're on your own I suggest you do the same. Bears may be destroyed legally in self-defense, but this should only be done as a last resort. If you are unfamiliar with firearms, I suggest that you plan your wilderness adventure in some place other than Alaska. For more information on this subject, write for a brochure titled "The Bears and You," produced by the Alaska Department of Fish and Game.

An encounter with a bear is a possibility when fishing a stream full of migrating salmon, but getting chewed up by biting insects is almost a certainty. They're found throughout the state but are particularly abundant in damp tundra areas in the interior, in certain coastal regions, and along major river systems.

Mosquitoes are plentiful in Alaska, and they're said to be large enough to carry people off. As one old sourdough advised, when you go to sleep at night be sure to zip up your tent fly or keep the cabin door closed.

No-see-ums are so tiny that they're difficult to see, but their bite certainly isn't. More plentiful in some places, and in the early part of the season, these little flies are real pests.

Blackflies, or their relatives, are also found throughout Alaska and are particularly numerous in June and the early part of July.

Most of these biting insects can be controlled with a good insect repellent, but early in the season you may need a head net also. Shoo-fly jackets are another possibility and are recommended for many parts of Alaska. Wind, of course, is a deterrent, and thankfully a breeze blows most of the time throughout Alaska. Insects are also less of a problem in late August and September, and at higher elevations.

Biting bugs are a part of Alaska, and a price we have to pay for the fabulous fishing in this state. My advice is to take plenty of repellent along, and don't pay any attention to them.

How to Get There

A number of domestic airlines offer daily service to Alaskan gateways, and a half-dozen foreign airlines provide additional service. The major Alaskan gateway is Anchorage, located in populous southcentral Alaska on Cook Inlet. Anchorage has a population of around 175,000 and is this state's largest and fastest-growing metropolis. Because of its location, it is the gateway to Bristol Bay, the Bering Sea Coast, the Kenai, and the Alaskan Peninsula, areas where most of the angling action is in Alaska. Anchorage is where it all begins.

Southcentral Alaska is served by Ketchikan in the south, and by Juneau, somewhat farther to the north. The latter city has a population exceeding 20,000 and is the capital of the state. Both of these cities offer access to the excellent saltwater salmon fishing in this part of Alaska and are served by frequent flights from the continental United States.

Gateway to the vast Alaskan interior is Fairbanks, a town that was founded during the gold rush and is now a commercial center with 25,000 inhabitants. Fairbanks is also served by commercial carriers, but not with the frequency that Anchorage is.

By road, Fairbanks is 3,800 miles from Chicago and 1,500 miles from Dawson Creek via the Alaska Highway. Much of this highway is gravel, although it is well maintained. There are gas stations, garages, and other facilities for meals and overnight accommodations at reasonable intervals. If you plan to drive to Alaska, expect the trip to take a week or more and do your traveling from the middle of May to October. Flying gravel can be a problem, so you may wish to outfit your car with plastic headlight covers and shield the bottom of your gas tank with rubber. The Alaska Highway is also hard on tires, so make sure that yours are in good condition before attempting the trip. For current details on the Alaska Highway and its facilities, write to the Milepost, P.O. Box 4–EEE, Anchorage, AK 99509.

The Alaskan Marine Highway System provides another way to get to Alaska and consists of car ferries operating from Seattle and Prince Rupert, British Columbia. These ferries provide an inexpensive and practical way to visit southeastern Alaska, which is otherwise accessible by road, and as an alternate method of seeing the rest of Alaska as well. You may want to drive the Alaskan Highway one way and take the ferry the other. Ferries operate several times each week during the summer months and have overnight staterooms for passengers. Reservations are required for these facilities, so planning is recommended. For details, write to the Division of Marine Highway Systems, Pouch R., Juneau, AK 99811.

What to Bring

What you bring with you to Alaska will be more or less determined by where you go and what you intend to do. For example, if your destination is the Arctic region, rain gear won't be a priority. If you're going elsewhere in Alaska, however, a good rain suit is the first thing you should stow in your duffel bag. In the clothing line, also include the following: an insulated parka, long-sleeved wool or flannel shirts, two pairs of trousers, long underwear, a wide-brimmed hat, a windbreaker, a sweater, waterproof camp shoes, wool socks, and a pair of gloves.

Unless you plan to confine your fishing to saltwater trolling, you'll need a pair of hip waders or chest waders. The latter will give you more fishing latitude, but they're bulky and will add considerable weight to your luggage. For this reason, you might want to give some consideration to one of the extremely lightweight stocking foot waders on the market. Red Ball makes a pair that weigh less than a pound, yet they're very durable. Wear them with sneakers or the wading shoes made to go with them. How about felt soles? You'll find them invaluable when fishing some streams, and unnecessary when wading others. In the process of planning your trip, make certain that you ask whether felt soles are needed.

One of the most important things you can take along is a good insect repellent. Deep Woods Off is good. So is Cutters. Muskol is also extremely effective. Vitamin B–1 is also reputed to repel insects, and everything else you may come in contact with. If you don't mind being shunned by friends as well as mosquitoes, give it a try. Take a daily dosage of 50 mg for at least a week before heading into the bush. In some cases, a head net is also recommended.

Follow your outfitter's recommendations concerning tackle to bring along, but remember that king salmon are big fish that may require heavier rods and larger reels than you may be used to using. Large, gaudy wet flies take plenty of kings, but records indicate that most king salmon are taken on lures and bait fished with spinning or casting tackle. Don't settle for anything less than twenty-five-pound test line when fishing for these big fish, however. Other salmon, trout, and steelhead are commonly taken on lighter spinning gear or perhaps a 7-weight fly fishing outfit. Include lures and flies, fishing vest, extra line, pliers, a line clipper, and a sharpening stone. If you're going to be on your own, add a first-aid kit, compass, fillet knife, rifle, matches, and other survival items. Polarized sunglasses always come in handy for spotting fish.

If you have a large tackle box, leave it at home. Pack reels, extra spools of line, and other small items in with your clothing. Transfer lures into small plastic boxes that can be carried in your vest or in a shoulder pack. All of this, clothing and fishing tackle, should be packed in one or more soft duffel bags that can be easily stowed aboard float aircraft. Rods are an exception. These should be packed in sturdy tubular cases that will withstand the type of rough treatment that airline luggage frequently receives.

Unless you're going to spend some time in one or more Alaskan cities, wear the same clothing that you'll be fishing in. This practice is perfectly acceptable and does not require you to lug dress clothing out in the bush, or find a place to stow it while you're there. Try to limit your clothing and other gear to fifty pounds, remembering that you may wish to bring home some smoked salmon or a few frozen fillets.

Fly-Out Fishing

A number of fishing camps in Alaska, particularly in the Bristol Bay region, include the use of a float plane in the price of their angling packages. With this arrangement, camp guests pile into float planes each morning and fly to a predetermined spot for a few hours or for a day of fishing. One day, their destination may be a river known for its trophy-sized rainbow trout. On another, grayling could be the objective, or one of the several species of salmon that ascend the streams in this part of Alaska.

This erratic schedule results from the fact that the quality of the fishing can vary from week to week or from stream to stream in the same region. One week the Brooks River may be jammed with spawning runs of king salmon and the next week most of the action could be on the nearby Naknek. Because there are no roads in this wilderness area, the only way to get from one spot to another is by pontoon aircraft. Consequently, patrons of fly-out fishing camps spend a lot of time crawling in and out of float planes.

They also catch a lot of fish. Having a float plane at your disposal means being in the center of the fishing action at all times. It also provides an opportunity to catch a greater variety of fish than might be available in one river. Considering everything, fly-out fishing can be very productive.

There are a couple of disadvantages, though, and one of them is price. It costs money to buy and maintain pontoon aircraft, and fly-out camps naturally have to pass these costs along to their patrons. As a result, a seven-day package that includes fly-out service may cost $1,000 more than one that does not offer this service. Under normal circumstances, paying an extra $145 per day might be worth it. But if the weather sours, grounding all aircraft for several days, the situation changes drastically. This happens frequently, too. Coastal areas of Alaska are subject to a lot of cloud cover, rainfall, and ground fog, and pontoon aircraft just cannot fly under these conditions.

Another possible disadvantage of fly-out fishing is that aircraft frequently crowd together in one place if a certain stretch of river has a better salmon run than others. When the word gets out, aircraft drop out of the sky like vultures, and fishing becomes an elbow-to-elbow proposition. Everyone may still catch fish under these conditions, but some may wonder if the hassle is worth it. After all, the average angler goes to Alaska to smell pine needles and watch soaring eagles, not get jammed up on a gravel bar with a dozen other anglers.

With so much elbow room in Alaska, this type of crowding can be avoided, but unfortunately not when the weather is bad. In western Alaska, where the majority of the fly-out camps are located, it is logical to expect a day or so of fog and rain each week. Weather is changeable in this part of the world. Grounded aircraft are part of the scene here, but no one talks much about the subject.

Fly-out camps offer the ultimate in Alaskan fishing, but you should anticipate that there will be days when the planes can't fly. This is no problem if good fishing is available in the vicinity and your camp has the equipment to exploit it. But, it can be exasperating if you're paying $300 per day and have no place to fish. This is the case with some fly-out operations, and you should be aware of this fact.

A word of warning, as a result: Before booking a fly-out camp, ask about the fishing when the planes are grounded.

BRISTOL BAY

The famed Bristol Bay region of Alaska is a stretch of coast fronting the Bering Sea, which extends from the Alaskan Peninsula 150 miles north of Cape Newenham. Included is the Wood River/Tikchik region, which is a 3,000-square-mile chunk of scenic wilderness containing fourteen major lakes and numerous crystal-clear rivers. This vast watershed is considered one of the fishiest spots in Alaska, and perhaps in the world as well.

King salmon begin to ascend Bristol Bay streams in the middle of June, muscling native trout and grayling out of the way as they push their way inland to their spawning areas. These burly Bristol Bay kings will average twenty to twenty-five pounds but go to fifty pounds or more. On the way

The Bristol Bay region is a 3,000-square-mile chunk of wilderness dotted with lakes and laced with hundreds of rivers and streams.

upstream, they'll take a variety of angler offerings and put up a hard-fought battle when hooked.

The Bristol Bay region is perhaps best known for its sockeye salmon run, which is the world's largest. Late in June, millions of these silvery fish leave the cold waters of the Bering Sea and commence their upstream pilgrimage. On the way their body coloration changes and the streams appear to be stained with crimson as the huge schools of these red salmon migrate inland. These sockeyes average six to eight pounds and can go to thirteen pounds or more. Frequently difficult to hook, they are valiant fighters on the end of a line, leaping repeatedly and making long powerful runs. Pound for pound, this salmon may be one of Alaska's greatest gamesters.

The sockeye run is followed closely by humpback and by the larger chum salmon. The former average three to five pounds and will strike both flies and artificial lures as fast as they are presented to these aggressive fish. On light tackle, humpies (also called pink salmon) are extremely fun to catch. Chum salmon average seven to nine pounds in Bristol Bay waters, with trophy-sized fish weighing twelve pounds or more. Not as plentiful as the pink and red salmon, the chum is considered a good game fish.

Silver salmon make their spawning run in August and are present in Bristol Bay rivers until the latter part of September. Considered an excellent gamefish, this salmon averages less than ten pounds but can go to twenty pounds. Silver salmon strike artificial lures willingly and are particularly susceptible to a well-presented fly.

Bristol Bay's freshwater gamefish are rainbow trout, Arctic char, Dolly Varden, Arctic grayling, lake trout, and northern pike. They're available from early June through October and furnish Bristol Bay anglers with plenty of action when the salmon bite slacks off. Lake trout are most aggressive in June, before the water begins to warm. Fishing for trout and char is best in late August and September. Grayling and pike are around all year.

A première fishing area like Bristol Bay might be expected to have a number of fishing facilities, and this is exactly the case. Here's where some of the state's first fishing camps were built, and here's where others have been added in recent years. There are plenty of fish to go around, though, and the camps are scattered far enough apart to assure anglers lots of elbow room.

Golden Horn Lodge is a good example. It is located on one of the Wood River lakes, and when I was there a few years ago there wasn't another lodge within miles. From this lodge we explored the surrounding wilderness by boat and float plane, caught lots of fish, and never saw another soul. Golden Horn is a first-class facility. Nicknamed "the wilderness Hilton," Golden Horn offers accommodations for twenty angler guests in the main lodge. This lodge, one of the largest log structures in the state, is impressive. Features include a spacious lounge with a large stone fireplace, a dining room that serves hors d'oeuvres, gourmet-class meals, complimentary wine with evening meal, and a variety of other goodies. This is a fly-out lodge. It maintains three DeHavilland aircraft that fly angler guests to a different spot each day of their week-long stay. On some occasions pilots stay with their passengers and act as guides. On others, guides go along or meet clients at wilderness locations. Outboard-powered boats or inflated rafts are frequently used to fish these remote waters, but wading is also a preferred fishing method. At the end of the day, guests fly back to the lodge for a hot tub or sauna, cocktails, and an excellent dinner. On the days when the aircraft can't fly, anglers scatter out in boats and fish a variety of waters teeming with trout, grayling, or whatever species of salmon is running at the time. Golden Horn is located fifty-five miles north of Dillingham and is accessible only by float plane.

Bristol Bay Lodge is another area fishing camp with impeccable credentials. This first-class fishing facility is located on Lake Aleknagik, some sixty miles northwest of Dillingham. It, too, has accommodations for twenty guests but houses them in attractive log cottages clustered around the main lodge. Sleeping quarters are heated and attractively furnished, and each has a private bath. The main lodge houses the kitchen, dining room, and great room. The great room features a big stone fireplace, bar, library, fully equipped fly-tying bench, and game table. Meals, served in the dining room, are hearty, and dinner includes complimentary wine. For the use of its guests, Bristol Bay maintains a fleet of three DeHavilland float planes. Some mornings pilots will fly anglers to wilderness streams where guides with boats are waiting for a day's fishing. On other occasions, aircraft will fly anglers to several streams, affording them an opportunity to fish a variety of spots for a different gamefish. When the planes can't fly, the Agulowak River and nearby Rainbow and Icy Creeks provide excellent fishing locally. Should guests desire, they can spend a few days fishing from out-camps established in wilderness locations.

These two camps are typical of the better fly-out fishing facilities available in the area. Both operate from the middle of June through September, on a Saturday-to-Saturday basis. Including charter air fare from Dillingham, the approximate price for a week's fishing at either of these two Bristol Bay camps is $2,800 per person.

For more details on fishing at either place, write to Bud Hodson, Golden Horn Lodge, P.O. Box 6748, Anchorage, AK 99502, Tel: (907) 243–1455; or Maggie McMillan, Bristol Bay Lodge, P.O. Box 6349, Anchorage, AK 99502, Tel: (907) 248–1714.

LAKE ILIAMNA

Lake Iliamna is Alaska's largest lake, located some 200 miles southwest of Anchorage, at the base of the Alaska Peninsula. The lake is seventy-five miles long and twenty miles wide, and it was once thought to be inhabited by some mysterious giant fish that have been spotted but never caught. The lake and its surrounding network of wild rivers, including the Kakhonak, Copper, Gilbratan, Kukaklik, and others, constitute a 2.75-million-acre wilderness region that is one of the most scenic in the state. To the north, the waters of Lake Clark flow into Iliamna via the Newhalen River and are a part of the Lake Clark National Park, which encompasses several million or more acres of wilderness terrain.

This is rainbow trout country.

In the late 1960s the Alaska Fish and Game Department recognized this fact and made the Iliamna area a "Trophy Fish Area." In 1978, the name was changed to "Wild Trout Area," but not the concept. To promote the propagation of rainbow trout in this region, the following restrictions were imposed:

1. Bag limits now allow only five fish with one over twenty inches. From a practical standpoint, this regulation suggests that all trout be released except one trophy fish for mounting.

The author admires a nice Copper River rainbow before releasing it.

2. Only artificial lures are allowed.
3. The season is closed on rainbow trout during their spawning season (April 10–June 7).
4. Subsistence gill net fishing by natives is regulated to reduce the take of rainbow trout to a minimum.
5. Stocking hatchery-reared trout in these waters is forbidden.

As a result of these regulations, and the cooperation of camp owners and fishing guides, the population of trophy-sized fish in these waters has increased dramatically. Anglers anticipate good trout fishing when fishing these lakes and streams, and they usually get it. Ten-pound fish are not uncommon here, especially in June and September. Rainbows in the five-pound category are commonplace.

Iliamna waters teem with other species of gamefish, too. The run of sockeye salmon in these rivers is phenomenal and lasts from late June through early August. King salmon enter these rivers a little earlier and are present during a part of the sockeye migration. Iliamna kings go to sixty pounds or more. Chum and humpback (pink) salmon follow the sockeyes, and when their run begins to taper off, the silver salmon show up. August and September is the time to catch this gamester. In addition, lake trout abound in area lakes, grayling are found in the rivers, and Dolly Varden trout are around all of the year.

A number of good fishing camps are located in this region, one of which is Valhalla Lodge. This camp is located on Six-Mile Lake, which lies between Lake Clark and Iliamna. This operator has more than a decade of experience in the sportsfishing business and uses float planes, jet boats for surface transportation, or rafts for daily float trips. The camp consists of a new main lodge and several new cabins offering completely modern guest accommodations. Hearty meals are served in the attractive dining room. Operated by the Gay family, this is a first-class facility in every respect. Valhalla is open from June 1 to September 30 and operates on a Saturday-to-Saturday basis. The price for a week of fishing is $2,900, but this includes round-trip air fare from Anchorage.

Van Valin's Island Lodge is an attractive fly-out fishing resort located on Lake Clark, within the national park of the same name. Accommodations for twenty guests are provided in five cabins with carpeted floors, comfortable beds, and private baths. The main lodge is large and attractively furnished. Meals are served family style and are tasty and well prepared. Management is excellent. Glen and Sharon Van Valin have been catering to anglers for more than twenty years and come highly recommended. This package includes the use of a float plane for daily fly-outs to surrounding hot spots, which makes fast-paced fishing almost a certainty. Pilots are trained fishing guides and stay with clients the entire day. The price for a week's fishing here is $2,500.

No See Um Lodge is a small lodge located on the Kvichak River, which drains out of Lake Iliamna and empties into Bristol Bay fifty miles farther downstream. Situated thusly, this fishing camp is in the path of some of Alaska's largest salmon runs and can offer good fishing throughout the summer. The operator owns a float plane, river boats, and rafts and is prepared to fish guests in any way they desire. Guest capacity is limited to seven, and a staff of five is available to cater to their needs. Options include daily fly-outs, floating streams otherwise inaccessible, or fishing the eighty-mile stretch of the Kvichak by jet-powered river boat. Accommodations here are new and completely modern. The main lodge houses the lounge and dining room, where well-prepared meals are served family style. This camp operates from the middle of June until the middle of October, on a Monday-to-Monday basis. It is reached from King Salmon, which is serviced by Wien from Anchorage. Price for a week's fishing is $2,700.

Iliamna River Lodge is located on the Iliamna River, in the heart of the Iliamna Wild Trout Area, and is surrounded by scenic wilderness. The region offers some of the finest rainbow-trout fishing in the state, and anglers fishing these waters frequently catch trophy trout. Itinerary features a combination of daily fly-outs, fishing floats, and fishing the Iliamna and surrounding waters by boat. Accommodations for twelve guests are provided in four cabins surrounding a main lodge. Some units have private bath facilities; others have adjacent bath facilities. Food service is first class and includes complimentary wine with evening meals. Noon meals are prepared by guides and usually consist of a shore lunch cooked over a campfire. The staff-to-guest ratio is almost one to one. This camp operates from early June to the middle of October and is priced at $2,600 for a week of fishing. Price includes air transportation from Iliamna.

For information about fishing at any of these camps, write to Glen Van Valin, Van Valin's Island Lodge, Port Alsworth, AK 99653, Tel: (907) 345–1160; Kirk Gay, Valhalla Lodge, P.O. Box 6583, Anchorage, AK 99502, Tel: (907) 276–3569; John Holman, No See Um Lodge, P.O. Box 935, Palmer, AK 99645, Tel: (907) 745–5347; or Paul Jobe, Iliamna River Lodge, 8536 Hartzell Road, Anchorage, AK 99507, Tel: (907) 349–9111.

KATMAI WILDERNESS

The Katmai National Monument, located 300 miles southwest of Anchorage, is a four-million-acre wilderness region of incomparable beauty. The backbone of the Aleutian Range with its 7,000-foot snow-capped peaks traverses the area. Nearby are the steaming fumaroles of the Valley of Ten Thousand Smokes, massive glaciers, a rugged coastline of mist-shrouded bays and surf-battered beaches, lush conifer forests, jewel-like lakes, and plunging brooks and rivers.

Here are such famed fishing waters as the Brooks River, Lake Naknek,

Katmai streams like Brooks and Kulik have long been acclaimed as some of the best in Alaska.

Grosvenor Lake, the Kulik River, and the King Salmon, Rainbow, Savonski, and Ukak Rivers. So fabulous is the rainbow-trout fishing that the area has been acclaimed as a "trophy trout area." Rainbows average slightly under five pounds, but slab-sided bows in the ten- and twelve-pound category are caught with regularity. These fish are wild, a natural strain of rainbow trout that remains untainted by mixing with hatchery strains, and they are great fighters.

The Katmai region is also host to Alaska's largest sockeye salmon run. Even in the off years, these river systems are jammed with thousands of sockeye salmon, clad in red spawning raiments, averaging six to twelve pounds. Although this species of migrating salmon is sometimes difficult to coax into taking a fly or lure, it is probably the best gamester of all the Pacific salmon. When hooked, a sockeye has the muscle for long-reel screaming runs and is considered as good an aerial acrobat as the silver salmon.

But this isn't all. Katmai streams and lakes play host to Alaska's other species of salmon, to Arctic grayling, Dolly Varden, and lake trout. The timetable is similar to that of other Alaskan streams, with the kings showing up first, followed by runs of sockeye, humpies, chum, and silvers. Lake-trout fishing is best during the first two weeks in June. Rainbows, Dolly Varden, and grayling provide the action early and late, and in between salmon runs.

The strategically located Brooks River is less than two miles long, but it is one of the most renowned angling streams in the state. This river is restricted to fly fishing only and features rainbow trout, sockeye salmon, and grayling. The first runs of sockeye arrive around July 4, and the majority of them are through spawning by the middle of September. Trout and grayling are present throughout the summer with the best trout fishing occurring before and after the salmon runs. In late August and September, Lake Naknek rainbows also enter the river to feed on salmon eggs.

Two facilities are located here, Brooks Lodge and Brooks Camp. The former is a wilderness lodge offering accommodations for forty-five guests at a modest price. The latter is a campground with ten sites, three of which contain shelters. The price for these sites is an even better deal (they're free), and they're available on a first-come–first-served basis, with a limit of ten days per stay. This campground contains a food cache in the form of a storage shed built twelve feet above the ground. Campers are urged to store food and cooking equipment in this cache to discourage marauding brown bears. There is a store where campers can purchase fishing supplies, some food, and other necessities. Incidentally, because this is a national park, no firearms are allowed. Fishing guides can be hired, and float planes can be chartered in order to fish surrounding streams and lakes. No roads reach into this area, so the only access is by float plane. Peninsula Airways offers daily service from King Salmon.

A few miles away, located between Coville and Grosvenor Lakes, is Grosvenor Camp. Not a pretentious camp, Grosvenor offers accommodations for a maximum of eight guests—basic cabin housing with shared bathroom and shower facilities. The package price of $1,500, for a week's fishing, includes meals and guided fishing by boat, but not daily fly-outs. These are available at extra cost but are not necessary.

One of Alaska's most expensive camps, Kulik Lodge is located just outside the monument, at the mouth of the Kulik River. This camp, accommodating twenty-five or so guests, offers modern accommodations and excellent fishing and has been serving discriminating fishermen since 1950. Here, the daily price includes daily fly-outs to rivers and lakes within a one-hundred-mile radius of the lodge. When the aircraft can't fly during periods of inclement weather, this lodge offers excellent local fishing.

Located near the village of King Salmon, on the Naknek River, is a new and modern camp named King Salmon Lodge. All the basic conveniences are here—wall-to-wall carpeting, indoor plumbing, laundry service, and freezer space for fish storage. Guest rooms are located in the main lodge, just steps

Remote wilderness streams, accessible only by float plane, are now floated on a regular basis.

away from the dining room and kitchen. Adjacent is a spacious lounge with a huge fireplace and bar. Meals, served family style, are gourmet quality and include complimentary wine. Incidentally, an open bar is included in the package price. The lodge has fishing licenses for sale, a camp store stocked with proven fly patterns and lures, and tackle to lend to guests who are in

need. This is a fly-out camp offering access to all of the better fishing waters of the region, but when weather is bad the Naknek offers excellent fishing locally. The price for a week's fishing at this camp is $2,500.

King Salmon is the gateway to the Katmai region and is located 300 air miles southwest of Anchorage. King Salmon is served daily by jet aircraft.

For information on Brooks Camp, write to the National Park Service, P.O. Box 7, King Salmon, AK 99613. For information about Brooks Lodge, Grosvenor Camp, or Kulik Lodge, write to Wien Air Alaska Airlines, Building G, Suite 8, 4797 Business Park Blvd., Anchorage, AK 99503. For information on King Salmon Lodge and its services and facilities, write to Mike Cusack, King Salmon Lodge, 3300 Providence Drive, Anchorage, AK 99504, Tel: (907) 562–2275.

KENAI RIVER

The Kenai River rambles for a distance of some eighty-five miles across the Kenai Peninsula to empty into Cook Inlet at the village of Kenai. Unlike most Alaskan streams, the Kenai isn't a thing of beauty. It's a big, rough river, discolored by glacier silt, with mud banks and choked with snags. Because it is one of the few places in Alaska where people can drive, anglers gather like gaggles of geese to cast globs of salmon eggs into its depths. Boats, trolling four or five lines astern, work their way back and forth through its swirling eddies. Here are people tracks, too—neon lights, motels, campgrounds, and hamburger joints. There is nothing unspoiled or virginal about the Kenai.

But despite these shortcomings, this Alaskan river is renowned worldwide. Here is where the big king salmon are. This is the place to go if you want to tangle with a 50-pounder and possibly hook into a monster king weighing eighty pounds or more. According to fisheries biologists, the Kenai has an excellent chance of breaking Alaska's present rod-and-reel record, because a fish caught in a trap a few years ago weighed 109 pounds. Kenai king salmon are consistently larger than other Alaskan salmon because they spend four years, instead of the usual three, in the ocean. This extra year in salt water certainly is a factor in these salmons' growth, and genetics possibly is too. For one or several reasons, the Kenai is the home of the world's largest king salmon.

Two runs of salmon occur here. The initial run commences around the first of June and consists of fish averaging around thirty-five pounds, with an occasional 50- or 60-pounder mixed in. This run lasts for about a month, and when it begins to taper off, a second run begins. This second run has larger fish, on the average, and is the one that attracts most of the attention. As an indicator of this popularity, it is estimated that nearly 40 percent of all sports-fishing in Alaska occurs on the Kenai Peninsula, and that the Kenai River alone accounts for 13 percent of it.

Fishing is big business on the Kenai. In 1978, there were only twenty fishing guides operating on this river, but this number has swelled to almost 200. They're successful, too. According to an Alaska Department of Fish and Game survey, professionally guided sports fishermen accounted for the majority of kings caught on rod and reel. Most of this fishing pressure occurs on the lower river below Naptowne Rapids because it's closer to civilization and has more facilities. Fishing action on the upper Kenai frequently is a little

Kenai River kings are consistently larger than other Alaskan salmon because they spend one more year in the ocean.

slower, but the area is more scenic, and there's a lot less boat traffic. But with more elbow room, I think the odds of landing a large salmon here are better than on the lower river.

Although wade fishing is a popular angling method on other Alaskan streams, most of the fishing on the Kenai is done from boats. Some anchor in likely-looking spots and still fish with salmon eggs. Others drift with the current, bouncing lures off the bottom. Still others back-troll four or five lines astern, with large flashy plugs wobbling in the current. All of these fishing methods are effective. Salmon stop feeding when they enter fresh water, but they become more irritable in this restricted environment and develop a strong territorial instinct. As a result, they attack everything that invades their migration path, or the territory that they've staked out for spawning, and this includes lures with treble hooks.

To fish the Kenai, make sure that your tackle is up to the task. This river has a six- to eight-knot current, and it takes a heavy rod and a lot of line to turn a fifty-pound salmon in a habitat like this. Furthermore, the Kenai has a lot of snags that a fish can wrap your line around. Landing a large king salmon with the proper tackle is difficult enough, so make sure that yours measures up. Rods should be a minimum of six-and-a-half feet long, constructed of fiberglass or graphite, and have enough backbone to fight a big fish. Use large-capacity spinning or casting reels (not spincast) loaded with high-visibility twenty-five-pound test line. Bring at least a pair of rigs like this, because equipment problems frequently occur when the quarry is a big fish. Lures for Kenai kings are so specialized that I recommend you wait until you get to Alaska to stock up.

From what I have been able to observe, the Kenai is subject to more fishing regulations than the average Alaskan stream. For example, in 1984 a portion of the river was closed to boat fishermen each Monday in July. Other parts of the river were restricted to single-hook lures only, and portions of Kenai tributaries were classified as fly-fishing-only waters. Last year's regulations differed from those of the year before, and they are not the same as those in effect now. Because the Kenai is heavily used and is a somewhat controversial fishery, it is doubtful that long-range regulations can be established and adhered to. It also is difficult to forecast how much longer these super-sized salmon will continue to return to the Kenai in the numbers that are present today.

The Kenai River is located 150 miles south of Anchorage and can be reached by driving to Soldotna or flying to Kenai. A variety of restaurants and motels is available in these two towns, and several campgrounds are present as well. In addition, some of the Kenai guides also offer accommodations and meals for their clients. Because a good fishing guide is essential in order to fish this river properly, I'm going to suggest several. Chris Goll, for example, is an Anchorage sporting goods store owner who provides varied facilities and services on the Kenai. Larry Suiter, who operates a local guide service and fish camp, is a first-class operator. Harry Gaines is another man in the same category, providing first-class services for a fair price. These are three good men, and they're worth looking up. The price for a day's fishing will be from $125 to $150 per person, with services varying from guide to guide.

For details on fishing the Kenai, get in touch with the following: Harry Gaines, P.O. Box 624, Kenai, AK 99611, Tel: (907) 283–4618; Larry Suiter, P.O. Box 454, Sterling, AK 99672, Tel: (907) 262–5685; or Chris Goll, 6425 Colgate Dr., Anchorage, AK 99504, Tel: (907) 333–8654. The Alaska Fish and Game Department, Subport Building, Juneau, AK 99801, can also provide additional information about this fishery. The telephone number is (907) 465–4100.

KOBUK RIVER

The sheefish, also called inconnu, is little known outside of Alaska, but it is a gamefish worthy of worldwide renown. Throughout its limited range (northern Alaska and the Yukon), this species of fish averages around ten pounds, but in the Kobuk River system it is known to reach a size of sixty pounds or more. In body conformity, the sheefish looks like a snook, but it actually is a predatory species of the whitefish family. Its body is silvery on the underside, darkening to dark silver on the back. When freshly caught it may have a purplish sheen. Its teeth are small but numerous. The scales are large like those of a tarpon. There are no spots, prominent lateral lines, or other markings.

Sheefish are anadromous, like salmon. They spend winters in the Bering Sea, and shortly after ice-out they enter one of a half-dozen rivers and begin to make their way upstream to their spawning grounds. In the Kobuk, this journey may last only a few weeks. Yukon sheefish, on the other hand, may travel 1,000 miles and spend all summer in the process. Sheefish spawn in late September and early October, laying anywhere from 100,000 to 350,000 eggs. The eggs are fertilized and sink to the bottom, where they lodge in

The sheefish is an excellent gamefish, but it also is highly prized as a food fish by Eskimo fishermen.

crevices between the stones. The eggs hatch during the long winter, and in the spring the young fry are carried downstreams, where they remain in salt water until they are old enough to migrate inland to spawn. Unlike the Pacific salmon, sheefish do not die after spawning. A sixty-pound fish, for example, may be twenty-five years old.

Because most strains of sheefish are migratory, good fishing depends on being in the right place at the right time. Early in the Alaska spring (mid-June), large schools of sheefish gather in the delta areas of such rivers as the Kobuk, Kuskowim, and Yukon, where they feed on enormous concentrations of smelt, also gathering for the run upstream. When fishing these tidal areas at this time, it is not unusual to catch more than thirty trophy-sized sheefish per day. The action is hot and heavy, but it lasts only ten days or two weeks. Mid-summer finds these fish in the middle or upper stretches of the river. Guides here follow the schools of migrating sheefish with aircraft and set up camps on gravel bars to fish these concentrations of fish. Others use rafts to float stretches of river inhabited by these fish. Later on, in August and September, schools of silvery sheefish concentrate in their spawning grounds and provide exciting sport at a scenic time of the year.

The strike of a sheefish is sudden and savage, and once hooked it puts up a spray-flinging aerial performance which rivals that of a tarpon. In this respect, it should be noted that a nickname for the sheefish is "tarpon of the Arctic." From every standpoint, the species is an outstanding gamefish.

Flashy spoons and spinning lures are attractive to sheefish and are responsible for most of the catches. But fly fishermen also do well. Medium-weight spinning and casting rods are recommended, with lure sizes dictated by the average size of the fish being caught. Reels should be loaded with twelve- to fifteen-pound test line. For fly fishing, a 9-weight rod is recommended, as is a sinking tip line and a multiplying reel spooled with 150 yards of backing. Large, gaudy flies work best. Sheefish occasionally feed on the surface in the spring, but when rivers are low and clear, they are usually taken on or near the bottom of deep pools. Lures, therefore, should have the capability of plumbing these depths.

Other species of fish are also found in the Kobuk. Grayling abound in these waters and may be taken on flies or small spinning lures. Arctic char, averaging four to ten pounds, are also present. Lake trout and northern pike are two other species of fish found in this river, in its tributaries, and in surrounding lakes.

The Kobuk River spills out into Kotzebue Sound, some 500 miles north of Anchorage. Approximately 200 miles in length, it snakes along the southern slope of the Brooks Range through some of Alaska's wildest country. For fishing the lower Kobuk, the village of Kiana is the place to go. Kiana is accessible from Kotzebue, which is served by regular flights from Anchorage. Bettles is headquarters for the middle and upper Kobuk and is best reached from Fairbanks.

Prices for fishing in this part of Alaska will vary from $150 to $300 per day, depending on to what degree float planes have to be used. Pontoon aircraft are not required in the Kiana area, but they will be necessary in order to properly fish the upper Kobuk. In the latter area, a certain amount of floating may also be required. The best time to fish the lower Kobuk is in mid-June (check with your outfitter for exact dates), and from mid-August through September farther inland.

For details on fishing the lower Kobuk, write to Lorry Schuerch, Kiana Lodge, P.O. Box 671, Kiana, AK 99749, Tel: (907) 475–2149. For the upper and middle stretches of this river, write to David Ketscher, Sourdough Outfitters, Bettles, AK 99726, Tel: (907) 692–5252; or Bernd Gaedeke, Alatna Guide Service, P.O. Box 80424, Fairbanks, AK 99708, Tel: (907) 479–6354.

KUSKOWIM BAY

Lying between the Kuskowim River and the Kilbuk Mountains is a wilderness area that is fished by probably fewer than one hundred anglers each year. Dillingham is the closest contact with the outside world and is located one hundred miles to the south. Prominent rivers are the Goodnews, the Kanetok, and the Eek, but more than a dozen other streams traverse this region, which includes the beautiful Togiak National Wildlife Refuge.

All five species of salmon ascend these rivers, offering nonstop fishing action from the time the first kings enter the streams in mid-June to the golden months of autumn when migrating silver salmon are the big attraction. Rainbow trout abound in these rivers, averaging four pounds, but are present in the ten- to twelve-pound category. Arctic grayling go up to three pounds and provide fast-paced fishing action for anglers with light fly or spinning outfits. Eight-pound Arctic char are common in June and in the fall. These aggressive gamefish eagerly take both flies and spinners, with the latter lures possibly being the most effective.

Fishing operations are few and far between in this out-of-the-way region, and one of the better ones is Ron Hyde's Alaska Rivers Safaris. Each year, Hyde sets up a posh tent camp on one of these rivers and fishes the surrounding waters from rubber rafts and jet-powered boats. This method of operation was chosen for a good reason. Alaskan rivers vary from season to season and sometimes from month to month. Last year's hot river could be slow this season, and a former average fishing stream could suddenly be the most productive in the area. A tent operation, rather than a permanent camp, allows maximum flexibility in adjusting to varying fishing conditions and assures top-notch fishing action at all times. Because Hyde selects his sites with care, the best fishing in the area frequently occurs in the pool a few yards from camp.

This tent operation is patterned after African safari setups and is first class

The rivers in this region are fished by fewer than one hundred anglers per year and contain a variety of Alaskan gamefish.

in every way. The tent is a large 25- × 40-foot dining tent that also serves as a gathering place for the camp's dozen angler guests. It is heated, of course, and comfortably furnished. Spacious 8- × 15-foot sleeping tents are designed for two persons. They're screened, have floors and doors, and are heated as well. Sanitary facilities, including hot showers, are also provided. The camp employs an experienced chef who puts out meals comparable to the best you'll ever eat at a fishing resort. Included in the menu selection are large cuts of top-quality meats, fresh salads, and home-baked breads and pastries. Noon shore lunches are prepared by guides over a fire, and freshly caught fish is usually on the menu.

Peak runs of king salmon occur the last week in June through July, and these fish average fifteen to twenty pounds in weight. Kings go to sixty pounds or more in these rivers and are frequently caught in the fifty-pound category. Occasionally these heavyweights will respond to large streamers fished deep and slow, but the majority are taken on spoons fished with spinning or casting equipment.

Silver salmon are more cooperative. They tend to hold in shallower water, can frequently be spotted with the aid of polarized sunglasses, and rise aggressively to flies. In this respect, silver salmon aren't too particular. Even poorly presented flies will be engulfed by this gamefish. Silver salmon average around ten pounds, but occasionally they are taken in the twenty-pound category. The best fishing is from the middle of August through September.

The other three species of salmon do their spawning between the king and silver runs and provide anglers fishing these waters with outstanding fishing action.

There's lots of elbow room in this part of Alaska. Fishing camps are few and far between, and most of the rivers are too small to accommodate float planes. Many of these waters might be classified as classic fly-fishing streams, easy to wade and fish with a flyrod. There is also something special about hooking a fifteen- or twenty-pound fish in a pool that looks as if it wouldn't hold a twelve-inch brookie. This is a probability when fishing these waters, and it provides a new angling dimension that is difficult to describe.

In this part of Alaska, daytime temperatures average in the 50s to mid 70s during June, July, and August. In September, the temperature averages ten degrees cooler, so warmer clothing is called for. Rain can occur at any time, so a poncho or rain jacket is indispensable. Biting insects are almost certain to be encountered, so bring plenty of repellent.

This isn't a cheap way to fish Alaska. Operator Ron Hyde doesn't have much of a fixed capital investment, but his location, limited capacity, and method of operation require substantial operating expenses. As a result, the tab for a week's fishing here is approximately what it will cost at one of Alaska's more plush fishing camps.

The gateway for this region is Dillingham, which is reached by jet flights from Anchorage. Because space is limited, make reservations as far in advance as possible.

Information on this type of fishing can be obtained from Ron Hyde, Alaska River Safaris, 4909 Rollins Drive, Anchorage, AK 99504, Tel: (907) 333–2860. For information on other camps in the area, write to the Alaska State Division of Tourism, Pouch E–28, Juneau, AK 99811.

NATIONAL FORESTS

Some of Alaska's national forests are worthy of inclusion here because they offer quality accommodations for the unheard-of price of $70 per week. In a party of two, this is $35 per head—$17.50 each if the group numbers four persons.

The Forest Service facilities are well-built cabins tucked away on wilderness lakes and streams. They're equipped with rudimentary furniture and stoves that suffice for heating and cooking, they have outhouses, and most of them include a small boat for fishing. Sure, they're rustic, but they're bug-

Comfortable Forest Service cabins, available throughout much of Alaska, are this state's best vacation bargain.

and bear-proof and are located in spots noted for good fishing and scenic beauty. You also have to admit that the price is right.

Thirty-five of these cabins are located in the Chugach National Forest, which occupies almost five million acres in southcentral Alaska. This chunk of government property includes part of the Kenai Peninsula, a stretch of coast fronting Prince William Sound, and the delta of the glacier-spawned Copper River. The Chugach Mountains lie immediately to the north, forming a scenic backdrop to a one-hundred-mile-long stretch of wilderness. Anchorage, of course, is the gateway to this region.

One example of what's available here is a 12 x 14 foot log cabin located on Hawkins Island in Prince William Sound. This is an A-frame structure, with two double bunks that will comfortably accommodate four persons. It is accessible by both boat and float plane, and its location offers excellent fishing for several species of salmon, and stream fishing for rainbow trout and Dolly Varden. The closest town is Cordova, located twenty miles to the east.

The Tongass National Forest, the nation's largest, occupies 16 million acres and includes the majority of southeastern Alaska. A pristine wilderness, it is a morass of forested islands, secluded bays, mist-shrouded fjords, rugged mountains, and living glaciers. Several towns, including Ketchikan and the capital city of Juneau, are included within its borders. Major islands are Admiralty, Baranof, and Prince of Wales. A total of 135 Forest Service cabins are available for rent here.

Located thirty-five miles from Juneau, on the north end of Admiralty Island, is the West Turner cabin. This facility is a log chalet, furnished with four bunks and both a wood-burning stove and a fireplace. Excellent fishing is available for cutthroat and Dolly Varden trout, and a skiff is included in the rental price.

The Helm Bay unit is located some distance to the south, and approximately twenty-four air miles from Ketchikan. This is a spacious 16 x 20 foot log cabin, built in 1978, that can accommodate four persons. A variety of fishing is available here. Bugge Lake offers fishing action for western brook trout (a brook and Dolly Varden hybrid), and other lakes in the area are populated with cutthroat. Helm Lake offers excellent sockeye fishing in the summer and a run of silver salmon in early fall. Crab fishing at the upper end of Helm Bay is productive, as is fishing for red snapper near the bay's entrance.

The Shipley Bay rental unit is located on Prince of Wales Island, eighty-five miles from Ketchikan. It is a 12 x 14 foot precut cedar cabin equipped with a stove and two double bunks. Shipley Creek and Lake have good cutthroat, rainbow, and Dolly Varden fishing, plus runs of pink, chum, and sockeye salmon. This facility is accessible by both boat and air. A fourteen-foot aluminum boat is included.

These are just a few examples. In these two national forests, there are a total of 170 Forest Service cabins available for rent for a fee of $10 per night. Stays are limited to one week.

When renting one of these units you have to pack in everything you'll need, including the following: food for seven days, foam pads for the wooden bunks, sleeping bags, tableware, cooking utensils, fishing tackle, boat cushions, and life preservers. You might also consider bringing a small outboard for the boat, and enough gas to power it for the time you'll be there. Some of the cabins have oil-burning stoves, and if you rent one of these you'll have to bring in a quantity of heating oil. Oil use will vary from between a half-gallon to five gallons per day, depending on the season.

Because you'll be on your own, I suggest that you equip yourself for possible emergencies. Bring a large-scale map of the area, a compass, a waterproof container of matches, a strong knife, a first-aid kit, a space blanket, candles, an axe, and even a gun. If the firearm is a rifle, make it no less than 30.06 caliber. A twelve-gauge shotgun loaded with slugs is equally comforting to have along. Make sure you include a fillet knife to clean your fish, and plenty of everything because schedules frequently go awry in Alaska. Inclement weather can delay a pickup by aircraft and turn a week's wilderness stay into one of ten days or more.

Most of the expense involved with one of these wilderness stays will be in transportation, and this cost can be split up among all members of your party. Whether you get to your cabin by boat or air, the cost is going to be a fraction of that of a normal week's fishing trip in Alaska. Figure several hundred dollars per person for supplies and transportation, instead of the usual thousand or so.

The Forest Service makes it easy to rent one of its cabins. On request, the Service will send you an information packet containing colorful literature, including maps, site descriptions, access information, and a list of the species of fish available in the area. Included will be a permit application on which you'll list three choices of cabins desired, and the date you'd like to rent one. When you mail this permit you'll include the rental fee. If one of the cabins you've requested is not available when you want it, this fee will be returned. Once you have your permit, you can then make access arrangements with one of the operators whom a local Ranger District office might recommend. In actuality, booking a trip of this nature is not much more complicated than making a reservation at a conventional Alaskan fishing camp.

For complete details on the Forest Service's rental cabins in the Tongass and Chugach National Forests, write to the Forest Service Information Center, Centennial Hall, 101 Egan Drive, Juneau, AK 99801.

PAINTER CREEK

The Painter Creek watershed is a chunk of wilderness that most Alaskans don't even know about yet. It is tucked away between two mountain ranges far out on the Alaskan Peninsula, 450 air miles from Anchorage and one hundred miles south of King Salmon. It is a region of untouched wilderness, laced with sparkling streams that offer untouched fishing.

Painter Creek gamefish are not only numerous, they also come in man-sized packages. King salmon reach fifty pounds in this watershed, and the silvers will top out at around seventeen pounds. Trophy-sized rainbows abound here, and steelhead average eight pounds. Arctic char, Dolly Varden, and Arctic grayling inhabit all of these streams, too, and they reach trophy proportions.

The best trout fishing occurs in the spring (June), before the salmon enter the streams. At this time the rainbows are concentrated, and anglers can experience strike-per-cast fishing action for as long as their arms can take it. According to those who have experienced it, this may be the hottest rainbow-trout fishing in the state.

King salmon begin to arrive in this region the first of July and remain until the middle of August. Char, Dolly Varden, and grayling provide fishing action through September and share these waters at this time with schools of red,

Painter Creek salmon are abundant and come in man-size packages.

pink, and chum salmon. Then, in September, the runs of silver salmon begin to arrive, and the rainbow trout return to feed on their spawn and compete for anglers' lures.

The only camp in the entire region is Painter Creek Lodge, which is tucked away in a sun-kissed valley between two ranges of mountains. Painter Creek is new and will accommodate only a half-dozen guests. But it is a first-class fishing camp in every respect. Guests are housed in comfortable cabins with private baths, and a spacious main lodge provides space for lounging and dining. Meals are excellent and include dinner wines.

In addition to the main lodge, the management has located wilderness camps on other streams in the area. These camps consist of 10 x 12 foot sleeping tents, a shower tent with hot and cold running water, and a large tent that houses both the kitchen and dining facilities. Guests can fish at two different wilderness camp locations during the week for a variety of fish species and angling experiences. Each camp has a capacity for six guests.

Lodge guests fishing these waters will see no other anglers during their stay, because the camp's private airstrip offers the only access in and out of the region. This is the case because the streams in the area are too small and winding for float planes to land on.

Painter Creek is owned and operated by J. G. Smith, a former Fish and Wildlife Officer with sixteen years of professional experience. An ardent angler, Smith has explored and fished all of Alaska's waters and feels that his location on the Alaska Peninsula represents the ultimate Alaskan angling experience. At any rate, Smith is a highly competent camp manager, and he provides first-class administration and service.

Despite its remote location, Painter Creek is reasonably accessible. To get there, take one of a number of commercial flights to Anchorage, and then a connecting flight to King Salmon. From there, the lodge will provide transportation the remaining one hundred miles to the camp airstrip.

Temperatures on the Central Alaskan Peninsula range from the mid 40s to the high 70s from June through September, and somewhat lower in October. From late June through July there are more than twenty hours of daylight per day. Coastal influences may create rapid weather changes, including wind, rain, and low-lying clouds. Anticipate some rain during your stay in this part of Alaska.

In the clothing line, bring lightweight chest waders, rain gear, long underwear, an insulated jacket, wool shirts and sweaters, socks, walking shoes or boots, a hat and gloves, and a sleeping bag (for wilderness camps). Include a fishing vest, camera and film, plenty of insect repellent, polarized sunglasses, and a belt knife.

For king salmon, bring 9-weight fly outfits with both sinking and floating lines; bring lighter gear for trout and other salmon. Popular fly patterns include muddlers, polar shrimp, sculpins, and bright-colored streamers. For spinning, bring at least two outfits capable of handling the type and size fish you'll be fishing for. Bring extra line and a selection of spinners and small spoons. The management, or its representative, will send you a complete list of tackle and clothing recommendations when you make your reservation.

Painter Creek Lodge offers Saturday-to-Saturday fishing packages from the middle of June through the first week in October. The price is $2,700 and includes lodging, meals, complimentary wines, and daily fishing using the camp's equipment, aircraft, and boats.

For details, write to Bob Edwards, Edwards Outdoors, 601 N.W. Loop 410, Suite 110, San Antonio, Texas 78216, Tel: (512) 349–3791. For general information on Alaska and its fishing potential, write to the Alaska State Division of Tourism, Pouch E–28, Juneau, AK 99811.

THE PANHANDLE

Southeastern Alaska is a narrow strip of coastline stretching from the Malaspina Glacier southward for a distance of 500 miles to Ketchikan. A maze of islands, channels, and bays, it is one of the least known and most beautiful regions in North America. Thick stands of tall spruce, nurtured by bountiful rainfall and mild winters, cloak the islands and mountain slopes. Glaciers glisten like jewels in the backs of the fjords; crystalline streams tumble down from inland heights. Wildlife abounds here—eagles, shorebirds, bear, moose, and graceful Sitka deer. Huge schools of salmon clog the streams on their spawning runs. No roads connect the towns and villages of this region, but it's very accessible, much closer to the lower forty-eight than the rest of Alaska.

This part of the state is steeped in history and legend, of colorful Chilkat and Tlingit Indians, former Russian rule, Juneau's romance of the Gold Rush. It's interesting and different, offering much to see and many things to do. But, once you've seen the Indian totem poles, viewed the awesome glaciers at Glacier Bay, and toured the waterfront in Ketchikan, it's time to get down to some serious fishing. Southeastern Alaska is the place to catch king and silver salmon before they ascend rivers to spawn, it's the place to do battle with giant halibut, and it offers excellent trout and steelhead fishing as well.

I first got acquainted with halibut at Glacier Bay. We had caught and released hundreds of salmon while fishing the Talchulitna several days earlier, and now we were on our way home. Glacier Bay looked like a good place to see a glacier, pick up a few salmon to take home for the freezer, and relax for a day or so. We had accomplished these objectives. The previous day we had boarded the *Thunder Bay* launch for a cruise to Muir, and today we already had our limit of salmon in the stern box.

"How about halibut?" the skipper asked.

"What about 'em?" I replied. I had heard of the species but never realized it was much of a gamefish.

The skipper grinned, gold tooth flashing in the sunlight. "I'll show you," he said.

A half-hour later we were back in a deep bay, bouncing heavy yellow jigs off the bottom, munching on ham sandwiches and sipping a little beer. Suddenly, my friend's rod was almost jerked out of his hand, and he dropped beer and sandwich to keep his rod from going over the gunwale. Now, with the rod butt buried in his midsection, all he could do was hold on as the line melted off the reel. Finally, as the spool slowed, he grunted, "What the hell."

The skipper's gold tooth glittered again as his thin lips parted in a grin. "Halibut," he announced. "Could be a nice 'un."

My friend's catch was hardly of barn-door proportions, but it did top the scales at sixty-pounds, and it kept him busy for half an hour. Gaffing the fish at the side of the boat, the lean skipper worked it over pretty well with a club before hoisting it aboard. Later I learned that a live halibut in the boat is bad news.

In these waters Pacific halibut average less than fifty pounds, but catches between 100 and 200 pounds are rather common. The largest taken on a rod and reel weighed 400 pounds and was caught in 1980. Halibut are gamefish.

Saltwater fishermen catch king and silver salmon and halibut up to one hundred pounds.

Their strike is sudden and savage, and they put up a tough fight before they can be beat. Equally important, I don't think there's a better food fish in the Pacific. In this respect, the halibut is superior to salmon.

A check of these waters reveals that all species of salmon spawn here, with the most action coming from the silvers and kings. Fishing here is done by trolling in salt water, which means that the fish are still feeding, are in good fighting form, and are excellent table fare. Look for kings up to sixty pounds but averaging thirty, silver salmon in the twelve-pound category, and other species of salmon in their normal size range.

A two-pound grayling is a good fish in this part of Alaska, and rainbow trout are somewhat smaller than they are in the Katmai region. Steelheading is good, however. Prince of Wales streams offer excellent late-fall steelhead fishing with catches averaging seven pounds. Farther up the coast in the Yakutat vicinity, rivers like the Situk and Alsek offer even faster-paced action with fish going up to seventeen pounds. Cutthroat trout are present also but average less than three pounds. Like Dungeness crabs? Come in July and August and harvest your own.

Bell Island used to be one of the best fishing spots in the Panhandle, but recently the only resort on the island was turned into a private club and thus is no longer available to the public. If you can wangle an invitation, though, be sure to go.

Although Glacier Bay Lodge is visited primarily by lookers instead of doers, it maintains a fleet of good fishing cruisers operated by experienced skippers. Salmon and halibut are both plentiful in these waters, and excellent fishing results can be anticipated. This resort, incidentally, is located within the Glacier Bay National Monument and is a first-class facility in every respect. Including transportation from Juneau, the tab for a fishing package here is less than $250 per day. Accommodations are included in this package deal, but not meals. They're available from a varied menu in the lodge dining room.

Another good fishing spot is Prince of Wales Lodge, located near the village of Klawock on Prince of Wales Island. This is a quality facility offering modern accommodations, tasty meals, and both saltwater and freshwater fishing. For salmon and huge halibut, anglers are fished in cabin cruisers operated by experienced skippers. Rainbow, Dolly Varden, and cutthroat trout abound in all of the island streams, and these spots can be reached by both boat and land vehicle. Tackle, technique, and fishing methods are a matter of choice at this camp, with each day's activities tailored specifically to a guest's desires. This camp can accommodate twenty-four guests and is accessible by float plane from Ketchikan. A choice of three-, four-, and seven-night fishing packages is available, with the seven-night trip priced at less than $1,600 from June through September. The lodge is also open in April and May, and in October, which are prime fishing periods for trophy-sized steelhead. Silver-salmon fishing is good in the early fall, and the best fishing for chinooks (king salmon) is in May. The price for early and late fishing is considerably less.

Also located on Prince of Wales Island is the Waterfall Resort, which formerly was the largest salmon cannery in this part of Alaska. Now completely remodeled into a posh fishing camp, Waterfall has all of the ingredients of a first-class angling facility. Living accommodations are modern and attractively furnished, and meals are tasty and well prepared; there's a bar and lounge, a billiard room, exercise facilities, and after-dinner movies. This camp offers saltwater fishing only and uses twenty-foot outboard-powered cruisers for this purpose. King, silver, sockeye, and pink salmon are the featured gamefish here, with a certain amount of attention given to halibut as well. Five days of fishing costs $1,600 here, but this price includes charter air transportation from Ketchikan. The season is from June 1 through August.

Alaska Sportfishing Packages operates Glacier Bay fishing packages and acts as a booking agent for Prince of Wales, Waterfall, and a number of other Alaskan camps. Write to this firm at 1500 Metropolitan Park Building, Seattle, WA 98101, Tel: 1–800–426–0603. Waterfall Resort can be reached direct by writing Waterfall Resort, P.O. Box 6440, Ketchikan, AK 99901, Tel: 1–800–544–5125. Prince of Wales Lodge can be contacted at P.O. Box 72, Klawock, AK 99925, Tel: (907) 755–2227. Additional details on fishing in southeastern Alaska can be obtained from the Alaska Department of Commerce, Division of Tourism, Pouch E, Juneau, AK 99811.

UNALAKLEET RIVER

The streamer fly landed on the surface of the water and slowly began to drift downstream into the long pool. As it passed a submerged boulder the size of a living room, a torpedo-shaped salmon came up from the depths and engulfed the gaudy fly. I set the hook instinctively, and a silver-sided salmon immediately became airborne.

Jumping once, twice, three times in succession, the salmon then steamed downstream, scattering other fish in its path. With the backing on my reel showing, I knew that the fish would be lost if it made the white-water chute below the pool. So I followed, booted feet stumbling over boulders strewn along the bank, arched rod held over my head, muscles straining, perhaps uttering a few expletives in the process. A half-hour later, I beached the salmon, scaled it at eighteen pounds, and released it to continue on its mission upstream.

The Unalakleet River possibly has the most intense silver-salmon run in Alaska. Around the first of August, multitudes of these fish enter the river and remain there until the middle of September. During this period, these salmon virtually jam the Unalakleet in schools of thousands. They strike flies and spinning lures with savage abandon and put up a powerful fight each time they're hooked. Unalakleet silvers average between eight and twenty pounds.

Chum salmon are present in the river prior to and during the early stages of

Located apart from other Alaskan fishing waters, the Unalakleet River has the most intense silver-salmon run in the state.

the silver-salmon run and also make a contribution to the Unalakleet's fishing action. Chum are strong fish, fighting a dogged battle when hooked, difficult to handle when they get in a current. These fish average between seven and ten pounds.

Pink salmon, also called humpbacked salmon, commence their spawning run the latter part of June and provide fast-paced angling action through July. Humpies average less than five pounds and so should be taken on fly equipment or light spinning gear. In the Unalakleet, they strike everything that hits the water, allowing anglers to catch fish until their arms ache. For their size, these pink-fleshed salmon are strong fighters.

King salmon arrive on the scene first, providing angling action from early June to the middle of July. Powerful fish, these Unalakleet kings can go up to sixty pounds and average half this size.

The Unalakleet has no rainbow trout, but it is populated with grayling, Arctic char, and Dolly Varden. During the first week of August, when the pink salmon are on the spawning beds, char jam the Unalakleet by the thousands. These fish weigh four to six pounds and readily strike both lures and flies. Want to catch a fish on every cast? This is the place and time to do it.

Located apart from most of Alaska's other salmon rivers, the Unalakleet empties into Norton Sound some 400 miles north of Anchorage. As a result of this remote location, these waters have little fishing pressure. No float planes land here. There is only one fishing camp on the entire river.

Silvertip Lodge is located ten miles from the mouth of the Unalakleet and is one of the state's most attractive fishing facilities. Situated on a knoll on a bend of the river is an eighty-foot-long lodge built of spruce logs. This large structure houses a spacious lounge with a fireplace, a bar, and dining and kitchen facilities. Guest accommodations are provided at the foot of the hill in cabins. A centrally located bath house has shower and toilet facilities. The food is excellent at this well-managed fishing camp, and a well-stocked open bar offers a new dimension in hospitality. Wine is served with the noon and evening meals. As mentioned previously, the main lodge is one of the most attractive in the state. Regrettably, the camp's guest accommodations are not comparable. Guests are limited to twenty.

This is not a fly-out camp, and it doesn't need to be one. As I have pointed out, gamefish are present at all times and are usually located a short distance up and down the river from camp. Because salt water is so close, the salmon caught here are usually in good condition and put up a hard fight. Boats are used to get from one fishing hole to another. An experienced guide is provided for every two anglers.

A week of fishing at Silvertip costs $2,500 and includes lodging, all meals, an open bar, transfers from the village of Unalakleet (ten miles downstream), a guide for every two persons, use of a fishing boat, fishing license, use of hip boots, fishing equipment, flies, and spinning lures. Unlike most other fishing camps, Silvertip provides fishing tackle, and from what I could observe the quality of this gear was good. I still recommend bringing your own equipment, however. Needed is a heavy fly or spinning rod for king salmon, and lighter gear for other Unalakleet fish. Hip boots are provided by the lodge, but I found that chest waders allow more latitude in fishing the pools of this river. Particularly recommended are the lightweight stocking foot waders (made by Red Ball), which are more comfortable to wear than normal waders. The Unalakleet has a gravel bottom, so felt soles are not necessary. Bring plenty of warm clothing, rain gear, and insect repellent. Because mosquitoes abound in the low-lying cabin area you may want to burn a small quantity of Buhack in your cabin before retiring. The smoke from this pyrethrum product kills mosquitoes on contact.

For information on fishing the Unalakleet, write to Silvertip Lodge, P.O. Box 6389, Anchorage, AK 99502, Tel: (907) 243–1416.

WILDERNESS FLOAT TRIPS

You stand a chance of getting wet or having a brush with a brown bear, but a float trip is the best way I know of to savor Alaska's true wilderness and catch a lot of fish.

It all starts at some remote lake where a float plane lets you off and then departs in a roaring rush of spray. You're alone except for a guide and perhaps a friend. On the rocky lake shore is a hillock of gear—food for seven days, tents, sleeping bags, cooking equipment, a rubber raft to be inflated, fishing tackle of every description. An eagle soars overhead, replacing the aircraft, which has disappeared behind a cloud-shrouded range of hills. A few raindrops patter on your shoulders, and you realize that it's time to get going.

It doesn't look as if all that gear and three people will fit in the raft, but somehow it and they do and you're paddling for the stream spilling out of the little lake. The current grips the rubber doughnut, and as you shoot your first foam-flecked rapids you realize that your Alaskan floatfishing adventure has begun.

Three riverbends downstream, at the junction of another stream, the guide beaches the raft on a gravel bar, and you reach for your fishing rod.

"First things first," he warns. "Let me take a look first."

"For what?"

"Bear tracks," he replies. Clambering up the gravel slope in booted feet, he adds, "If the place is occupied, we'll stop someplace else."

In this case it wasn't, and in a few moments you're fast to a silvery-colored salmon that vaults two feet out of the water in a shower of spray. He's a bright fish, still fresh from the sea and full of fight. All around are other salmon that are not, though. They have donned their spawning colors of reds and browns, and their jaws have become hooked and adorned with snaggled teeth. You can see them working in the shallows, distributing their spawn over the gravel bottom, fulfilling their mission and destiny. You're still fast to your fish, though, and when you finally bring him gasping up on the bar, you gently extract the rose-colored fly and nudge the fish back into the water again.

At the end of the day, your guide stops to make camp. After he inspects the bar for possible bear signs, the raft is unloaded, tents are erected, a fire is built, and the evening meal is prepared. After the thick steaks have been grilled and consumed, there is the murmur of the river in the background, flickering northern lights, the warmth of the fire, and lots of conversation about fish caught and lost. And, after a day on the river, sleep comes easily, despite the rumble of thunder in the distance or the thought that a marauding bear might visit the camp during the night.

Depending on the stream being floated, some outfitters float a specified distance each day, fishing as they go, pausing for lunch, and changing camp-sites each night. On other occasions, more permanent camps may be set up and two or more nights spent there. Length has something to do with how a stream is floated also. Floats of almost any length are possible, I suppose, but the most popular are the five-, seven-, and ten-day trips.

One outfitter, Paul Holland, floats a number of streams, depending on the species of fish desired and the time of the year. During the first two weeks in June, trophy-sized rainbow trout and grayling are the quarry. For the next six weeks, available species of fish include trout and grayling with the addition of king and sockeye salmon. During August, another river is used, and it yields char, lake trout, and chum salmon, as well as trout and grayling. And in September, the accent is on the big rainbows that have followed the spawning salmon upstream, grayling, and silver salmon that spawn at this time of year. The rivers that Holland floats include the Gulkana, the Kanektok, the Chilikadrotna, the Talachulitna, and Talachulitna Creek. Other good streams are the Goodnews, the Togiak, the Brooks, the Mulchatna, and the Naknek.

Floating is not for everyone. Ice cubes won't be available for your pre-dinner cocktails, and there won't be any ice cream or freshly baked apple pie for dessert. Meals will be bountiful, but because they're prepared over an open fire, don't expect gourmet cuisine. The opportunity to be wet and cold exists on every float. The temperature can drop suddenly with the passage of a cold front, gale-force winds blow frequently, and rain is always a possibility. Tents are small in size and offer little protection from wind, rain, and biting insects. When you're at the mercy of the elements, inclement weather can be downright unpleasant.

On the other hand, I think that a float trip is the ultimate way to see and savor Alaska with a fishing rod in hand. It offers an opportunity to get off the beaten path and fish waters not accessible by any other means. It usually means great fishing action. A person is gambling, of course, but the weather can be perfect. A float trip is also one of Alaska's biggest bargains, and they're hard to come by in this part of the world.

Most outfitters furnish everything—float plane transportation in and out of

Remote waters, like this small lake, are accessible only by float plane and are frequently overlooked by anglers.

the wilderness, rafts for floating, competent guides, tents, sleeping bags and foam pads, cooking and camping equipment, and all food. The price for a week in the field will vary from outfitter to outfitter, and possibly with the river floated, but anticipate paying from $1,500 to $1,700 per person in a party of two or more. Anchorage is the gateway for most of Alaska's best float streams. Figure on going from the middle of June through September.

For more details on floating a number of Alaskan streams, write to Paul Holland, Alaska River Guides, Star Route C, Box 8867, Palmer, AK 99645, Tel: (907) 345–1160. For details on floating the Talachulitna and Chelatna Rivers, get in touch with Silvertip Lodge, P.O. Box 6389, Anchorage, AK 99502, Tel: (907) 243–1416. An economical Lake Creek float is available from Lake Creek Lodge, P.O. Box 8–229, Anchorage, AK 99508, Tel: (907) 333–7692. For floats in the Iliamna region, write to Wildalaska Outfitting Co., 8536 Hartzell Road, Suite 32, Anchorage, AK 99507, Tel: 349–9111.

Canada 3

Canada is a sizable chunk of real estate. It occupies 3,851,809 square miles at the top of the North American continent and, as countries go, is second in size only to the Soviet Union. It fronts three oceans, is traversed by a dozen great river systems, and is dotted by thousands of lakes. It is a land of mountains, forests, vast stretches of tundra, and a slab of glacier-scarred granite known as the Pre-Cambrian Shield. Because most of this nation's 22 million people are clustered along the U.S. border, wilderness and plenty of elbow room abound elsewhere.

More than a million Americans cross the Canadian border each year with a fishing rod in hand. Some wing their way northward to the Northwest Territories in pursuit of trophy-size lake trout. Others probe foam-flecked rapids for

The incomparable shore lunch can be one of the highlights of a Canadian fishing trip.

grayling, rainbows, and slab-sided brookies. Most cast or troll for popular species such as northern pike, walleye, or smallmouth bass. Facilities vary greatly. There are deluxe fly-in lodges, inexpensive housekeeping camps, outpost facilities, packages built around aircraft, houseboats, or canoe treks. From every standpoint, Canada is an angling-oriented tourist destination unequaled elsewhere in the world. ✎

Northwest Territories

The Northwest Territories, an Arctic region, occupies more than a million square miles of forest and tundra and stretches 2,000 miles from one ocean to the other. It's the land of the great white bear, the Eskimo, and migrating herds of caribou. It also is the place where anglers gather each summer to do battle with Arctic gamefish.

Lake trout abound in these frigid lakes and are caught on or near the surface throughout the season. Lakers average around ten pounds in this polar habitat, but larger trophy fish are plentiful. A record 65-pounder was taken from Great Bear Lake a few years ago, and larger fish will undoubtedly be caught as anglers continue to explore these far-north waters.

Arctic char are found in the clear, turbulent streams that spill into the Arctic Ocean, and they grow to trophy proportions. For example, one river has set five world records in the last several years and now holds it with a fish exceeding thirty pounds in size. Beautiful, wild, the crimson-sided char is an outstanding gamefish.

Graceful Arctic grayling are found in most Northwest Territory streams, where they are readily taken on flies and small spinning lures. Most average less than two pounds, but trophy fish exceeding five pounds are known to exist here.

Northern pike don't receive the angling attention that they do in other provinces, but trophy-sized pike still inhabit some of these waters.

Western Canada

Canada's western provinces have more in common with Alaska than the rest of the country. This is mountainous terrain, a scenic region of snow-capped peaks, lush forests, and high-country lakes. It is the land of the grizzly bear, elk, and mountain lion, but it also belongs to Pacific salmon, cutthroat, and Kamloops trout. Like the rest of Canada, this is fishing country.

All five species of Pacific salmon ascend British Columbia streams and are taken by sports fishermen in both salt and fresh water. Steelhead, which are sea-going rainbows, average sixteen pounds in some rivers and are renowned for their fighting ability. High-country streams and lakes offer world-class fishing for several species of trout.

Central Canada

The unspoiled wilderness region of central Canada is traversed by several large river systems and dotted with thousands of pristine lakes. It is the land of the moose and the bear, the domain of eagles, a place of scenic splendor. Unspoiled fishing country, this is the part of Canada that most American anglers visit when they head north.

The northern pike is the principal gamefish in this region, and it is known to attain a size of forty pounds or more. Weed beds are favorite places to catch pike, and there is no shortage of this type of habitat in this part of Canada.

Almost as popular is the walleye, which averages less than five pounds but can go to twenty pounds or more. A favorite food fish for Canadian shore lunches, walleye tend to gather in large schools and are relatively easy to catch when located.

Muskellunge, weighing up to sixty pounds, occupy a limited range in the sourthern and western part of Ontario. Muskies have much in common with northern pike, but they are considerably more wary and difficult to catch.

The smallmouth bass is native to parts of Manitoba and Ontario, and pound for pound it may be this continent's best gamefish. The smallmouth prefers rocky shorelines and the connecting waterways between lakes. Average catch is around three pounds.

Lake trout and grayling, both coldwater fish, are most abundant in the northern reaches of this region, with grayling frequenting the streams, and lake trout deeper lakes. Best fishing for lake trout is early in the season, before they retreat to the depths.

More common farther east, brook trout are found in some central Canadian streams and grow to trophy proportions in these waters.

Eastern Canada

Although a multitude of people reside in this region, or adjacent to it, the northern reaches of Quebec and Labrador are still wild and beautiful. Some streams in this region offer the best Atlantic salmon fishing in the world. Lake trout and char are native to these waters, and the brook-trout fishing can be sensational in some of this area's streams and lakes. Quebec also offers angling for pike, walleye, and smallmouth bass.

Fly-In Fishing

Because roads are few and far between in the northern portions of Canadian provinces, fishing camps located here are accessible only by float plane.

What does this mean?

Fly-in waters normally receive less fishing pressure than those that can be reached by car, so one would think that the fishing would be better in the more remote locations. By and large this is true, but the big difference usually lies with the size of fish caught, not the actual number boated. Fishing pressure may or may not thin the ranks of certain species of fish, but it certainly does reduce the number of trophy-sized specimens. If you're primarily interested in catching a large pike or lake trout for your den wall, I suggest that you consider a fly-in fishing camp.

Fly-in fishing camps have a few disadvantages, however, and the primary one is cost. It costs more to construct a remote fly-in camp, for instance. And because everything must be flown in by aircraft, it costs more to equip it, too. A fly-in camp has to generate its own electricity, operate with a radio communication system, and spend more money on sales promotion and advertising.

A ten-ounce steak that has a $2.50 price tag in your local supermarket will cost a Cree Lake camp operator a minimum of $10 before he can serve it to a customer. A fishing lure that you can buy for a few dollars will probably be sold for twice that amount if the camp store is to realize a profit on the transaction. Guides are more expensive in remote locations, so are boats, motor repairs and parts . . . everything.

These additional costs have to be passed on to the customer, so fly-in camps are necessarily more expensive. Some cost twice as much as a drive-in operation, some even more than that.

Does the difference in fishing justify the extra cost? The answer to this question is both yes and no. If money is no object and the trip can be written off as a business expense, a fly-in trip is recommended. The same situation is true if you want a trophy fish suitable for mounting, or you're looking for a once-in-a-lifetime outing. Want to catch Arctic char, grayling, Atlantic salmon, or lake trout in shallow water? You have no option other than a fly-in trip.

Resorts and lodges accessible by road still do a lot of business, though. One example is Forest Lake Lodge in Ontario. At this comfortable anglers' resort, our family of four enjoyed a week of fishing for what a comparable stay would cost one person in a Northwest Territories camp. The facilities were first class, the food was great, and the service was superb. Perhaps we had to work a little harder for our fish, but we still caught our limit of walleye and had a little action with muskellunge as a bonus. For a relaxing family vacation, this was the ticket.

Bugs That Bite

Canada has 'em, a host of biting insects that includes blackflies, oversized mosquitoes, and both deer- and horseflies. All of them are pests, and on occasion they can be a downright nuisance.

Blackflies are the worst, in my opinion. These tiny winged insects arrive on the scene shortly after ice-out and make their presence known for a period of several weeks. Mosquitoes and other biting bugs are around for the entire summer but appear to be particularly voracious early in the season.

Anglers fishing central Canadian lakes should experience few problems with insects, because most of their time is spent in boats on the water. Portages are an exception, expecially those that wind their way through dark, damp stands of thick timber. On occasions such as this, hiking anglers are so laden down with tackle and equipment that they don't have a free hand to defend themselves with. Fishermen wading forest or tundra streams or fishing for salmon, grayling, or trout are also easy marks for biting bugs.

As a result of this potential insect problem, most fishing camps are located on islands or the points of peninsulas, which have water on three sides and are thus relatively insect free. On an unusually still night, a few mosquitoes may do a little foraging around camp, but this is the exception, not the rule.

Don't go to Canada without insect repellent, though. Little bottles of cream repellent, Off!, Cutter, Bens, and the others are handy to carry in a pocket or keep in a tackle box. Spray cans are more suitable for evening application or in preparation for a foray into mosquito territory.

Head nets may also be helpful in warding off biting insects. I don't like the darn things, but then I've seen times when the mosquitoes were thick enough to make one welcome.

That Shore Lunch

Some people believe that the best thing about a Canadian fishing trip is that daily shore lunch, and I'm inclined to agree with them.

Fishing guides, whether they are Indian natives or fast-learning college students, are usually adept at filleting fish and frying them to perfection over an open campfire. It's another reason for hiring a guide, and unless you like slaving over a hot bed of coals, it's a valid one.

A primary prerequisite to this happening is catching enough fish to eat for lunch. Fail to do this, and the meal may consist of an onion sandwich, a helping of pork and beans, and perhaps half of a canned peach . . . slim pickin's for a hearty appetite spawned by a morning on a Canadian lake.

For two anglers and a guide, several three-pound walleye are just about right. Trout are also shore-lunch fare, and a seven-pound northern pike will do just as well. These fish are transformed into boneless fillets with a few strokes of the guide's knife and when dumped into a brown paper bag containing salt, pepper, and a cup of flour. In the meantime, coffee is boiling in a fire-blackened pail, and a half-pound of lard (that's right, lard) is melting in the heavy cast-iron skillet. When the grease is hot, the flour-coated fillets are placed in the skillet with a sharpened stick and come out minutes later as crisp, golden-brown delicacies that would be impossible to duplicate in a modern kitchen. Add a helping of pork and beans, a slice of sweet onion, and a piece of bread toasted over the coals, and you have a feast beyond compare.

Several factors contribute to the perfection of this gastronomic happening.

Perhaps it's the taste of freshly caught fish. Perhaps it's the scent of spruce needles in the air, the sight of an eagle soaring overhead, a ravenous appetite, or the scenic surroundings. Most likely it's all of these things added together. Regardless, this experience is one more reason to head north on a Canadian fishing trip, and I heartily recommend it.

Wind and Weather

Canadian weather, particularly above the 50th Parallel, has many moods and dimensions. What may begin as a cloudless day with a glassy calm lake surface can be overcast and spitting rain by noon, and cold enough for an insulated jacket when you head for camp at the day's end. Frontal movements march across the horizon with regularity, draping the sky with ever-changing cloud formations and bringing about wide fluctuations in barometric pressure and wind direction. According to the locals, if you don't like the weather in these parts, wait five minutes.

Because rain can occur at any time during a Canadian fishing trip, a quality rain suit is a must. Take it along on each day's outing, whether the morning sky has a cloud in it or not. Make sure you have it when the wind is blowing, because windblown spray can get you wetter than a summer shower.

Although it is more comfortable to fish a lee shore when the wind is blowing, the best fishing usually occurs on the opposite side of the lake. The wind blows insects in this direction and flushes baitfish out of their weedbed habitat. Gamefish congregate, and fast-paced fishing action usually results. Fish the windward shore of a lake when the wind is blowing—it pays off.

Your guide may not be aware of this fact or may choose to ignore it. Handling a boat in the wind and waves can be difficult, so the guide may elect to take the easy way out and fish only protected waters. Suggest a different tactic if you aren't getting as many strikes as you think you should be getting.

But strong winds, especially those accomplished by storms, can prove hazardous to small boats. Bear this in mind if you're fishing a Canadian lake without a guide. If a storm is coming up, don't allow yourself to get trapped in open water without nearby shelter to head for.

I prepare for the vagaries of Canadian weather by taking along a small tote bag filled with various items of apparel. Included is a good rain suit, an insulated vest, an extra long-sleeved shirt, and a pair of rubber totes that I can slip over my shoes when rain or heavy spray is present.

CHANTREY INLET ● Northwest Territories

The Arctic char is one of North America's most exotic gamefish. This beautiful salmonoid is closely related to the brook trout and ranges throughout the Arctic regions of Alaska, Canada, Baffin Island, and areas farther east. The

Chantrey, a far-north spot, offers world-class angling for both char and lake trout.

char is also somewhat controversial. The experts agree that this fish spends its summers grazing in rich ocean pastures, and that is ascends certain rivers in the fall to spawn. But it doesn't die from the effort as the salmon does, and it is believed to winter inland.

Let's leave the char's private life to the experts. More important to us is the fact that it is a splendid gamefish. It attacks flies and spinning lures with savage abandon, strips line from reels in long runs, and fights with a tenacity few other gamefish possess. Equally important, the char comes in man-sized packages, averaging from five to thirty pounds.

One spot to fish for this species is Chantrey Inlet, where the mighty Back River spills out into the Arctic Ocean. Char and lake trout gather here in large numbers to create a fishing mecca that almost defies description. During the first half of July, it's possible to hook both species of fish on successive casts—a situation I haven't seen duplicated elsewhere. Char average twelve to fifteen pounds in these waters, and the lakers are somewhat larger. When the char run tapers off (usually by the latter part of July), the lake trout increase in number, and a number of forty- and fifty-pound fish have been reported here. An average catch is fifteen to twenty pounds, with thirty-pound fish being relatively common.

Chantrey Inlet Lodge, a fishing camp located on the bank of the Back River, offers accommodations for eighteen people in cabins surrounding a main building for dining and lounging. Although somewhat rustic, the camp is comfortable and well managed. Equipment is first class and well maintained. Guides are local Indians familiar with the waters and how to catch fish.

Most of the fishing is done a few minutes from the dock, thus obviating the need for long boat rides across windswept waters. Most of the char are caught in the river; casting is from the bank. Lake trout are caught by the same method, or by trolling or casting from a boat. These fish are not deep; many are taken from shallow rapids or wrestled from the eddies on the edge of this fast water. The result is sporty fishing by anyone's definition.

Chantrey Inlet Lodge has no camp store, so you'll have to bring everything you need. This includes tackle, lures, film, insect repellent, liquor, suntan lotion, and cigarettes. On the other hand, you also have to travel light. Because Chantrey Inlet is reached only by charter aircraft, luggage is limited to forty pounds per person.

For trout fishing, I recommend both casting and trolling rods with two-hand handles and enough muscle to handle a forty- or fifty-pound fish. Large-capacity reels, either casting or open-face spinning, should be loaded with twenty-to thirty-pound test line. For char, use somewhat lighter equipment that can be cast with more ease. Spool these reels with fifteen- to twenty-pound test line. Because submerged boulders, slashing fish, and rough waters can take a toll on line, I strongly recommend that you bring along several extra spools. Again, note that there is no camp store here.

In the lure line, bring large Dardevle spoons in the five of diamonds and potato bug colors, magnum Hellbenders, large-size Mepps spinners, Creek Chub Pikies, magnum Rapalas, and a variety of jig heads with white and pink plastic tails. Burke Wig Wags prove to be most effective. These lures are all you'll need in order to take Chantrey Inlet trout, and the same lures in smaller sizes are equally effective for char. Restrict your selection of lures, but bring several of each because big fish and boulders will separate you from a lot of them. As a further precaution, let me suggest that you fish with the best snap swivels you can buy, and that you use either short wire leaders or a few feet of thirty- or forty-pound test shock leader at the end of your line. Either one of these precautions will save a lot of lost fish and lures.

In the clothing line, bring insulated underwear, two warm fishing shirts, two pairs of trousers, one insulated vest and jacket, rubber boots, wool socks, a hat or cap, two pair of gloves, and a good rain suit. Plan to travel in part of this clothing, and pack the rest, along with your fishing gear, in one large or two small duffel-type bags. Carry rods in a sturdy tubular rod case marked with your name and address.

In these cold Arctic waters it takes seventy years to produce a thirty-pound lake trout, so fish are not killed indiscriminately. Only fish that are badly injured will be retained for eating. All others, except for one trophy of each species for mounting, will be released. Guests do not bring back boxes of fillets from this camp.

Chantrey Inlet Lodge offers a six-day package that includes charter air transportation from Fort Frances, Ontario (1,500 miles). These trips are all inclusive and are priced at $2,300 for the first several weeks of the season and several hundred dollars less for the last.

For additional information on fishing at Chantrey Inlet, write to the Chantrey Inlet Lodge, P.O. Box 637, Fort Frances, Ontario P9A 3M1, Tel: (807) 274–3666.

GREAT BEAR LAKE • Northwest Territories

Great Bear Lake, Canada's largest, straddles the Arctic Circle and is considered one of the best lake-trout fisheries in the world. This largest of the trout family grows slowly in this far-north environment, but it lives for a long time and reaches behemoth proportions. Great Bear holds the current world record with a 65-pounder taken in 1970, and there is reason to believe that some angler will eventually turn up an even larger fish here. Each year, several 50-pounders are caught, and trout in the thirty- and forty-pound class are commonplace. Incidentally, Great Bear is one of the few large Canadian lakes that have never been fished commercially.

Most of these big gray trout are taken by trolling, but not deep. Lures that dig down into these gin-clear depths rarely trail more than one hundred feet astern. Strikes may be accompanied by a swirl of water at the surface, and the resulting fight may be a savage slugfest that can last half an hour. And the fight is not always won by the angler. When fishing for fish this size, lots of things happen to tackle. Hooks straighten out, swivels tear open, lines snap, rods break. As a result, a fish on the other end of the line does not always mean a fish caught.

Most anglers fishing for trophy-sized lake trout use either open-face spinning gear or casting equipment. Bass rods with pistol-grip handles are not recommended, however. Make sure you have a handle you can get both hands on, one that you can occasionally stick into your midsection to get a little more leverage. Revolving spool casting reels are recommended, not spincast reels. The Abu 7000 is ideal. Load reels with twenty- to thirty-pound test line, and bring along an extra spool or two.

When packing for a fishing trip up in this part of the country, leave your big tackle box at home and take along only those lures that are known to take lake trout. This selection should include a number of magnum Hellbenders, deep running Rebels or Rapalas, a selection of big spoons, and some big jigs. Formerly, Bass Buster maribou jigs were the best available, but now there are a number of plastic tails on the market that are equally effective. Big spinners, like the Mepps Giant Killer, are also recommended.

Great Bear Lake is one of the best lake-trout fisheries in the world.

Great Bear's grassy bays also have northern pike in the twenty-pound category, but few people fish for them. It's also grayling country. The Arctic rivers that flow into Great Bear are prime habitat for this beautiful gamefish, and the species gets particularly large in these waters. Grayling catches in the three-pound category are fairly common here, and fish four pounds or larger are a possibility. If this doesn't sound like much of a fish, bear in mind that a one-and-one-half-pound grayling is average in most places, and that the current world record weighed only five pounds and fifteen ounces.

For this type of fishing bring a flyrod, or at least a light spinning outfit. With tackle like this along, keep an eye open for the gravelly bays, which frequently have insect hatches when the water is calm. On these occasions, lake trout feed on the surface and can be taken on dry flies. Talk about action—this is it.

In this land of the midnight sun, the summer is short. Here, the ice goes out around the end of June, and the first signs of winter begin showing in September. As a result, Great Bear trout feed voraciously during this period. This is the time when food is the most plentiful and is the time when they put on most of their annual growth.

Several fishing camps are located on this vast body of water, and one of the best ones is Plummer's Great Bear Lake Lodge. This camp is located on a tiny island in the Dease arm of the lake and consists of a cluster of cabins surrounding a main lodge. Accommodations are first class and satisfy the most discriminating angler. Excellent meals are served in the main lodge, which also has a spacious lounge and a camp store. Large aluminum boats, powered with twin outboards, are used for fishing. Indian guides are skilled at finding fish and in preparing shore lunches. This camp is not particularly scenic, but its island location does provide relief from marauding squadrons of mosquitoes, and the Dease area is recognized as excellent fishing water.

This Winnipeg-based operation offers Saturday-to-Saturday trips during July and August, including round-trip jet transportation from Winnipeg. Incidentally, the lodge has a private air strip long enough to accommodate jet aircraft. Price for these all-inclusive trips is slightly more than $2,000 per person.

Great Bear Lake Lodge maintains float aircraft that provide fly-out side trips to the Tree River for char fishing. This turbulent Arctic stream, which empties into Coronation Gulf, 232 miles to the northwest, is recognized as one of the world's best char fisheries.

Also providing first-class accommodations and fishing facilities is Great Bear Lodge. This camp offers a similar package priced about the same, but it includes charter air transportation from Edmonton instead of Winnipeg. Meals are excellent here, as are facilities and services.

A special government regulation stipulates that only one trout over twenty-eight inches fork length, and only two trout in total, may be taken from Great Bear Lake on any one fishing trip. The regulation is a wise conservation measure designed to preserve Great Bear fishing for decades to come.

For information on fishing Great Bear Lake, write to Great Bear Lake Lodge, 1110 Sanford Street, Winnipeg, Manitoba, Canada R3E 2Z9, Tel: (204) 774–5775; or to Great Bear Lodge, 2701 W. 7th Street, Sioux Falls, SD 57104, Tel: (605) 336–2008.

TREE RIVER • Northwest Territories

The sunlight reflecting off of the surface of the river makes the guide squint as he raises his arm and points. "There," he grunts, "deep."

You cast the glittering spoon into the middle of the river and let it settle into the foam-flecked depths. When you feel it nudge a boulder on the bottom, you raise your rod tip to make it flutter like a wounded thing in the swiftly moving current. It encounters an obstacle that sends vibrations up the line. Bottom again? No, this is different. Fingers grip the rod handle a little tighter, arm muscles contract, and the bowed rod begins to buck. In the middle of a swirling eddy, a crimson-sided fish explodes to the surface, shakes his hook-jawed head, and then shoots out into the teeth of the current. You hang on, with arms straining, beads of perspiration popping out on your forehead. That's all you or anyone can do. When a twenty-pound char makes its initial run, all you can do is hang on.

The Tree River is located above the Arctic Circle, 232 miles east of Great Bear Lake. As wild as its surrounding terrain, the Tree plunges along a watercourse strewn with boulders, some as large as houses, others the size of watermelons, through narrow spray-draped gorges, tumbling downward in thundering waterfalls to finally embrace the placid waters of the Coronation Gulf. There are no trees along this river's sixty-mile course, only barren plain and eskers of glacial rubble, all covered with a knee-high growth of lichen, moss, and stunted alders. This is tundra country—vast, lonesome, the land of the caribou, the great white bear, and the Arctic char.

Char grow large in Tree waters. The world record for this species has been broken by Tree anglers five times within the last several years, with the largest being a burly 32-pounder. From a practical standpoint, the Tree has proven to be one of the finest char rivers in the Arctic.

The Tree River Camp consists of a half-dozen walled sleeping tents and a larger structure that houses the camp's cooking and dining facilities. Add a few outhouses, several boats pulled up on the river bank, and a radio tower, and there you have it. The place isn't fancy, but it is sufficient for an overnight and two days of fishing.

Boats are available for fishing the quieter stretches of the lower river, but most fish are caught by fishing from the bank. Eskimo guides are provided for every two anglers, and these locals are familiar with the river and where the char are. As might be expected, fishing is good. Char are found in the river throughout the summer, and they are generally receptive to anglers' offerings. As a consequence, most anglers who fish this spot for two days get about all of the action they want or can handle.

Because it takes so many years to produce a trophy fish in these Arctic waters, Tree River guests are asked to release virtually all of the fish they catch. A trophy fish may be taken home for mounting, and occasionally a deeply hooked fish may be injured too badly to safely release. These wounded fish are eaten, and in this case it should be noted that char are excellent table fare.

Tree River is owned and operated by Great Bear Lake Lodge and is available only to Great Bear guests as an overnight side trip. On this trip, priced at $300, guests get to fish one afternoon, that evening, and the next morning.

For details on Tree River fishing, write to C. M. Plummer, Great Bear Lake Lodge, 1110 Sanford St., Winnipeg, Manitoba R3E 2Z9, Tel: (204) 774-5775.

Ed Eppinger with a trophy-size Tree River char.

GREAT SLAVE LAKE • Northwest Territories

"Are you sure about Great Slave?" I asked Ed Eppinger.

Ed manufactures Dardevle spoons, and because these lures are synonymous with lake-trout fishing, he's considered an authority on the subject.

I had reservations about Great Slave Lake because this big Arctic lake has been fished for decades and logically should be past its prime. Great Slave has been commercially fished for as long as I can remember, too.

"But not McLeod Bay," Eppinger said. Then he went on to tell me that he considered Great Slave's Taltheilei Narrows one of the première fishing spots in Canada.

He's right, of course. The Narrows is a constriction (more than one hundred miles long) that separates McLeod from the rest of giant Great Slave Lake, and it is the path that roving schools of trout must traverse as they migrate back and forth between the two bodies of water. There's current here, revolving eddies, and a deep rapids that attracts a concentration of baitfish. Trout like the food supply and the habitat, and they hang around in large numbers. This area has another advantage, too. Wind is usually a fishing factor up in this far north, frequently blowing anglers off the lake or keeping them pinned back in sheltered bays that are nonproductive from a fishing standpoint. Such is not the case here, because the Narrows is protected from wind from all directions.

Situated on this famous rapids, only fifty feet from the water's edge, is Great Slave Lake Lodge. This fishing camp features modern accommodations, excellent meals, well-maintained equipment, and good guides. It is a first-class operation from every standpoint. It also has something that most other camps don't—here, the fishing is located right in front of camp. No long boat rides are involved, no portages through forests or swamps buzzing with mosquitoes. Here you can be fishing within minutes of leaving the dock. Should you want to do some fishing after dinner, on your own, you can do so. With the best fishing grounds so close at hand, more time is spent fishing here than at the average northwoods camp.

Fishing results bear this statement out. Anglers catch lots of thirty-pound trout in these waters, fewer in the forty-pound category, and an occasional one considerably larger. For a number of years, anglers who fished this spot regularly felt that the next world's record would come from the Narrows. This hasn't happened yet, but who is to say it won't?

Great Slave is renowned as a grayling fishery, too. In the nearby streams that spill into this large lake, Arctic grayling grow to trophy proportions and provide a pleasant change of pace for the average sports fisherman. Want a really large grayling for your den wall? I can't think of a better place to get one than right here.

Good northern-pike fishing is available in Great Slave, but it's not conve-

Bill Cullerton hefts a trophy-size lake trout before releasing it.

nient to this camp. To tangle with pike in the twenty-pound category requires a short float plane flight or an hour-and-a-half boat ride. As a result, most of the anglers fishing out of this camp concentrate on trout and grayling.

This is catch-and-release water. Because it takes so many years to produce a trophy-sized trout in these cold waters (ten years for a two-and-one-half-pound fish), the possession limit is three fish, with only one over twenty-eight inches long. Grayling are limited to five in possession, and the same limitation applies to northern pike.

Great Slave Lake Lodge has a 5,200-foot private air strip that can accommodate a 737 jet, and the lodge offers a pair of packages that include air transportation to and from Winnipeg. One is an eight-day trip that offers six days of fishing with boat, motor, and guide and is priced at $1,800. A shorter five-day trip offers three days of fishing and has a $1,200 price tag.

For details on this camp and fishing Great Slave's Taltheilei Narrows, write to C. M. Plummer, Great Slave Lake Lodge, 1110 Sanford St., Winnipeg, Manitoba R3E 2Z9, Canada, Tel: (204) 772–8833. Another source of information is TravelArctic, Yellowknife, N.W.T., X1A 2L9, Canada.

KASBA LAKE • Northwest Territories

Kasba, a one-hundred-square-mile lake located just above the Saskatchewan border, is approximately fifty miles long and has more than 1,000 miles of shoreline. Renowned as a lake-trout fishery, Kasba also produces a number of trophy-sized pike each year and offers some of the best grayling fishing in Canada.

Anglers have plenty of elbow room here. Kasba Lake Lodge is the only fishing camp on this large lake, and it limits its guests to forty per week, from the middle of June to the first of September. Doug Hill and his two boys opened this camp in 1975 and immediately established a "trophy only" policy that has remained in effect ever since. Other camp owners initially raised their eyebrows at this move, but most have now followed suit, as has the Northwest Territorial government. This policy, which encourages barbless fishing and the release of virtually all fish caught, will assure quality fishing in Kasba for decades to come.

How good is Kasba?

I talked to one angler who claims to have caught and released one hundred trout in a day, and he admitted that his arms were sore as a result. During the 1985 season, more than 350 lake trout between eighteen and forty-two pounds were caught and released by Kasba guests. Since the camp opened in the summer of 1975, anglers have caught and released more than 700 trophy-sized trout. Because accurate records are kept of these catches, all these claims can be documented.

On this far-north lake, the ice is out only twelve weeks of the year, and the trout feed actively throughout this period. Most of them are taken by trolling at depths of less than ten feet or less, but casting also works well for those who try it. In casting for surface-feeding Kasba lakers, use lighter spinning or casting gear than normally used for trolling, or a #10 or 12 fly outfit. Dry flies work well at the beginning of the season, and large streamers seem to be better in late July and August. Want a supreme angling thrill? Land a thirty-pound great gray trout on a fly rod.

Fly fishermen should also be alerted to the fact that the Kazan River, fished out of Kasba Lodge, is considered one of the best grayling streams in the

Renowned as a lake-trout fishery,
Kasba produces trophy-size pike as well.

country. Here, a three-pound fish won't raise any eyebrows, and fish in the four-pound category are taken each season. The present world record of 5 pounds, 15 ounces is expected to be broken here, because experts believe that the Kazan contains grayling exceeding six pounds. Only time will determine if this speculation is correct.

Kasba's weedy bays are full of northern pike, and each year explorative anglers catch and release pike exceeding twenty pounds in weight.

Kasba Lake Lodge is a first-class operation. Guests are awakened each morning with a hot cup of coffee delivered to the cabin, and they find a bowl of ice and a tray of snacks waiting for them when they return from fishing. Guest accommodations are provided in modern cabins acccommodating four to six guests each. A main lodge building houses the kitchen, dining room, and lounge. Equipment is relatively new and well maintained. Food service and camp administration are excellent.

Unlike other far-north camps, Hill does not use native Indian guides. Canadian youths do the guiding here, and many of them have college degrees. Most have several years of guiding experience, are talented shore-lunch chefs, and are knowledgeable concerning the history of the region and its wildlife. From what I have been able to observe, Kasba guides get high marks from guest anglers.

Bring a couple of spinning or casting rods for trolling and a lighter outfit for casting to schools of surface-feeding trout. This latter outfit will suffice for big pike as well. All reels should be loaded with at least twenty-pound test line. Include a light fly outfit or spinning gear to fish for grayling in the Kazan. For grayling, bring your own waders, preferably the lightweight stocking-foot type. In the lure line, include a number of large Dardevle spoons, a selection of large Mepps spinners, a few Flatfish, and magnum-sized Hellbenders. The Hellbender, a deep-running lure, has a lot of flashy action and is extremely effective for lake trout suspended at ten or fifteen feet deep. Include weedless spoons for pike and a variety of trout flies for grayling. Woolly worms, muddler minnows, and black gnats work well. Spinning lures for grayling should be little spoons, spinners, and some brightly colored jigs.

In the clothing line, include warm shirts and trousers, an insulated vest and parka, good-quality rain gear, a change of clothing to wear around camp, waterproof boots, a hat or cap, gloves, wool socks, and insulated underwear. Bring sunglasses and plenty of insect repellent.

Kasba Lake Lodge usually opens during the latter part of June and closes the last day of August. During this period it offers a dozen week-long packages that include round-trip air transportation from Saskatoon, seven nights' accommodations, all meals, and fishing with a boat, motor, and guide for each two persons. Price for this all-inclusive package is $1,800.

For more information about fishing Kasba Lake, write to Doug Hill, Kasba Lake Lodge, P.O. Box 96, Parksville, British Columbia V0R 2S0, Canada, Tel: (604) 248–3572.

MACKENZIE RIVER • Northwest Territories

The mighty Mackenzie is one of the world's largest rivers. It is miles wide in some places, drains one-fifth of Canada, and flows a distance of 1,200 miles from the bottom of Great Slave Lake to the Arctic Ocean. Rich in both legend and history, this great river of the north is also one of the better pike fishing spots on this continent.

Why this is so is something of an enigma.

I say this because both Great Slave and the river it feeds are both located above the 60th Parallel, a region normally noted for its population of lake trout, grayling, and Arctic char. Pike are found in these cold Arctic waters— anglers fishing for trout and grayling occasionally catch them. But they're not particularly abundant, and they rarely reach the trophy proportions that they do a few hundred miles south.

But where the Mackenzie spills out of Great Slave Lake is an exception. This area is a morass of islands, reed-studded reefs, and grassy bays, and it teems with northern pike from ice-out until the end of the Arctic summer. The pike are not only thick here, they're also large. Catches from these waters average ten pounds or more. Twenty-pound fish won't raise an eyebrow, and pike in the twenty-five- and thirty-pound class are taken each season.

For a change of pace, these waters also offer excellent fishing for Arctic Grayling. Here, these beautiful little gamesters average around two pounds, but trophy fish in the three-pound category are also caught frequently. Occasionally difficult to locate, schools of trophy-sized walleye and whitefish also abound in these waters and are caught by anglers who run into them.

Anglers fishing these waters usually seek and catch trophy-size pike. Most are released.

Accommodations are provided by Brabant Lodge, which is located on an island in the middle of the river. An extremely attractive and well-managed camp, Brabant offers accommodations for thirty-four guests in comfortable log cabins with carpeted floors and private baths. The main lodge has a dining room, a spacious lounge, and a bar that provides complimentary drinks to Brabant guests. Hearty meals with a home-cooked flavor are served family style in the dining room. A camp store sells lures that are most productive in these waters. The fleet of outboard-powered boats is well maintained and always available for guest use. Everything considered, this is probably one of the best-equipped and -managed camps in the country.

In a departure from the norm, Brabant does not include guide service in the camp's regular fishing packages.

"Why not?" I asked John Pollard, the manager.

"Because they're not necessary," he replied. Then he went on to explain that the camp was located in the middle of the region's best fishing grounds, that no long boat rides were necessary, and that everyone caught fish. He was right. Huge pike have been caught by anglers fishing from the camp dock, and records indicate that most guests have about all the fishing action they can handle. Initial guide service is provided to show newcomers around the area, and a full-time guide is available at extra cost for those who request it in advance.

Brabant has a catch-and-release policy that has been in effect for several years, and it might be responsible for the large numbers of trophy-sized pike in these waters. Guests are instructed on how to release pike and grayling unharmed, and they're encouraged to use barbless hooks in order to facilitate this process.

Because you'll be handling a lot of fish while fishing these waters, I suggest that you take along a few extra pieces of equipment that will come in handy. One is a wire mouth spreader, which will make it easier to hold the toothed jaws of a big pike open while you're removing the hooks. The other is a pair of long-nose pliers, or a twelve-inch gadget called a Hook Out, to actually do the job with. Add a towel for wiping the fish slime off your hands, and you're in business.

Recommended tackle for Mackenzie pike is a stiff casting or spinning rod, its reels loaded with monofilament line testing at least twenty-four pounds. Even with thirty-pound test line, you'll lose a lot of big fish here, because this water is full of weeds, snags, and other underwater obstructions. Use a short wire leader and quality swivels to further reduce the number of lost fish. I suggest that you fish with a pair of rigs like these and also bring along a spare outfit. Include a light fly rod or an ultralight spinning outfit for grayling.

For pike, bring a number of large Dardevle or Thompson spoons in red and white, yellow and red, and so on, several magnum-sized Hellbenders, similarly sized Rapalas, a few large surface lures like the Creek Chub darter, and a few buzz baits. Make sure that some of your spoons are equipped with weed guards for fishing in the weeds. Standard trout flies will work for grayling. For spinning, include a selection of small spoons, Mepps spinners, and small brightly colored jigs. In case you run into a school of walleye, bring along a few larger white-and-yellow jigs and several smaller Hellbenders. Leave your big tackle box at home. Bring these selected lures packed in a small plastic container that you can pack in your luggage.

Pack clothing in a duffel bag and limit your total to forty pounds. Include long underwear, two pairs of warm shirts and trousers, an insulated vest and a parka, gloves, wool socks, waterproof shoes or boots, a hat or a cap, quality rain gear, and comfortable clothing to wear around camp.

Brabant Lodge offers several package trips ranging from three days to a week, priced at approximately $250 per day. These tours include round-trip fare from Hay River, all meals, accommodations, use of a boat and motor for fishing, a fishing license, cleaning and freezing of catch, and complimentary cocktails. Guides are not included, but they are available at extra cost. The lodge operates from the middle of June to the middle of September.

For more information on fishing this area, write to Brabant Lodge, L-2, 6 Heritage Drive, S.E., Calgary, Alberta T2H 2B8, Canada, Tel: (403) 253-4343.

HAKAI PASS ● British Columbia

I could see the first faint flush of dawn through patches of morning mist as I eased the outboard-powered skiff along the edge of the kelp bed. The tide was running full, swelling the height of the waves that crashed upon the rocky shore. My rod was in its holder, tip bowed by the drag of the lead weight and cut-herring plug. Ron Martin crouched on the bow seat, riding herd on a pair of rods.

"It's time," he observed.

I nodded in reply, anticipating a strike at any moment. Suddenly, one of Ron's lines went slack, and the bow went out of his rod. He stared dumbfounded at it for a moment before he realized what had happened. Then he grabbed the rod and started frantically to reel. When the line soon went tight, he pointed the rod tip downward and struck upward with all his strength. The twin hooks struck home, and the torpedo-shaped salmon bored into the depths.

I managed to get the other two rods in as Ron held onto his bucking rod. At that point, there was nothing he could do except hold on. A half-hour later, I would lift the landing net around the big chinook salmon (called a tyee here if more than thirty pounds, and the fish would weigh forty-seven pounds when we finally got it on the scales).

Hakai Pass is located on the British Columbia coast, far north of Campbell River, just northwest of Rivers Inlet, and immediately south of some islands called "Nalau." It's a fishing hotspot, a staging area where schools of salmon troop past prior to their spawning runs up British Columbia streams. The

In British Columbia, chinook salmon are called tyee if they weigh more than thirty pounds.

Hakai Pass area plays host to most of the salmon heading into Fitzhugh Sound, as well as many destined for Rivers Inlet, just to the southeast.

The pattern begins in May, when billions of tiny euphausid shrimp, called krill, swarm those waters. They are preyed upon by vast schools of herring, which in turn are pursued by the predator salmon. The early chinooks, commonly called spring salmon here, range from ten to thirty-five pounds and are present through July. Later that month, forty- and fifty-pound tyee begin to show up, and they hang around through August. August, then, is tyee time, a period awaited eagerly by anglers up and down the British Columbia coast and even all over the world. Schools of hard-fighting coho salmon, ranging above twenty pounds, follow from August to October.

"Mooching" (slow trolling or drifting) is the favored way to fish Hakai waters and is basically a fishing method using not only the slow-trolling techniques but even deep jigging as well.

Live herring are sometimes used, but a piece of cut, frozen medium-size herring works as well and is much easier to obtain and keep. Fishing depth varies with the species of salmon sought. Big chinook are usually hooked at depths of forty or more feet, while coho are found shallower. In late summer, when the latter species of fish is abundant, faster trolling at lesser depths is successful.

A typical salmon rod is eight to ten feet in length with plenty of strength in the butt section but with sufficient tip-bending capacity to absorb the shock of a tyee strike. Most are made of graphite or fiberglass and should have a double handle for good leverage. Reels may be single-action "knuckle busters," spinning or revolving-spool casting models. Large-capacity spools are mandatory, loaded with 300 yards of twenty-pound test line. Most popular bait for mooching is the plug-cut, eight-inch herring. Two single hooks, either 4/0 or 5/0, used in tandem, are preferred with such baits. Depending on the tides, trolling speed, and other factors, a four-ounce weight is usually sufficient to get a bait down to the proper depth. That is the type of equipment furnished by the outfitters I'll describe later, and it is well suited for that type of fishing. If you wish lighter gear, bring your own and include a selection of spoons and wobbling lures as well.

Unlike Campbell River and Rivers Inlet, there are few lodges or fishing camps at Hakai Pass. Instead, accommodations and fishing facilities are provided by comfortable cruise ships like the *S.S. Thorfinn*, a converted Norwegian steam-driven whaler, 170 feet long with a thirty-foot beam. She accommodates twenty-six guest anglers in comfortable double-berth staterooms and features a spacious bar and lounge, a sun deck, and a dining room. The *Thorfinn*'s kitchen staff serves gourmet-class cuisine with complimentary wine at lunch and dinner. Among the dishes served are crabs and prawns that are caught at the locations the ship stops at.

For fishing, the *Thorfinn* provides fourteen-foot outboard-powered boats, well designed for those waters. Because the ship literally anchors on top of some schools of salmon, fishing often is done within sight of the ship. No long boat rides are necessary. Fishing equipment, including hooks, weights, and bait, are all provided. Guides are not regularly provided and are not necessary, but some briefing on tackle and technique is readily available.

Ships like the *Thorfinn* follow the schools of salmon from one location to another and can virtually guarantee quality fishing, regardless of the season. In the *Thorfinn*'s case, the season lasts from June 10 until the middle of October, with the latter part of the season spent in the Queen Charlotte Islands, farther north.

The *Thorfinn* is reached by flying boat from Vancouver and offers guests a choice of four- or five-day packages, priced at approximately $235 per day. Special charter air transportation from Vancouver is extra, around $250 per person.

Coho and chinook salmon caught in the sea are firm fleshed and make excellent table fare. For that reason, most of the anglers taking these trips bring home a box of frozen salmon or salmon fillets. The flesh of chinook salmon is indistinguishable from that of Atlantic salmon or summer steelhead.

For more information on fishing Hakai Pass or other British Columbia hot spots, write to the following: Seaward Holdings Ltd., 62N Ft. of Carrall St., Vancouver, B.C. V6B 2H6, Canada, Tel: (604) 687–1651; Oak Bay Marina, 1327 Beach Drive, Victoria, B.C. V85 2N4, Canada, Tel: (604) 598–3366; or Skippers Salmon Charters, P.O. Box 1821, Victoria, B.C. V8W 2Y3, Canada, Tel: (604) 682–7284.

OMINECA MOUNTAINS ● British Columbia

It's not necessary to go to New Zealand, Alaska, or Argentina to experience first-class mountain trout fishing. It's available in Canada, in the Omineca Mountains of British Columbia.

There is a difference in trout.

Eastern brookies have inspired lots of poetic prose, and they're fun to stalk

in pastoral surroundings. But they don't grow very large, except in Quebec and Labrador. They don't often put much of a bend in a fly rod.

Hatchery-reared fish are also another breed. I once caught a ten-pound rainbow in an Ozarks River, and it didn't put up near the fight that a smaller wild trout will.

I'm even of the opinion that mountain trout are superior gamesters to their flatland kin. I can't prove that, of course, but I think that mountain-bred trout jump a little higher, make more powerful runs, and have more staying power. In my opinion, there's a difference in wild trout, too.

Omineca Lodge is a fly-in camp located on a wilderness lake in British Columbia's remote Omineca Mountains. It's a first-class facility, constructed of peeled birch logs, and features carpeted floors, a central heating system, a dining room, a spacious lounge with a large fireplace, and four guest bedrooms. Meals are served family style and are bountiful and well prepared. The staff-to-guest ratio is almost one to one, which means that guests receive personalized service.

Tutizzi Lake and its tributaries provide anglers with eight miles of lake fishing, two miles of small-stream fishing, and another twelve miles of river fishing. Boats are used to fish the lake and some river pools, and to float some sections of the Tutizzi River. For those who want to fish certain stretches of river early or late, overnight tent facilities are set up. Other rivers are floated in inflatable rafts or fished by wading or walking the bank. In addition, the lodge maintains a float plane for fishing other waters in the area.

Snow-draped mountains surround Tutizzi Lake and Omineca Lodge.

All of these lakes and streams teem with wild rainbow trout that readily take wet and dry flies and average better than two pounds. Rainbows in the eight-pound category are caught on occasion, and 5-pounders are taken frequently. Lake trout abound in the same waters and are even taken on flies. Those fish average around seven pounds and go to twenty-eight. Dolly Varden are plentiful and have been caught in the seventeen-pound category. Arctic grayling and mountain whitefish are two other species of gamefish available in those high-country lakes and streams, and they provide excellent sport on fly or light spinning equipment. When the chinook are running in the nearby Meziadin River, anglers may elect to fish for that species also. In this river, those salmon can weigh between forty and fifty pounds and add another dimension to fishing there. For fly or spin fishermen, the high-country lakes and streams are an angler's paradise.

For rainbow trout, Dolly Varden, grayling, and whitefish, bring a light- to medium-action fly rod with a matching line. Include floating, sink-tip, and sinking varieties, and plan on using a $3\times$ to $5\times$ leader. If you prefer, use a light-action spinning rod and a six- to eight-pound test line. For larger salmon, steelhead, or lake trout, use a heavier fly rod with a reel capacity of 150 yards of fifteen- or twenty-pound test backing. Include both floating and sinking lines, with weight-forward types preferred. Spinning rigs should be medium action, with reels loaded with sixteen-pound test line. The outfitter will send you a list of tackle and lures for sale at the lodge.

Since Omineca Lodge is a fly-in camp, limit your total luggage to fifty pounds and pack it in a duffel bag. Take along chest or hip waders with felt soles, a fishing vest, a rain suit, a broad-brimmed hat, waterproof boots, warm fishing togs, and comfortable clothes to wear around camp. Travel in your fishing clothes to avoid bringing extra clothing. Include suntan lotion, insect repellent, a camera, and plenty of film.

The lodge offers a seven-day package priced at $1,600, which includes float plane transportation from Smithers, lodge accommodations, all meals, fishing guide for each two anglers, boats, motors, and two aerial side trips during the week's stay. Additional flying side trips are usually available for salmon and steelhead at an extra charge. The tour operates from late June until mid-September.

The little town of Smithers is located on Highway 16 and is accessible by automobile from Alberta on the east and from Vancouver, 750 road miles to the south. Smithers is also served by daily commercial jet from Vancouver.

For additional information on fishing in that area, write to Dana Cole, 801 P Street, Lincoln, NE 68508, Tel: (402) 477–9249.

BOW RIVER ● Alberta

The Bow River is spawned in the glacier-strewn heights of Banff National Park and winds its way in an easterly direction for a distance of more than 300 miles. Above Calgary, the Bow is an alpine stream, very much in a hurry, and generously laced with white-water rapids. Below this oil-rich city, the Bow turns into a flat prairie stream with an average width of 400 feet and a current of seven miles per hour.

This is where the action is, though. Above the city, the Bow is a good trout stream, but below, for a distance of some forty miles, it's one of the best rainbow-trout fisheries in North America. Here, stretches of river are virtually alive with trout, with most of them exceeding sixteen inches in length and many weighing five pounds or more.

Ironically, much of the lower Bow's acclaim as a trout fishery results from municipal pollution that is discharged back into the river. Treatment plants remove harmful substances from the effluent, but they do not eliminate the nitrates or phosphates. These fertilizers enrich the water and stimulate a fantastic growth of weeds and aquatic insects. The latter provide a food

The author with an average-size Bow River rainbow.

bonanza for feeding trout, while the weeds provide cover for small fish and other aquatic life. As might be expected, the growth rate of the trout in this nutrient-rich stretch of river is nothing short of phenomenal.

Bow River trout run large. Most average sixteen inches or more in length, with catches in the three- to five-pound category being rather common. This is fly-fishing-only water, and a good many large trout are taken on tiny dry flies. As a consequence, little hooks pull out, and gossamer-fine leaders snap. Many of the larger fish, rainbows and some browns, are lost.

Because this forty-mile stretch of river runs through private property, river access is limited, and it is difficult to get to. Certainly, the lower Bow is not a wading stream, because the banks are either too steep or are impassable muck. Floating is the only feasible way to fish this stream, and this is the method that the outfitter uses.

For the past half-dozen years the Bow River Company has been operating day floats on this river, fishing approximately ten miles of river in a day's float. Fourteen-foot John boats are used for this purpose, and they're operated by a guide with oars. Two anglers are assigned to each boat. With forty miles to float, it is possible to have a three- or four-day float on this stream, with the nights spent on gravel bars in comfortable tent camps. Many anglers, however, want day floats only and spend their nights in Calgary motels. The latter method is the comfortable way to fish the lower Bow. The overnight version is favored by some because it offers an opportunity to fish late-evening and early-morning risers.

Either way, the trout fishing is outstanding. Hatches of Mayflies, caddis, and stoneflies occur throughout the day, and as a result the trout feed voraciously. Foraging trout do it the easy way, though, holding in the slowly revolving eddies, waiting for insects to collect in pockets. These schools of feeding trout are not difficult to locate because insect-feeding gulls also gather for the feast and are accurate indicators of fish activity. Watching the birds is just as applicable here as it is in salt water.

Anglers are advised to bring rods eight or nine feet in length, and both sinking and floating lines. Both are usually used throughout most of every day. Fly boxes should contain dry flies tied on #12 to #18 hooks with some of the most popular patterns being the Letort Hopper, Light Cahill, Adams, Blue Wing Olive, and poly-winged spinners. Favorite nymph patterns on the Bow are yellow and black Stoneflys, the Bitch Creek, and Hare's Ear nymphs. All should be tied on #4 to #6 hooks, with the latter flies somewhat smaller. In the streamer line, include the Maribou Dace, Maribou Muddlers, Leeches, Sculpins, and Matuka Streamers in sizes #2 and #4. Additional flies may be recommended by the outfitter at the time of booking or may be obtained locally on arrival.

Chest waders are recommended, and since you'll have to be getting in and out of the boat, they should be comfortable and relatively lightweight. In this respect, Red Ball makes a stocking-foot wader that weighs less than a pound and is ideal for clambering in and out of boats and float planes. Use it with wading shoes or sneakers, with felt soles preferred. Include a fly fishing vest, a warm jacket, rain wear, wool socks, and a broad-brimmed hat. Include sunglasses, insect repellent, and suntan lotion. Days can be extremely warm on the river, but the weather can change suddenly and be wet and cold. On these day floats, and especially for floats of longer duration, be prepared for any contingency. For overnight trips be sure to also bring along a sleeping bag and foam pad.

Bow River floats are priced at $150 per day per person and include a boat and guide for each two anglers and transfers to and from the river. For overnight floats, meals and tent accommodations are also provided. The season is from June 15 through September.

Calgary is a booming city with more than 600,000 inhabitants and is loaded with good hotels and fine restaurants. It also is the gateway for visits to Lake Louise, Banff, or Jasper Park. Calgary has a modern jet airport and is served daily by a number of air carriers.

For additional details on fishing the lower Bow River, write to the Bow River Company, Box 57, Okotoks, Alberta T0L 1T0, Canada, Tel: (403) 938–3259.

STONY RAPIDS • Saskatchewan

Based upon personal experience, I have to rate Riou Lake as one of the finest pike fisheries in Canada.

Certainly it was on that day. A friend and I had flown into Riou, and when the float plane had disappeared over the horizon we both began to lob weedless spoons into the weeds that lined the edge of the bay. Both lures were attacked the moment they splashed into the water, and each of us was fast to a pike that was somewhere between ten and fifteen pounds. That's the way the entire afternoon went. Cast after cast produced strike after strike, and all of them were good fish. We caught and released eighty-seven northerns on that rainy afternoon, and several of them were trophy fish in the twenty-pound category. It was a fishing experience to remember, one I'll never forget.

That happened a few years ago, but the situation hasn't changed. Because most of the pike caught in this lake are released, Riou continues to produce fast-paced action for just about everyone who fishes it. Riou is located a dozen miles south of Stony Rapids and is accessible only by float plane.

Selwyn Lake, a larger body of water located seventy-five miles north of Stony Rapids, is now producing larger fish, though. An angler from Arizona caught a 41-pounder here a year or so ago, and each year Selwyn continues to produce a number of fish in the twenty- to twenty-five-pound category. From what I have been able to ascertain, Riou is the more consistent of the two

Margie Rogers took this Fond du Lac grayling on a small marabou jig.

lakes and can be counted on to produce plenty of action for those who visit it. Selwyn is supposed to have larger pike, but they aren't always cooperative. In this respect, it should be noted that Riou is a pike lake and that Selwyn is also a trophy-trout fishery. Lake trout exceeding thirty pounds are caught in it each season, and a large percentage of anglers concentrate on this species when they visit Selwyn.

Black Lake is a forty-mile-long lake located fourteen miles southeast of Stony Rapids. This productive fishery is fed by three major rivers, including the Fond du Lac, and has been making angling history for years. Black is 180 feet deep in some places and is an outstanding trout lake. But because it lies above the 59th parallel, the water remains cool and the trout remain active all summer. In 1984, for instance, a lodge guest landed a 48-pounder here, and he hooked it in fifteen feet of water. Black Lake also produces lots of trophy-sized northern pike (twenty pounds or larger) and braggin' size walleyes.

The place to stay in the Stony Rapids area is Morberg's Black Lake Lodge, located on the Fond du Lac River, where it spills out of Black Lake. This spot, a beautiful location for a fishing camp, is an outstanding place to catch trophy-sized grayling. These gamesters abound in the river in front of the lodge and can be taken on both flies or spinning lures almost anytime. Guests staying at this lodge frequently fish for trout and pike during the day and then take an after-dinner stroll along the river bank to catch grayling. This species grows large in these waters, up to four pounds.

Morberg's is a first-class fishing camp. It consists of an attractive main lodge surrounded by log cabins that provide guest accommodations. The cabins have carpeted floors and are well furnished and completely modern. Meals at the lodge are excellent, as is camp administration and all other services. Guides, some who have been guiding here for twenty years, are top notch.

To eliminate time-consuming long boat rides on Black Lake, Morberg's uses a fast nine-passenger boat to transfer anglers to and from the other end of the lake. Tent outpost camps are established there for guests who want to spend the night and fish these productive areas a second day. A float plane is retained at the lodge to provide fly-outs to Riou, Selwyn, and other surrounding lakes. An extra charge is made for this service.

The lodge is open from early June through mid-September and offers a seven-day/six-night package that includes charter airfare from Saskatoon, six nights' accommodations, all meals, and fishing with a boat, motor, and guide for five full days. This package is reasonably priced. Private-aircraft package rates are also available.

For additional information on fishing Black, Riou, or Selwyn Lakes or other waters in the Stony River area, write to Grande Domain Retreats, 801 P St., Lincoln, NE 68508, Tel: 1–800–228–4333 or (402) 477–9249.

HATCHET LAKE • Saskatchewan

Hatchet Lake is located 475 miles north of Saskatoon, in the shadow of the Northwest Territories border. The lake is ten miles wide and eighteen miles long and is a part of the Fond du Lac River, which flows between Wollaston and sprawling Lake Athabasca to the west. Nearby are a dozen other lakes, all accessible from Hatchet by boat or a short portage.

Hatchet is far enough north to be considered a good trout lake, and from ice-out to the end of June anglers enjoy good surface fishing for lakers. During July and August, the trout retreat to deeper water and are taken mostly by deep jigging. Trophy-sized northern pike abound in Hatchet's numerous weed-filled coves and bays, and occasionally they are caught lurking near schools of walleye and whitefish congregated below river rapids. Each year, pike in the twenty-five-pound category are taken from these waters. Although it is not renowned as a walleye lake, anglers fishing for this species catch a lot

Fishing a few days after ice-out, Homer Circle caught this lake trout on the surface.

of 5-pounders and occasionally net a ten-pound walleye. Hatchet is grayling country, too. This beautiful little gamefish is native to the Fond du Lac River system and is popular with light-tackle fishermen.

There is only one fishing camp on this lake, and it's a first-class facility. Hatchet Lake Lodge is located on an island in the north end of the lake and features a recent 3,600-square-foot addition to its main lodge. Guests are housed in cabins surrounding this building, which are completely modern and tastefully furnished. The food at Hatchet is considered first class, as is the equipment maintenance and the performance of guides and staff. The camp is owned and operated by George Fleming, a Scot who has a love affair with bagpipes. At Hatchet, a kilted piper announces both breakfast and dinner with a lilting Highland tune.

To get the day started right, guests awaken to a hot cup of coffee. When they return to camp after a day out on the water, they find a bucket of ice and a tray of snacks awaiting them in their cabin. Hatchet guides offer anglers a choice of how they want their fish prepared for shore lunch—pan fried, baked in foil, or skewered on a sharp stick and cooked over the coals. Should guests desire, they can use boats and motors for after-dinner fishing. Dusk, at this latitude, occurs just before midnight, so there is plenty of daylight after the evening meal is finished.

Like other Canadian camp operators, Hatchet has a trophy policy which decrees that fish weighing more than twelve pounds will be released for future sport. There is one exception: If a guest catches a trophy fish and wants to have it mounted, he or she may do so.

Hatchet has a 4,000-foot air strip and includes charter air transportation from Saskatoon with its regular packages. Special rates, which do not include air transportation, are offered to guests who have their own aircraft. Fleming's regular-week package operates on a Saturday-to-Saturday basis and includes an airport reception at Saskatoon, charter air transportation from Saskatoon, accommodations, all meals, fishing with a boat, motor, and guide provided for each two guests, and cleaning and freezing of catch. The price exceeds $1,700.

For information on fishing this area, write to George Fleming, Hatchet Lake Lodge, Sub Post Office 55, Calgary, Alberta T3B 0H0, Canada, Tel: (403) 286–2717. For additional information on Hatchet or on fishing in Saskatchewan, write to Tourism Saskatchewan, Bank of Montreal Bldg., 2103 11th Ave. Regina, Saskatchewan S4P 3V7, Canada.

CHURCHILL RIVER ● Saskatchewan

The Churchill River begins near the Alberta border and meanders across Saskatchewan and Manitoba to empty into Hudson Bay at Churchill. Although called a "river," this watercourse is actually a series of lakes linked together by waterfalls and white-water chutes. A part of the Pre-Cambrian Shield, it is carved out of granite and dotted with spruce-covered islands. It is perhaps one of the most scenic regions in Canada. Equally important, the Churchill is a sports fishery beyond compare.

This is big-pike country.

I can remember easing into a secluded bay on McIntosh Lake one summer afternoon hoping to catch a few pike. We surprised a hen mallard and several offspring, and as the trio paddled hurriedly across an opening in the lily pads, the whole bay seemed to explode beneath them. The mother became airborne in a shower of spray, but the two ducklings disappeared into the maw of a giant pike.

With trembling hands, I transferred my favorite weedless lure to a heavier rod and reel, which was loaded with thirty-pound test line. As the guide eased the boat closer with his paddle, I checked the snap on my wire leader and

Trophy-size pike like this are common in the Churchill River watershed.

inspected the front several feet of line for nicks and abrasions. Then I sat with sweating palms until we maneuvered close enough for a cast. Within minutes of the pike's attack on the duck and her brood, I had a large surface lure limping across the surface of the same pool and was holding my breath in the process. Nothing touched it the first and second times, but on the third cast the water erupted again, and I set the hooks on one of the largest northern pike I have ever encountered.

But, despite my preparation, it was no contest. My drag was set at the limit, and the thirty-pound test line was strong enough to mow down an acre of lily pads as the pike steamed out of the bay. I was unable to stop the fish, and for some reason my guide couldn't get the motor started in time to take up the chase. Helplessly, I watched the line melt off of the reel, and it parted with a loud pop when it reached the end. My monster pike was gone.

That pike is probably still living in the Churchill lake chain. Although the system annually produces trophy northerns in the twenty-five- and thirty-pound category, I haven't heard of anyone's catching a 40-pounder since my encounter. That pike is one of the reasons I keep going back to the Churchill as often as I can.

Other popular species of fish here are lake trout and walleyed pike, with the latter being most in demand. Highly prized as a food fish, Churchill walleye are also considered good gamefish because of their habitat. In this watercourse, the species schools up in the eddies below waterfalls and rapids, where they are primarily caught on white or yellow jigs. In this fast water, they put up a good fight and are exciting to catch. Lake trout are found in most of the lakes and average from ten to thirty pounds. Most are taken early in the season.

To catch walleye, I prefer a light-action spinning or spincast rod with the reel loaded with eight- or ten-pound test line. Walleye have teeth, but I still don't recommend the use of a wire leader, which I think deters strikes. I lose an occasional fish as a result of not using a wire leader, but because they're plentiful I don't let this worry me. For lake trout, I suggest using a stiff trolling rod with a reel spooled with eighteen-pound test line. Wobbling spoons are the most common lures used, but other deep-running lures can also be effective. Because any strike can be a trophy fish, I recommend a stiff casting rod and a revolving spool reel laced with twenty-five- or thirty-pound test line. The best lures are spoons, buzz bait, and other weedless lures.

La Ronge is the gateway to the Churchill and is a sprawling frontier town located just above the 55th Parallel, on the shore of Lac La Ronge. This town is accessible by road from Prince Albert and other cities farther south. It also is serviced by air from Saskatoon. From La Ronge, Churchill River lakes are reached by a half-hour float plane flight on farther north.

The best camp in this region is Sportsman's Lodge, which is located on a mosquito-free peninsula on McIntosh Lake. This camp can accommodate more than fifty guests in modern cottages that surround a spacious main lodge, and it is a first-class facility in every respect. Meals are excellent, equipment is new and well maintained, and native guides are as good as you'll find in the country. Prices are on a par with those of other fly-in camps. A four-night all-inclusive package, for example, is priced at less than $250 per day, and longer stays are even more economical on a daily basis. Youngsters under twelve stay for free. The season is from May 25 to late August.

Tom Pierce is the owner of Sportsman's Lodge and can be reached at Box 20212, Oklahoma City, OK 73156, Tel: (405) 843–7235.

NUELTIN LAKE ● Manitoba

Nueltin, a 125-mile-long lake that sprawls across the Northwest Territories border, is located 200 miles west of Hudson Bay and is a two-hour flight by DC3 from Thompson to the south.

Nueltin is where the big lake trout are coming from these days. In the last three years, this lake has annually produced 150 trophy lakers (more than twenty pounds) and a number of considerably larger fish. Notable catches were a 52½-pounder taken in 1982 and a 56-pounder caught the following year.

Because Nueltin's cold waters never warm up during the brief summer along the 60th Parallel, trout remain near the surface and feed voraciously throughout the long Arctic days. Most are taken in less than ten feet of water by casting or trolling.

For a change of pace, anglers can fish the numerous rivers that run into the lake and catch grayling, some in the trophy class. Nueltin has an abundance of sheltered weedy bays that contain northern pike, and more and more anglers are spending a day or so of their stay here to fish for pike. Ten- to fifteen-pound pike are numerous in these waters, and several have been caught in the twenty- to twenty-five-pound category.

Anglers wishing to fish this lake have a choice of three facilities. One is Treeline Lodge, an American Plan facility that accommodates twenty guests in eight cabins. The main lodge houses a family-style dining room and lounge. Centrally located is a bath house that has lavatories, showers, and flush toilets. Guides are provided here, and they are experienced in boat handling and in finding fish.

Two outpost camps are also located on Nueltin. One is situated on the narrow section of lake separating north and south Nueltin through which schools of trout migrate. It's a natural feeding ground for big lakers, an ideal site for a fishing facility. The Narrows Camp, as it is called, can accommodate ten anglers in two large tent cabins. Two other similar facilities are provided for cooking and dining. At this camp, anglers do their own cooking, operate their own boats, and look after themselves. A camp manager is provided to keep the place neat and tidy and to make sure that the equipment is well maintained.

Windy River, located in the Northwest Territories eighty miles north of Treeline, offers guest accommodations in one large building and might be considered more of a housekeeping facility than an outpost. Ten anglers are accommodated here, and a camp manager is on hand to maintain the equipment and keep the place clean.

All of these facilities are owned and operated by Bill Bennett, who has a reputation as a first-class operator and rather strong beliefs concerning conservation of Nueltin's fish population. Recognizing that it takes a half-century

Nueltin produces more than 150 trophy trout each year for the anglers who fish it.

to produce a trophy-sized laker in these waters, Bennett operates by a "trophy only" policy that allows guests to kill only one trophy fish of each species during their week's stay. Others are released to be caught again. Anglers are encouraged to fish with barbless hooks. Only small fish are used for shore lunches.

Most anglers fishing for Nueltin's trophy trout use revolving-spool casting outfits or comparable open-face spinning rigs. Rods should have enough backbone to handle a fifty-pound fish. Reels should have large-capacity spools and be loaded with eighteen- or twenty-pound test line. The same equipment will also suffice for pike fishing in Nueltin's weedy bays. Grayling are another matter. Since these beautiful little fish rarely go to more than two pounds, use ultra light spinning gear or a flyrod suitable for small trout. Grayling strike a variety of flies or tiny crappie jigs. Small spoons and spinners also work well.

Treeline Lodge has an air strip and is reached by a DC3 from Thompson. This flight operates each Saturday throughout the season, bringing in a load of new anglers each week and taking others out. Windy River and Nueltin Narrows camps also operate on a Saturday-to-Saturday basis but use float planes based in Lynn Lake. Both Lynn Lake and Thompson are reached by commercial air carrier and by road from Winnipeg. Treeline's 4,000-foot strip is suitable for most private aircraft, but pilots are advised that the lodge is 200 miles north of the closest navigational aid or other landing strip.

Bennett offers seven-day package trips for all of these facilities, and the price includes air transportation from Thompson and Lynn Lake. Prices are quoted in Canadian funds and are extremely reasonable when the location of these camps is considered. A week at Treeline, for instance, is less than $2,000. Windy River is $1,500 for a comparable week's stay. Nueltin Narrows is an economical $1,300.

For information on fishing at one of these three camps contact Bill or Beth Bennett at the following addresses. Summer: P.O. Box 1229, Thompson, Manitoba R8N 1P1, Canada, Tel: (204) 677–3507. Winter: P.O. Box 935, Campbellford, Ontario K0L 1L0, Canada, Tel: (705) 652–3280.

SICKLE LAKE ● Manitoba

If you're interested in catching a trophy pike to hang on your den wall, Sickle Lake could be the place to get the job done.

This scythe-shaped lake is located in the western part of Manitoba and is accessible by float plane from Lynn Lake, thirty miles to the north. Not a large body of water by Manitoba standards, the lake is less than a mile wide and only eighteen miles long. But because Sickle offers access to a dozen other surrounding lakes, the overall area becomes a fishery of note.

Only one camp is located in this region. Sickle Lake Lodge was opened in 1980, and anglers fishing these waters promptly began to catch pike twenty pounds or larger. Instead of decreasing as a result of fishing pressure, the number of trophy pike caught in these waters has increased each year ever since. Today, a glance at Manitoba's Master Angler Awards book reveals that Sickle is dominating the northern pike division with catches exceeding twenty pounds. In this case, the records prove that this fishery is everything that anglers claim it is.

Brian McIntosh, owner of this fishing camp, attributes Sickle's continuing success as a big fish producer to the trophy policy that he established when his camp was first opened. This policy is simple. It allows a guest to kill one trophy-sized fish if he or she wants to have it mounted. Otherwise, all fish weighing more than eight pounds are released to furnish sport for some angler in the future.

Anglers fishing Sickle Lake are allowed one trophy-size pike per stay. Others are released.

This camp policy doesn't affect the time-honored "Canadian shore lunch," however. Walleye are used for this purpose, as are small trout and occasionally small northern pike. Should guests desire, they also can take a box of frozen fish fillets home with them. Again, only small fish are used for this purpose.

Because the camp's anglers are spread throughout the Sickle Lake chain, fishing pressure is greatly reduced, and all angler's have an opportunity to catch that trophy fish they're looking for. Some of these lakes are accessible by boat, others are reached by an all-terrain vehicle, and still others require a short portage. Fly-out trips to other lakes are also available for a reasonable additional fee.

Sickle Lake Lodge is a modern camp featuring a spacious main lodge and several surrounding cabins offering all amenities. Meals served in the dining room are tasty and well prepared. Equipment is well maintained, and the service of management, guides, and staff is excellent.

In addition, McIntosh operates several outpost camps located varying distances north of Lynn Lake. These comfortable camps consist of large two-person walled tents with wood floors, plus an even larger tent for cooking and dining. Guests have a choice of several options concerning guides, food preparation, and other services, and in all cases a camp manager is provided to solve any problems that might arise.

The price for a week's trip to Sickle Lake Lodge is less than $1,700 and includes round-trip air transportation from Lynn Lake, all meals, seven nights' accommodations, boats, motors, and guides. Prices for the outpost camps are considerably less and vary with services offered. These prices also include float plane transportation.

For more information on fishing Sickle Lake and surrounding waters, write to Brian McIntosh, Box 551, Dyersburg, TN 38024, Tel: (901) 627–3228 or (901) 285–0915.

GUNISAO LAKE ● Manitoba

Gunisao, a thirty-eight-square-mile lake located 250 miles north of Winnipeg, is considered one of the best walleye fisheries in Manitoba. Catches in the twelve- or thirteen-pound category occur annually here, and fish half this size are common. Northern pike, lake trout, yellow perch, and whitefish are also present in this lake, but here the accent is on fishing for large walleye.

A part of the Gunisao River system, this fishery comprises several island-dotted lakes, stretches of river, waterfalls, and rapids. A half-dozen smaller tributaries spill into Gunisao and also contribute to this lake's fishing potential. Walleye habitat abounds, and it is for this reason that the lake is so productive.

Gunisao Lake Lodge is the only fishing camp in the area. Formerly a small Indian settlement, this facility is completely self-contained. It includes a large building that houses lounge and dining facilities, as well as four guest cottages. The cottages are completely modern, heated with electricity, and attractively furnished. Meals are tastily prepared and bountiful in size, and they always include home-baked bread. Equipment is well maintained, and native guides are skilled at finding fish, boat handling, and the preparation of tasty shore lunches. Gunisao also has a 3,600-foot all-weather air strip, which makes it accessible by wheeled aircraft.

Like some other Canadian fishing camps, Gunisao has a policy that encourages anglers to release walleye over four pounds and pike over eight pounds. If a trophy fish is desired for mounting, it may be killed. Smaller walleye are used for shore lunches or taken home.

Because this lake is located below the 54th Parallel, summer temperatures may have more effect on the fishing than they do farther north. Catching pike in Gunisao during July and August should pose no problem, and perhaps the same can be said for small walleye. Trophy-sized walleye in the ten- to twelve-pound category are another matter, however. If I wanted to catch a fish of these proportions, I'd plan my fishing trip for the first two weeks in September or the last two weeks in May. Records indicate that these are the times when most of the trophy walleye are taken at this latitude, and this situation is almost certainly related to water temperature and its effect on both predator and food fish.

Gunisao Lake Lodge offers a choice of three-, four-, and seven-day packages, all of them priced at $200 or more per day. Prices include accommodations, meals, and fishing, with boat, motor, and guide provided for each two anglers.

For more information, write to Jim and Marlene Gulay, P.O. Box 100, Fisher Branch, Manitoba R0C 0Z0, Canada, Tel: (204) 372–6486.

White-water rapids and channels between lakes are prime walleye habitat.

OUTPOST FISHING • Manitoba

If you really want a wilderness experience and you don't mind doing a few camp chores, fishing from an outpost camp may be for you.

A typical outpost camp will consist of a walled tent or permanent cabin setup situated on a remote lake known for its fishing potential. Expect a wood stove for heat, a propane range for cooking, and logically a propane refrigerator and lights. It will be adequately furnished for four to six persons and be well equipped and supplied with food. There will be a supply of wood, plenty of gasoline, and a boat and outboard for each two angler guests. Miscellaneous other equipment like a landing net, life preservers, and boat cushions are also included. Outpost camps are usually checked twice weekly by float plane, and some of them have radio communications with the main camp as well. Running water will be a bucket that you can fill at the lake shore. Toilet facilities will consist of a conveniently located outhouse.

This type of operation offers several advantages. First of all, it costs less to stay in an outpost camp than it does to stay in a conventional fly-in lodge. It also offers the ultimate in fishing potential because yours will likely be the only camp on the lake, and the operation will probably be new. As a result, you'll be fishing unspoiled waters that will likely be teeming with fish. With a little luck, you should catch trophy-sized fish, and plenty of them.

But, there are always two sides of the coin. On this type of trip, you'll have to operate the outboard, net and handle your own fish, keep from getting lost, prepare the meals, wash the dishes, and tote water from the lake and logs from the woodpile. Know how to fillet a walleye? Someone in your party had better learn how before you book a trip like this.

Because there will be no guide along to locate your fish, some knowledge of walleye and northern-pike habitat should be a prerequisite for outpost fishing. Fish the shallow weed-filled bays for pike, paying particular attention to the type as well as the quality of vegetation sought. Walleye habitat is different; in this part of the country it will be the eddies below rapids and waterfalls, in the channels between lakes, and off rocky points or islands. Depending on the season, you'll find these schools of fish in fifteen to thirty feet of water.

What you take with you is more important on a trip like this than it is on a conventional Canadian fishing trip. If you run out of Dardevles or yellow jigs, for instance, you can't purchase more at a camp store. Should you break a rod, there will be fewer people around to loan you a replacement. You'll need to take long-nosed pliers to remove hooks from toothed jaws. Include a good fillet knife and a steel to keep it sharp. Plenty of insect repellent is a must, and so is a little emergency survival kit that might consist of matches, a signal mirror, flares, and a compass. Having a kit like this for each boat is a good idea in case an accident or storm leaves you isolated, away from camp for a period

If you don't mind handling your own fish and doing the camp chores, outpost fishing is the way to go.

of time. On a trip like this, you have to take along everything you might need. A little more pre-trip planning than usual is required.

But you also have to travel light because a float plane will be used to get you to your wilderness destination, and it will have limited space. In this respect, leave your big tackle box (jammed with bass lures) and take along those lures most attractive to the fish you'll be catching. For pike, I suggest three large Hellbenders to catch any fish lying deep. You'll need several Johnson spoons to fish the weedbeds, and more Dardevles (red and white, and yellow and red). Add a couple of large Rapala minnows and several yellow and black skirted buzz baits to fish the weeds along with your weedless spoons. Lures for walleye are even less complicated. Take a handful of smaller Hellbenders in a variety of colors and a bundle of plastic skirts in white, yellow, and hot pink. Match them up with jig heads in two different sizes. This limited selection of lures will take all the northerns and walleye you'll care to catch, and it can be carried in a small container.

Several camp operators in the province offer outpost fishing. Two that I can recommend specifically are those operated by Sickle Lake and Little Churchill Lodge.

The former offers several outpost camps in the Seal River area, north of Thompson. Spacious walled tents are used for living, with separate larger facilities for dining, cooking, and lounging. Equipment is excellent and includes electric-start outboards and trolling motors in some camps. Prices for each camp are the same but vary with services desired. Food packages are available, for example, and so are the services of a cook and guides. All are for the period of one week and include float plane transportation from Thompson. Trophy-sized northern pike are the primary species of fish sought at these camps, but it should be noted also that lake trout, Arctic grayling, and walleye abound here too. Some of the camps are limited to parties of six persons. Prices range upward from $850 per person, depending on the package desired.

Little Churchill maintains outpost camps on lakes surrounding Waskaiowaka, and all of them offer outstanding fishing for big pike and walleye. Each camp has a fully equipped cabin that can provide accommodations for from four to six persons. Prices for these weekly packages (food not included) are less than $600 per person. Another outpost camp operation on Holmes Lake, farther to the north, includes food and the services of a man to cut firewood and clean up, and maintain equipment. This seven-night outpost package includes air transportation from Thompson and is priced somewhat higher.

For details on these outpost packages, write to Brian McIntosh, Sickle Lake Lodge, P.O. Box 551, Dyersburg, TN 38024, or Mike Dyste, Little Churchill Lodge, 15410 Forest Land, San Antonio, TX 78232.

WASKAIOWAKA LAKE • Manitoba

Waskaiowaka Lake is a 75,000-acre expanse of fishing water located 550 miles north of Winnipeg and approximately eighty-five miles northeast of Thompson. Waskaiowaka is a part of the Little Churchill River and is recognized as a première northern-pike fishery. Pike grow large in these productive waters. Anglers fishing here annually catch and release trophy pike (twenty pounds and up) with regularity, and the average catch is around ten pounds.

If Mike Dyste has anything to say about it, Waskaiowaka is going to be prime pike water for years to come. Dyste is the owner of Little Churchill Lodge, located where this river spills out of Waskaiowaka Lake, and his is the only camp located in the area. According to this camp operator, it takes twenty to twenty-five years to grow a twenty-pound northern in his area, and he is aware of the fact that these big, aggressive predators are the first to be

The northern pike is the principal gamefish of the Little Churchill watershed.

cleaned out when anglers begin fishing a new lake. So, like other Canadian camp operators, Mike has instituted a "trophy only" policy that allows guests to kill only one large pike per stay, and it must be for mounting purposes. To make it easier to release these big fish, fishing with barbless hooks is recommended.

Although the average guest fishing these waters spends most of his or her time probing pockets in the weedbeds for large pike, Waskaiowaka and the Little Churchill have good walleye fishing as well. Creeks and rivers running into the lake, islands, and rocky points offer fast-paced walleye fishing throughout the season. As a result, this species of fish is the favorite for shore lunches and to take home at the end of the trip.

Little Churchill is a good camp. Guests are accommodated in spacious cabins featuring carpeting, flush toilets, comfortable beds, hot and cold running water, and other amenities. A larger lodge houses the dining room, and a comfortably furnished lounge with a large fireplace. Naturally, the camp has electricity. Experienced guides take good care of angler guests and equipment is maintained in first-class condition. The camp accommodates thirty-six persons.

Located as it is between the 56th and 57th Parallels, this camp opens after ice-out (in June) and is operational until September 15. Fishing is uniformly good throughout the season, although some anglers like to be on hand early when the pike are spawning in the shallows. This is a good time to catch a trophy fish, but so is the mid-summer period, when the pike are lurking in the weedbeds.

Currently, Little Churchill Lodge offers a weekly package on a Friday-to-Friday basis, including air transportation from Thompson, all meals, seven nights' accommodations, six days' fishing with a boat, and motor and guide furnished for each two persons. Price for this package is under $1,500. Thompson is accessible either by road (500-mile drive) or by jet from Winnipeg.

For information on fishing Lake Waskaiowaka, write to Little Churchill Lodge, Box 1191, Thompson, Manitoba R8N 1M9, Canada. Winter address is 15410 Forest Land, San Antonio, TX 78232, and the telephone number there is (512) 494-2638. For additional information about fishing these waters write to Travel Manitoba, 7–155 Carlton St., Winnipeg, Manitoba R3C 3HD, Canada.

EAGLE LAKE ● Ontario

Muskie fishermen are a breed apart.

Advocates of chalk stream trout fishing are dedicated; so are anglers dunking plastic worms for largemouth, men with sunburned noses stalking bonefish on Keys flats, bill-fishermen, almost anyone who'd rather fish than play golf or watch pro football on television.

But these anglers cannot compare to an avid muskie buff. I know men who have spent a lifetime trying to catch a trophy muskie. Another man called me at midnight recently to report that he'd had three "follows" that day. His voice was still trembling.

Muskellunge affect people that way. This North American gamefish attains a weight of seventy pounds or more (current record is 69 pounds, 15 ounces) and is a quarry worthy of any angler's skill and wiles. Muskie are big. They're mean. A big one can shatter a graphite rod or strip the line from a reel. They're also smart. To say that muskie are difficult to catch could be the understatement of the year.

People keep trying, though, and one of the best places to get the job done is on Ontario's Eagle Lake. This lake, located a few miles southwest of Dryden, holds the Canadian world record (61 pounds, 9 ounces), and many experts feel

The muskellunge is Eagle Lake's most sought-after gamefish, but other species abound too.

that the next record will come from these waters too. There's reason to believe that the fish are available. Muskellunge in the fifty-pound category have been caught here since this record was set, and anglers report encounters with monsters considerably larger. Discounting the fact that muskie fishermen occasionally stretch the truth, I am still of the opinion that Eagle is the place to go for muskie action.

Muskie spawn immediately after the ice melts and take up to two weeks to complete the process. When this chore is over, both the male and female retreat to deep water, where they are relatively inactive for a period of time. Afterwards, these big fish stake out territorial claims until the heat of summer drives them into deep water again. In the southern part of their range, muskie are difficult to locate in the summer. Autumn is different, though. As the water begins to cool, muskellunge move into the shallows again, where they feed heavily and become more aggressive. As a result, this is the best time to take a trophy fish. Incidentally, it should be noted that twenty-eight inches is the minimum size limit for this species, and that the legal muskie season is from the third Saturday in June through November.

But Eagle Lake also offers good fishing for other species of fish as well. On the two occasions I have fished this lake I found it an excellent walleye fishery, producing fish averaging three pounds or more. Larger walleye are present in these waters—each season a few trophy fish in the ten- to fifteen-pound class are taken. Eagle produces some fair lake-trout fishing early, and good smallmouth fishing throughout the season. Northern pike are plentiful, but because they have to compete with a large muskellunge population, the big ones appear to be few and far between.

Eagle lake is accessible from the south by new Highway 502 from Fort Frances (127 miles). Dryden, less than ten miles distant, has an airport capable of handling jets and is serviced by air carrier from Fort Frances.

Eagle Lake boasts one of Canada's best fishing resorts in North Shore Lodge. This first-class facility offers all the amenities one expects in a quality resort, plus good fishing equipment and experienced guides. Both American and Housekeeping Plans are available to guests, with the latter priced from $300 per week with boat, motor, and guide furnished. American Plan accommodations, which include a guide for each two persons, are available for slightly more than twice this amount. This price, incidentally, includes pickup at the Dryden airport. For more information, write to North Shore Lodge, Eagle River, Ontario P0V 1S0, Canada, Tel: (807) 755–2441.

On the opposite side of the lake is South Shore Lodge, which offers more primitive facilities at a slightly more reasonable price. This facility is not accessible by road. To reach it, you have to either drive to a boat landing or taxi to the same place from the airport. There, a boat will pick you up and provide water transportation to the lodge. This is strictly a fishing camp, but it is located in the middle of some good fishing water, and certainly the price is right. The last time I checked, a six-night package was available for less than $400 per person, and this included meals, boat, and motor for each two persons, as well as transfers. Not included was a guide (highly recommended) and gasoline. For more information on this spot write to South Shore Lodge, Eagle River, Ontario P0V 1S0, Canada, Tel: (807) 227–5553.

LAKE OF THE WOODS • Ontario

Lake of the Woods, a picture-post-card lake, sprawls across 2,000 square miles of wooded terrain on the Ontario–Minnesota border. It has 65,000 miles of shoreline, is dotted with 14,000 islands, and provides outdoor recreation for thousands of people each year.

Lake of the Woods is a composite of several different types of water and fisheries. The Minnesota portion, known as Big Traverse Bay, is best known for its walleye fishing. Here, the lake is an expanse of open water the color of tea and relatively shallow. Across the lake, to the east, Whitefish Bay is deep and clear and renowned as a muskellunge and trout fishery. Sabaskong Bay, to the south, is clear early in the year but has an algae bloom that clouds the water in late summer. This area offers good pike, walleye, and muskie fishing. Monument Bay, on the western side of the lake, is the place to go for muskie action.

This big northwoods lake is considered one of the best walleye fisheries in the world, and these fish are particularly active from ice-out through June. Guides fishing the Traverse Bay section of the lake expect all their clients to limit out during this period. In the island-studded remainder of the lake, the same situation is true. Later, the walleye schools migrate to deeper water, where they're slightly more difficult to locate but still catchable. Walleyes in this lake don't quite average three pounds, but large specimens are still around. Minnesota waters produce them, and so do Whitefish Bay and the Beacon and Chisholm Islands.

Anther species of fish common to these waters is the smallmouth bass, which is considered one of our hardest-fighting gamefish. I'm inclined to agree. This bronze-backed gamester strikes with sledge-hammer force and puts up a stubborn and powerful fight. In these waters, this northwoods bass averages around three pounds but can grow twice this size.

Smallmouth provide good fishing throughout the season, but the most spectacular action occurs in June, when the bass are in the shallows, spawning. On this occasion you can ease a boat along a boulder-strewn shoreline and productively cast surface lures and spinner baits up against the bank. The results are usually outstanding. Later in the year the smallmouth move into slightly deeper water, where they can be caught on jigs and deep-running lures.

Formerly a renowned northern-pike fishery, Lake of the Woods still has plenty of pike but may be short of trophy fish twenty pounds or larger. Fishing pressure tends to strip a lake of big, aggressive pike, and I think this is the case here. But this may not be a permanent situation. Anglers are more conservation-minded these days, and more and more of them are releasing their catch. Pike also grow faster in these waters than they do farther north, and the ten- and fifteen-pound fish now being released could reach trophy proportions in a few short years. As a result, I think we can be optimistic about this lake's future as a pike fishery.

Lake of the Woods is not short of big fish, though. It has a large muskellunge population, and the average size is eighteen pounds or more. Fish in the thirty-pound category are relatively common, and the largest fish taken from these waters weighed fifty-five pounds.

Muskie season opens in mid-June, and the fishing is good through the fall. August and September constitute perhaps the best period, though. As the summer draws close to a close, these big fish move into extremely shallow water and become very active. They'll strike surface lures at this time, but the best producers are bucktails and jerk baits. Earlier in the summer, these big

Sprawling Lake of the Woods offers quality angling and is easily accessible to American anglers.

fish may be found lurking near schools of walleye, which are their primary forage. As a result, a number of muskies are hooked by walleye fishermen, who have difficulty in landing these big fish on light tackle.

In some waters, trolling is a favorite muskie fishing method, but in this lake, casting is more effective. The middle of the lake, from Sabaskong across to Monument Bay, is a morass of islands, shallow water, rocky reefs, and weed beds. It's prime muskie water, ideally suited for casting.

Warroad, Minnesota, is the gateway for fishing the Traverse Bay section of the lake, and the guides here use good-sized launches to fish this open water. In Ontario, the primary access points are Nestor Falls, Sioux Narrows, and Kenora. All of these points of civilization are located on Highway 71, which runs north out of Fort Frances.

Lake of the Woods has every type of facility available to the visiting angler. Motel accommodations are located along the highway, and nearby marinas offer boat-rental and guide service. Fishing camps and resorts, some of them relatively posh, are dispersed along the shoreline and on the numerous wooded islands that dot this portion of the lake.

One example is Ash Rapids, which is located on an island twenty-two miles southwest of Kenora and is accessible only by boat or float plane. Ash Rapids can accommodate thirty persons and is an attractive, completely modern resort catering to fishermen and their families. Surrounding the lodge is a maze of islands, bays, and waterways that make for a pristine angling environment. All of the lake's species of gamefish are present here, and with guides to help locate them, anglers do rather well.

Rates are reasonable, too. An angling package here—which includes American Plan accommodations, fishing with a boat, motor, and guide, and cleaning and care of the catch—is priced at slightly more than $120 per day. Per-person price for a couple is even less.

Down the lake at Sioux Narrows, Red Indian Lodge offers a fishing package, including a guide, for approximately the same amount of money. The same situation applies to a dozen other camps offering quality facilities and services for reasonable prices.

For more information, write: Ash Rapids Camp, P.O. Box 1090, Kenora, Ontario P9N 3X7, Canada, Tel: (807) 733-2569—in winter, (807) 547-2723; Red Indian Lodge, Sioux Narrows, Ontario P0X 1N0, Canada, Tel: (807) 226-5616; Chamber of Commerce, Sioux Narrows, Ontario PNX 1N0, Canada; Northwest Ontario Travel Association, 127 Main Street, Kenora, Ontario P9N 3X6; or Ontario Ministry of Tourism and Recreation, Queens Park, Toronto M7A 2E5, Canada.

QUETICO PARK • Ontario

Ontario's Quetico Park and the adjoining boundary waters of Minnesota make up one of the largest water-based wilderness regions in either country. Set aside in 1926 as a roadless area to preserve its primitive character, the region occupies millions of acres of land and water and straddles the U.S.–Canada border for a distance of some 200 miles. More than a thousand miles of canoe routes are said to traverse this region, and the portages are worn deep from centuries of use by Indians and fur trappers.

The region is one of placid blue lakes, tumbling waters, and twisted rivers surrounded by tall stands of scented evergreen forest and dotted with muskeg bogs and outcroppings of weathered granite. Wildlife abounds here. This is moose country, the land of the black bear and the lean-flanked timber wolf. Here, eagles soar high overhead, beavers build their lodges, mallards raise their young, and the twilight silence reverberates with the eerie cry of a loon.

The fishing is good, too. Although thousands of canoeists dip their paddles into Quetico waters each summer, few are skilled anglers, and rarely do they

The Quetico Wilderness is canoe country, but its pristine waters offer good fishing as well.

stray far from established routes. As a result, much of the region's waters see very little angling pressure and some may never have been fished.

Northern pike in the thirty-pound category have been caught in Quetico lakes, and the species abounds here. Find a weedy bay or a submerged weedbed offshore, and you're almost certain to find pike. Schools of walleye inhabit most of the swirling foam-flecked eddies at the tail of fast-water stretches and usually can be induced to strike white and yellow jigs or deep-running wobbling baits. Lake trout are found in these waters and are easiest to locate at the beginning of the season. Quetico lakers average less than ten pounds and are most commonly taken on trolled spoons. Smallmouth bass abound here also and will strike surface lures when they're in the shallows, deeper running lures later in the season. While not as common, largemouth bass inhabit these waters too and may be caught while fishing for some of the other species.

Since no camps are allowed within the boundaries of this wilderness region, the only practical way to explore and fish it is to rent the necessary supplies and equipment and do some canoeing and camping. Such equipment will consist of a lightweight canoe that is easy to paddle and portage, paddles, carrying yoke, life vests, cushions, a lightweight tent that is both rain- and bug-proof, sleeping bags, foam pads, cooking sacks, and perhaps a camp stove.

Over the years, outfitters have worked out trail menus featuring the latest in freeze-dried meals, snacks, and dehydrated beverages. Also available are steaks, luxuries like bacon and butter, and fresh foods. All of this is packaged together in a portable food pack that has a minimum of bulk and weight. Both are important on a trip of this type, as participants will discover on their first portage. In this respect it should be noted that cans and glass bottles are prohibited in the Quetico Park. Plastic bottles make a suitable substitute.

Use equal care in selecting your own personal gear. Include a first-aid kit (if the outfitter doesn't include one), fillet knife and hone, insect repellent, suntan lotion, a compass, and a couple of small flashlights. Clothing should include an extra shirt and a pair of trousers, a warm jacket, a rain suit, waterproof boots, wool socks, and a broad-brimmed hat. If you go early in the season (May or early June), I suggest that you take along extra insect repellent to ward off the blackflies. Select lures with care, and pack them in a small plastic box. Limit yourself to three rods and three reels, and give some consideration to some of the new telescopic rods now on the market. Long rods, on some portages, can be a pain.

Most Quetico canoeists plan a trip that includes daily travel and a new camp each night. It may make more sense to canoe to a certain area, set up a permanent camp, and fish the surrounding waters. Consult with your outfitter on this subject. Explain that good fishing is your primary objective, and he or she will recommend an area one or more portages off of regular canoe trails. You'll be fishing waters that have seen little or no angling pressure.

There are several jumping-off places for a Quetico canoe adventure, with one of the most popular being Ely, Minnesota. A dozen or more Quetico outfitters are headquartered here, and all of them provide first-class services. To the west, an outfitter named Bill Zup has a camp on Ontario's Lac la Croix and outfits Quetico canoe parties as well. Zup also has a first-class operation, and the area he services may offer better fishing than the boundary water closer to Ely. Another possibility is to approach the Quetico region from the Canadian side, which sees even less traffic from U.S. canoeists. Atikokan is the jumping-off spot for these trips and has several quality outfitters.

These trips are a bargain. You can book a trip with any of the outfitters I've mentioned and be completely outfitted for less than $30 per day. This includes canoe, tent, food, sleeping bags, all equipment—everything you'll need besides your clothing, toilet kit, and fishing tackle. Most access to and from the park border is provided by launch, but float planes are also available to take you in and out. The price for this service will add $100 per person to a week's trip, but the difference in fishing potential might make the extra investment worthwhile.

For more information on fishing the Quetico Superior wilderness region, write to the following: Canoe Canada, Box 1810, Atikokan, Ontario P0T 1C0, Canada, Tel: (218) 365–6123 (807) 597–6418; Bill Zup, Lac la Croix Outfitters, Crane Lake, MN 55725, Tel: (218) 993–2273 and (807) 599–2710; or Chamber of Commerce, 1600 E. Sheridan, Ely, MN 55731.

BEAUCHENE LAKES ● Quebec

Known for their fine smallmouth-bass fishing, the Beauchene Lakes are located forty miles east of North Bay, Ontario, and are best reached by float plane.

These gem-like lakes encompass a 120-square-mile chunk of wilderness and provide a perfect smallmouth habitat—clean, cold water, a boulder-strewn shoreline, submerged timber, and aquatic weeds. Combine this ideal habitat with an abundant food supply and you have all of the ingredients for a productive northwoods fishery.

The smallmouth bass is one of North America's hardest-fighting gamefish.

Smallmouth, throughout their Canadian range, average less than two pounds, with an occasional trophy exceeding three. Beauchene bass come in larger packages averaging around three pounds and can go to seven pounds or more.

Lunkers in the five-pound category are relatively common in these waters.

Familiar with the smallmouth bass?

Bassers familiar with both species of black bass rate the smallmouth as much better gamefish than the largemouth. Other smallmouth devotees claim that the species is the best gamefish in North America. I'm not sure I disagree. This northwoods brawler strikes with the force of a sledge-hammer blow, leaps with wild abandon when hooked, and has a staying power that few other gamefish can match. From every standpoint, the smallmouth bass is an exciting gamefish.

The action here begins in late May and lasts until mid-September. During the early part of the season, the bass are found in the shallows and strike surface lures readily. Fly rodders use popping bugs to induce these strikes; bait casters or spinning enthusiasts use a variety of floating lures to stimulate action. At this season of the year, the bass are spawning, and anglers ease quietly along the shoreline looking for beds or fish. Once the target is spotted, an accurate cast is almost certain to produce a savage strike. It should be noted that all bass caught at this season of the year are released on the spot so that they can return to their nests. Even a trophy fish is illegal at this early time, because the season doesn't open until June 15.

After spawning, Beauchene bass move into four or six feet of water but remain along the shoreline. Here, they continue to respond to surface or shallow running lures until they leave the shallows in early August. At this season they can be taken by fishing submerged timber with black jigs or weedless worms. They return again to the shallows when the water cools in the fall.

These lakes are the exclusive domain of Club Beauchene, which has leased the property from the Quebec government since the early 1900s. Accommodations are provided in a plantation-type lodge that features bedrooms with private baths. Breakfast and dinner are served family-style in the dining room, with box lunches provided for the noon meal. Aluminum boats, powered with small outboards, are provided for fishing on a shared basis. Maps of the lakes are provided, but normally not guides. The latter are available at extra charge.

In addition to smallmouth, some of the Beauchene lakes abound with nice-sized walleye, ranging up to ten pounds. Lake trout, averaging less (around seven pounds), cruise the shallows in the spring and may be taken along with spawning smallmouth. They retreat to the depths in the summer and move back into shallow water in the fall. Brook trout are present in some of the lakes, as are northern pike, whitefish, and several varieties of panfish.

To preserve its trophy fishing, Club Beauchene management enforces a "trophy only" policy that restricts fish killed to one of each species. This conservation policy is to be applauded, because trophy smallmouth bass are difficult to find these days, and Club Beauchene provides evidence that such a policy works.

If you're thinking about fishing this part of Canada early in the season, bear in mind that blackflies are thick during the first three weeks of the season. Plenty of insect repellent is recommended, and perhaps a hooded Shoo-Fly jacket as well. Mosquitoes are around most of the season but are usually a problem only at night.

Smallmouth are great gamesters, but because they'll average less than four pounds I recommend relatively light tackle for fishing these waters. Bring a flyrod with a good supply of cork-bodied bugs. For spinning, I suggest Mepps spinners, a variety of surface lures, or Rapala minnow imitations. Add a few small spoons (weedless varieties for brush and weeds) and a supply of jigs, and you'll be in business. Smallmouth bass are easier to release than pike or walleye, but single barbless hooks will still facilitate the process.

Club Beauchene is accessible by road, but the last thirty miles is an extremely rough road. A better way is to fly to North Bay from Toronto and transfer to a float plane for a short twenty-minute hop to camp. The last I heard, Norland Air supplied this service.

Package trips operate on a Sunday-to-Saturday basis and are priced at approximately $725 in American funds. Included are accommodations, all meals, and fishing with a boat and motor for each two persons. Guides, if desired, cost an extra $60 per day.

For information on fishing Club Beauchene waters, I suggest you write to PanAngling Travel Service, 180 North Michigan Ave., Chicago, IL 60601, Tel: (312) 263–0328. For additional information on Quebec fishing, write to Ministere du Loisir, de la Chasse et de Peche, Direction generale des parcs et du plein air, 150 boul, Saint-Cyrille est, Quebec A1C 5R8, Canada.

GEORGE RIVER ● Quebec

The Atlantic salmon is a classic gamefish. Aggressive when hooked, this beautiful salmonoid leaps high in the air, makes long runs, and fights a bruising battle that is not over until the fish is finally tailed or netted. Throughout their range, these salmon average around ten pounds, but individual adults have been scaled in the seventy-nine-pound class (world record set in 1928). Fish weighing fifteen to twenty pounds are fairly common and are formidible combatants in this weight class.

Salmon fishing is unpredictable. Schools of salmon enter a stream when the water is high, and they may pass through the lower beats without pausing. On the other hand, low water can prolong a run and leave the upper stretches of a stream virtually fishless. Timing is very critical, but trying to predict weather

Jim Chapralis, of PanAngling, expertly tails this Atlantic salmon.

and water conditions is difficult. There is simply no guarantee that any given day or week is going to produce fishing action. As an indicator of this, it takes ten days of fishing Europe's better streams to produce one salmon. In Nova Scotia the average is seven rod days per fish, and about half that in New Brunswick. In contrast, the records show that isolated rivers like the George may yield as many as four or five salmon per day during peak weeks.

Quebec's Ungava Plateau is a vast expanse of sub-Arctic tundra blanketed with lichen and stands of stunted black spruce. The region is a part of the Canadian Shield, with low-lying terrain to the south and west and the mountains of Labrador to the east. Glacier-carved lakes and rivers crisscross the area, and one of these is the George. This stream drains a 400-mile-long watershed adjoining the Labrador border and is considered one of the best Atlantic salmon-fishing streams. Unlike other salmon rivers in this part of Canada, which primarily yield catches of small salmon (grilse), the George regularly gives up catches in the fifteen- to twenty-pound category. A 28-pounder is the largest salmon caught here, but thirty-pound fish are known to inhabit these waters.

The ice goes out in late June, and throughout July the George, swollen by melting snow and ice, is a white-water torrent. Fishing is good, though. Few salmon have entered the river at this time, but the George still abounds with trophy-sized brook trout (called speckled trout), lake trout thirty pounds or larger, Arctic char, and splake. Splake are a hybrid cross between a brook and lake trout that goes to twenty pounds or more.

Around August 1 the salmon leave the frigid waters of Ungava Bay and begin their migratory runs up the George. Tides at the mouth of this river are forty to fifty feet high, and their influence can be seen fifty miles island. These tides give the salmon a boost on their upstream journey and speed them to waiting anglers fresh from the sea, and in prime condition.

The last time I counted, a half-dozen fishing camps were strewn along the George River, offering accommodations and fishing facilities for more than one hundred persons. Typical of these is the George River Lodge, located 135 miles upstream and 150 miles from Schefferville to the south. The latter town, a mining community of some 5,000 persons, is the only semblance of civilization in this entire area.

The stretch of river fronting the lodge has been divided into three beats offering access to twenty-six pools that are natural holding areas for salmon and other species of George fish. Guests (twelve of them when the camp is full) fish these beats on a rotation basis, changing each day. At this season all fishing is limited to flies, fished by wading or from a canoe. Earlier in July there are no restrictions on fishing methods, and spin fishermen do better than the angler wielding a fly rod.

Spin fishermen are advised to bring medium-action spinning rods equipped with large-capacity reels loaded with twelve-pound test line. Favorite lures are Mepps spinners in several different sizes, and a variety of Dardevle spoons. Also bring a smaller spinning outfit or fly rod to fish for smaller char and brook trout. Fly rods for George salmon should be nine feet long and have reels loaded with WF 10F line and at least 200 yards of fifteen-pound backing. Leaders should also be heavy, testing at least twelve pounds. Expert casting is not a prerequisite for fishing this stream, though. A thirty-foot cast will take a salmon, and rarely will an angler have to cast sixty or seventy feet. A few favorite flies are Black Dose, Jock Scott, Blue Charm, and a variety of muddlers tied on 4, 6, or 8 size hooks. Some of the more popular dry flies are the Wulffs, Rat Face, and McDougal tied on 8–12 size hooks.

Bring felt-soled waders or hip boots (the latter are more comfortable on portages or for climbing in and out of canoes), a rain parka, and plenty of warm clothing. Consideration might be given to a jacket that fits snugly at the wrists to help ward off the hordes of mosquitoes and blackflies native to this region. Bring plenty of insect repellent, and perhaps a shoo-fly jacket as well. Include a pair of polarized sunglasses, suntan lotion, and comfortable clothing to wear around camp. During July and August the average temperature is 60 degrees, and slightly colder than that in September.

George River Lodge is remote and rustic, but it does have electricity, refrigerators and freezers, showers, and flush toilets. Neither camp management nor the Quebec government appears to have any concern for fish stocks, so take-home fish limits are generous. Bear this in mind when packing, because the luggage limit is sixty pounds and you'll be charged for any excess. George River Lodge offers a week's package (Thursday to Thursday) that is priced from $1,500 to $2,500, depending on the time period. July is the cheapest. The latter part of August and the first part of September are the most expensive.

Gateway for this part of the world is Schefferville, Quebec, which is reached by a 700-mile flight from Montreal, or from Sept-Iles. The latter town is accessible by both air and rail.

For more information on fishing the George River, write to the George River Lodge, 865 rue Duchesneau, Ste-Foy, Quebec G1X 2Z1, Canada, Tel: (418) 656–1550. Or write to Ministere du Loisir, de la Chasse et de Peche, Case Postale 8888, Quebec City, Quebec G1K 7W3, Canada.

MINIPI RIVER ● Labrador

"Best brook trout fishery in the world." This is the claim made for the Minipi River, and there is reason to believe that the statement is not an exaggeration.

The Minipi is located in the Labrador bush, seventy miles southwest of Goose Bay, and is currently accessible only by helicopter. Unlike many Canadian streams that are swift and turbulent, this river system consists of a series of small lakes connected by short stretches of fast water. These lakes are shallow, averaging less than five feet in depth, and are filled with lush aquatic growth. Brook trout abound in these pools, a special breed of Salvelinus fontinalis that grows to a huge size. These slab-sided brookies average more than five pounds and go to ten pounds or more in the lakes. Smaller trout, thought to be a different species, inhabit the riffles.

Can you imagine catching brook trout that average five pounds in size? The thought is mind-boggling, but it's true. Fisheries biologists who have studied these Minipi monsters believe that they grow a pound each year and live ten years or more. Equally important, these fish are insect feeders, deriving most of their annual growth from the mayflies, caddis, and stoneflies that they gobble up each summer. Hatches of these aquatic insects occur with regularity from late June until the middle of September, with the most intensity in July and early August.

These waters are restricted to fly fishing, and the fact that Minipi trout feed exclusively on insects makes them susceptible to a well-presented fly. Although some blind casting is done when a hatch is not on, trophy trout are frequently located in advance and cast to as specific targets. Minipi trout can also be wary. Particularly when the breeze stills, and the surface of the water becomes like a piece of glass, it is necessary to make forty- or fifty-foot casts to keep from spooking the fish. Except for the period of the main mayfly hatch in mid-summer, when large trout move out into the lake to take advantage of the abundant feed, most fishing is done in the river sections.

Large canoes, powered by 7.5 horsepower engines, are used for fishing. A good deal of fishing is also done by wading. An experienced guide is provided for each two fishermen. Guests have the option of taking a box lunch when they camp for the day, or they can enjoy a leisurely shore lunch if they want. In this case, a stop is made at one of the fast-water sections of the river, where small (twelve- to fourteen-inch) trout can be taken on almost every cast. These little fish are called "lunch trout" and are just the right size for eating.

Anglers wanting to fish the upper Minipi have a choice of two camps, both operated by Canadian Jack Cooper. One is Anne Marie Lake Lodge, which is located on the lake by the same name. The other is Cooper's Minoni Lodge, which is located in the headwaters of the west branch of the Minipi. Both facilities are rustic in construction and decor, but they provide all the necessary creature comforts. Beds are comfortable, there is inside plumbing, and savory meals are served in spacious dining rooms. There are no sheets, though—sleeping bags with freshly laundered liners are used.

According to Jack Cooper, the huge "Labrador reds" of the Minipi are not an inexhaustible resource and would not last long if anglers were allowed to kill their limit of these fish. As a consequence, Cooper has established a catch-and-release policy that limits guests to one trophy trout for mounting and those small fish that they may choose to eat while in camp. All the rest are released. Because only sixty anglers fish these waters each year, this conservation policy should assure that trophy-sized Minipi trout will be around for many years to come.

Northern pike, some reaching a size of twenty-five pounds, are found in these waters, and they occasionally attack large flies or streamers that are thrown too close to their weedbed habitat. Unless anglers are deliberately fishing for this species and using a heavy shock leader, most hooked pike will break off. Landlocked char are also found in these waters, are slightly larger than the trout, and put up an excellent fight when hooked.

Anglers fishing these waters will primarily use a floating line, but there are times when the fish are down and a sinking line is needed. The best fly patterns are those that approximate the shape and size of the large Hexagenia

Minipi brookies average five pounds and go to ten or more.

Mayflies, notably Wulffs, Humpies, and Irresistibles in #10 through #16 sizes. The muddler minnow, over the years, has proved to be the most successful wet fly in these waters; Matuka patterns and a Hare's Ear are also popular. Rods should include an eight-foot stick for normal fishing and a longer, more powerful one for use during windy days or when the fish are down. Reels should have at least twenty-five yards of backing.

Labrador has plenty of biting bugs, so come prepared with insect repellent and plan to use it. If you plan to fish these waters at the beginning of the season, consider a head net and a Shoo-Fly jacket.

Hip boots are considered adequate for these waters and are more comfortable when hiking between pools. Make sure that they have nonslip felt soles. Include a pair of polarized sunglasses, suntan lotion, plenty of warm fishing togs, and comfortable clothing to wear around camp. Limit your gear to forty or fifty pounds, and pack it in a duffel bag that is easy to stow in a small aircraft. Because you'll be wearing boots or waders while fishing, I recommend a hip-length rain parka instead of a conventional rain suit. Days will likely be warm, but cold snaps can occur at any time.

A week's fishing package (Sunday to Sunday) at Minipi costs $2,000 per person for a party of two, and $700 more on a single-supplement basis. This package price, however, includes round-trip air transportation from Goose Bay by helicopter. Also included are accommodations, all meals, a nonresident fishing license, and guided fishing services.

Eastern Provincial Airways operates regular air service to Goose Bay from Montreal and Halifax, with Montreal possibly being the preferred gateway to northern Labrador. A representative meets all Minipi camp guests in Goose Bay and supervises their transfer to the helicopter for the flight to camp.

For more information on fishing in this part of Labrador, write to Minipi Camps, P.O. Box 340, Happy Valley, Labrador A0P 1E0, Canada, Tel: (709) 896–2891; or Department of Development, Tourism Branch, P.O. Box 4750, St. John's Newfoundland A1C 5T7, Canada, Tel: (709) 737–3831.

The southern half of Tierra del Fuego is mountainous and heavily forested.

The Caribbean and Central and South America 4

If the paradise of the Caribbean islands were not enough, Central and South America is a paradise plus for sportsmen. This vast land mass is 5,000 miles long and is approximately 3,000 miles across at its widest point. It is comprised of the vast Amazon basin, which is almost as large as the entire continental United States; the 4,000-mile-long Andes Mountain range; other sprawling river systems like the Orinoco, the Magdalena, and Paraná; the llanos of Colombia and Venezuela; and the Patagonia region of Argentina. And except for a narrow strip of desert along the Pacific coast, all of this part of the world has something to offer the angler.

It also has an array of gamefish that have no peers elsewhere on earth. The dorado is a good example. This beautiful fish inhabits a far-flung area extending from the Magdalena River headwaters in Colombia to the mouth of the Parana River in subtropical Argentina. In its southern range it goes to seventy-five pounds or better and is every inch a gamester. In my opinion, the dorado strikes harder, jumps higher, and has more stamina than any other freshwater gamefish I have ever tangled with.

The payara is a savage saber-tooth fish that equals the dorado in jumping ability and grows almost as large. This silvery gamester abounds throughout most of the South American tropics but appears to grow larger in the Orinoco River system than it does farther south. The largest payara I have boated weighed twenty-eight pounds, but I have lost larger specimens and am of the opinion that the species can go to forty pounds or better. Actually, the payara is still something of a mystery fish. Only a handful of anglers have fished for payara, and to my knowledge there is no scientific data available on the species. Like dorado, this fish prefers white water and is usually found in this type of habitat.

The principal gamefish of the South American tropics is a bass-like cichlid called the pavon, or peacock bass. The pavon is a beautiful fish. Its eye, gill covers, and fins are crimson colored. It has a golden-hued body, with bluish-black bars on the sides and a spot on the tail resembling the eye of a peacock feather. This Amazon dandy is a great gamefish. It strikes lures with savage abandon, leaps frequently when hooked, and is so powerful that the average bass fisherman will have to catch one to believe the stories about it. One species, cichla temensis, averages around five pounds and probably exceeds thirty pounds in weight.

There are other gamefish in the Amazon basin: For example, one time something gulped down a surface lure I had thrown into a pocket in the lily pads, and I set the hook on a 250-pound pirarucu. I was familiar with this huge fish because I had seen specimens that natives had speared for food. But I never dreamed that the pirarucu would strike an artificial lure. It did, though, and three minutes later my reel was devoid of line.

On another occasion I was trolling a large Lazy Ike lure in the turbid waters of the Meta River when something almost jerked my rod out of my hands. I set the hook, and twenty yards away a large zebra-striped fish came climbing out of the water in a burst of spray. The colorful fish jumped a half-dozen times before it changed tactics and began to wage a dogged underwater contest that lasted many minutes more. When I finally beached it, I discovered that I had caught a catfish. It was a beautiful thing, with black and white stripes, and it had jumped like a tarpon. But it was still a catfish. Later on I learned it was called a suburi or suburim, depending on what country I was in. It's an excellent gamefish.

I've caught black piranha as large as ten pounds and consider them good gamefish too. Curbinata are silvery drum that look and fight like our stripers. Pacu are built like our bluegill but reach a size of twenty-five pounds or larger. The picuda resembles our northern pike or muskellunge and goes to six feet more. These fish jump like crazy and are extremely difficult to land. The trahira looks like a cross between our bowfin and a grayling. It is a savage-toothed predator and goes to fifteen pounds. But that's not all. I've caught a half-dozen other species of fish that I have been unable to classify. One was a six-foot greenish-colored fish that even my native guide was unable to identify. It was a good fighter, though, and when we steaked and ate it for dinner it was delicious.

The vastness of what I'm talking about staggers the imagination. There are thousands and thousands of miles of rivers in tropical South America, and each of these systems is studded with tributaries and ox-bow lakes. These lakes and streams teem with gamefish, and as I mentioned previously, the majority of these waters have never been fished.

The same situation is applicable to South American trout fishing. Virtually all of the lakes and streams in the Andes were stocked with trout more than fifty years ago, and these fish populations have thrived in their new environment. Rivers and lakes of Argentina and Chile, even the famous fisheries, see little fishing pressure as North Americans know it. Fishing is good, as a result, and comparable to fishing in wilderness Alaska and better than in New Zealand, in my opinion. Rainbows and browns grow to thirty pounds or better in the lakes, and almost this large in the streams. If you get away from the traditional fishing centers of San Martin, Bariloche, and Esquel in Argentina, the odds of catching trophy fish really improve. Patagonian rivers and streams remain virtually unfished, and the same situation applies to some of the less accessible fisheries in Tierra del Fuego. In these waters, magnificent sea-run browns exceed twenty pounds in size, and none of them has ever seen an artificial fly. Ten-pound brook trout are relatively common, and there are streams with runs of Atlantic salmon that are fished only by the natives.

To a lesser extent, the same situation applies to trout in the high, inaccessible lakes of Bolivia, Peru, Ecuador, and Colombia. No one has heard of these lakes, but I've talked to men who have fished them, and their stories are enough to make an angler's arm twitch.

South America has the fishing water and is blessed with some of the greatest gamefish in the world. Most of its countries are sparsely populated, and few of these people fish. As a result, most South American lakes and streams have little or no angling pressure. The result is a dream situation for those with the means and the inclination to take advantage of it.

Practical Matters

I've been poking around in South America for many years, and I can count on two hands all the snakes I've ever seen. One was a colorful emerald tree boa stalking a monkey high in a tree top, another was a sleeping anaconda, the other three were heading the other direction, and the rest were dead. I've seen more snakes while fishing in Florida or Arkansas. Although present in the South American tropics, they aren't a problem.

The Amazon caiman (alligator) is said to grow to a length of eighteen feet, but very few of them live very long these days: Today, forest Indians and mestizos, who live in the bush, hunt the caiman for its skin and have made the large ones wary. They're around, because you can see their glowing red eyes when you stroll along a river bank at night with a flashlight. But, I don't think they're as abundant as they are in Africa, and the Indians don't consider them to be a major threat to humans.

In my Latin American travels I've been involved in six revolutions, but in each case I never knew about it until I returned home and read the papers. Many of these government changes are bloodless coups, and in other cases most of the violence takes place within a few blocks of the government center. Contrary to what the press says, Americans are still warmly received in Argentina, and not every person in Colombia is in the drug business. I suppose that bad guys do exist down there, but the chances of meeting up with one of them are few and far between.

Piranha pose a potential threat to life and limb, but even the stories about this little fish have been exaggerated. I've seen Indian kids swimming in an Amazon lake or river and have caught piranha in the same waters a half an hour later. I once saw a school of piranha reduce a wounded crocodile to a skeleton in three minutes, but it should be noted that both normally co-exist in the same waters. Piranha will attack a hooked peacock bass, but not under normal circumstances. Jaguar swim in piranha-infested waters, and so do big anaconds and tapir. And I know of no case in which any of these animals have been attacked. As a result of these observations, I am of the opinion that the piranha isn't the villain he's purported to be.

Insects are another matter of concern. Amazon wasps sting as hard as our variety, but the average angler will never encounter one. Ants bite too, and this may be the reason why most Amazon natives sleep in hammocks. Depending on where you are, mosquitoes may or may not be a problem, but generally I haven't found them as large or voracious as the Maine or Alaska variety. The jejen must also be reckoned with. This is a tiny biting gnat, similar to the North American blackfly, and its bite can be equally painful. Happily, all of these insects are discouraged by insect repellent, and I highly recommend its use.

A change of water frequently affects intestinal functions, and this occurs with South Americans visiting our continent as frequently as it does with us visiting theirs. As a result, I try to avoid drinking water when I am traveling, and particularly when I am in the tropics. The tap water in the better South American hotels is usually safe to drink these days, but elsewhere I don't take chances. When I do drink it, I boil all water for a minimum of fifteen minutes, or I treat it with a Potable Agua tablet. These little tablets come fifty to the bottle and are very effective. Oh, yes, I always keep a bottle of Lomotil tablets in my toilet kit, too.

Spanish is spoken throughout South America except in Brazil, where Portuguese is the official language. I have never found this language barrier to be a problem, though. Most of the native guides I have fished with didn't know much Spanish either. As a result, we didn't talk much. They handled the boat and I caught the fish, which turned out to be a good arrangement. English is spoken widely in hotels, airports, and restaurants. Even if you can't say "buenos dias," language rarely will pose a problem.

If you plan to travel to Latin America, obtain a passport. Most Latin American countries also require a tourist card, but these are usually available from your airline at no charge.

Pay attention to the seasons and remember that they are the reverse of ours when you cross the equator. They ski in Chile in July, for instance. In tropical South America there are no seasonal temperature differences, but there are wet and dry seasons that have an effect on fishing and living. Generally, north of the Amazon the dry season is our winter, and south of the Amazon it is the opposite.

And if avoiding winter is your goal, or if you need some sun and warmth next January, you might want to plan a stop in the Bahamas before heading farther south. You'll see why, on the next page.

BONEFISH FLATS • Bahamas

In all the Caribbean, there's one destination that's especially alluring to fishermen: the Bahamas. Sprawling alongside the Gulf Stream, off the coast of Florida, the Bahamas Islands stretch for a distance of 700 miles. In between these islands, sand spits, and rocky cays are vast expanses of shallow flats dimpled with tailing bonefish.

The bonefish is a streamlined fish, sheathed with silver scales, with a turned-down snout that allows it to root around in the sand and marl for the small mollusks and crustaceans that make up its diet. Because the bonefish is vulnerable to both birds and sharks in this shallow water habitat, it is extremely wary. The shadow of a bird or flyline overhead, the motion of a casting angler's arm, the whisper of a pole rubbing against a boat's gunwale will stampede bonefish off of a flat like a covey of quail on the rise.

And when they move, it's with missile speed. Sink a hook into the jaw of a bonefish, and he'll push up a hump of ocean in front of him as he streaks through the shallows. The sound of a screaming reel drag adds credence to the belief that this denizen of the flats is one of the fleetest fish that swims. Probably isn't true, but it seems like it.

It's strong, too. Fly reels should have at least 200 yards of backing, and spinning reels an equal amount of eight-pound test monofiliment. So powerful is a bonefish that about all an angler can do is hold his or her rod skyward and hang on when the fish makes its first run. Then, when the fish finally slows, the battle just begins. Pumping a stubborn six-pound bonefish back across the flats can be both time-consuming and exhausting. And if there are very many little mangrove sprouts on that particular flat, it also can be an exercise in futility.

Bahamian bonefish average less than four pounds, but bigger fish are still around. Bonefish topping ten pounds are likely to be encountered on any flat in the Bahamas, and they come in considerably larger packages in spots like Bimini and the Berry Islands. The former has produced bonefish in the sixteen-pound category, and reputable anglers who fish the latter spot swear that there are twenty-pound bonefish cruising these remote waters.

Bonefish are taken with flies, small jigs, and bait, with the first fishing method being the most difficult. Long casts are usually required to place a fly in front of a fish without being seen, and accurate casting is a prerequisite as well. So is fast action, because feeding bonefish occasionally race across the flats in their eagerness to outstrip their companions. In these cases, an ability to strip in a line quickly or lay a fly a few feet in advance of the moving school is essential to getting a strike.

But Bahamas bonefish are not nearly as wary as those inhabiting the Florida Keys. On flats where fishing pressure is light, bonefish frequently react

Stretching for a distance of 700 miles, the Bahamas provide unlimited habitat for bonefish and other flats denizens.

aggressively to the offerings of even neophyte anglers. If you're new to bonefishing, this is the place to get acquainted with the sport.

Bonefishing is essentially hunting. Because the water on the flats can be extremely shallow, the best procedure is to spot your fish before making a cast. If the water is less than sixteen inches deep, the tails of feeding bonefish may actually protrude from the water and can be spotted from some distance away. Cruising bonefish are difficult to see because they are about the same hue as the glistening marl or sand flats they occupy. Polarized sunglasses are essential for this reason, and a wide-brimmed hat will also come in handy. So will the sharp eyes of a seasoned bonefish guide.

Bahamas weather is usually delightful, and this includes January and February. It should be noted however, that occasional winter northers drift this far south, and that bonefish are extremely weather sensitive. Winter fishing in the Bahamas can be excellent on occasion, but don't count on it. For optimum fishing conditions, plan your bonefishing trip for the spring and fall.

If you're a fly fisherman, bring along rods suitable for a 9- or 10-weight line. Weight-forward floating lines are best. Reels should have 200 yards of twenty-pound test backing. Nine-foot leaders should have an eight- to ten-pound tippet. For spinning, bring along a seven-foot medium-action spinning rod capable of casting 1/8- and 1/4-ounce lures. Load your open-face reel with 200 yards of eight-pound test line. I do not recommend closed-face spinning reels.

It gets very hot on these bonefish flats, so bring cover-up clothing, sun-screen, lip coat, and other fishing togs. Include sneakers for wading and boat use, a rain suit, and a variety of tropical-weight clothing for dining and evening wear. Don't forget insect repellent.

The best fishing camp in the Bahamas is probably Deep Water Cay, located at the east end of Grand Bahama Island. Strictly for anglers, Deep Water Cay provides accommodations for sixteen guests and offers package prices that include skiffs and bonefishing guides. Accommodations are first class, as are the food and the camp administration.

Surrounding the camp are thirty miles of lightly fished flats that offer a wide variety of fishing water. There are banks to drift across, flats to wade for the big loners, and creeks to fish on windy days. Bonefish in this area average five pounds or better, and they're plentiful.

Clustered near the northern tip of Andros is a handful of cays known as the Berry Islands. The flats here are extensive and are considered by Bahamian experts to hold some of the largest bonefish in the world. The Chub Cay Club is located here, but it caters primarily to big-game fishermen who gather here to fish for billfish and other saltwater heavyweights that abound in the tongue of the ocean fronting the Berry group. As a result, bonefishing in the area remains almost untapped and holds great potential. Chub Cay is a first-class facility, offering skiffs and bonefishing guides for hire.

Some of the finest bonefish habitat in the Bahamas is located at the Bight of Abaco. The Abaco Cays form a crescent on the eastern rim of the Little Bahama Bank, and tucked away in the center are several hundred unpopulated cays and one hundred square miles of bonefish flats. Here, particularly in a remote area known as the Marls, you'll find virgin bonefishing unmatched elsewhere in these islands. Bight bonefish average less than three pounds, but they're so plentiful that it's impossible to hold this against them. They're also aggressive, forgiving of a neophyte's sloppy cast, and brazen in their eagerness to please.

Treasure Cay is the place to stay here. Located at the center of the Bight, Treasure Cay is a modern resort featuring swimming pools, tennis courts, and eighteen-hole golf course, shopping, restaurants, a marina, skiffs, and bonefishing guides.

Prices are not cheap in the Bahamas, but neither are they particularly expensive. At Treasure Cay, for example, a double room goes for $95 to $150 per day, depending on whether it's the low or high season. The rates at Chub Cay are somewhat less, but the price for a day of bonefishing is the same ($150 per day). At Deep Water Cay, American Plan accommodations cost $100 per day, and a day on the bonefish flats goes for $175 for one or two anglers. This fishing camp also has a three-day all-inclusive fishing package (including air transportation from West Palm Beach) for $692 per person in a party of two, and $598 during the low season, which runs from the middle of July through February.

For information on these Bahamas fishing spots, write to the following: Deep Water Cay Club, P.O. Box 1145, Palm Beach, FL 33480, Tel: (305) 684–3958; Treasure Cay Hotel, P.O. Box 3941, Miami, FL 33101, Tel: 1–800–327–1584; or Chub Cay Club, P.O. Box 661067, Miami, FL 33166, Tel: 1–800–325–1490 or 1–800–327–0787. For more general information about fishing in these islands, get in touch with the Bahamas Sports Information Centre, 225 Alhambra Circle, Suite 415, Coral Gables, FL 33134, Tel: 1–800–327–7678.

LAKE DIAZ ORDAZ • Mexico

It's a new bass lake.

Diaz Ordaz, also called Lake Baccarac, was first opened to the angling public in 1983, with sensational results. During the first year, almost every angler averaged more than one hundred bass per day, and their stringers included several fish in the four- and five-pound category. The lake is still hot, too. I fished Ordaz last year and caught my limit each day I was on the water. These were good-sized bass, too. Most averaged around four pounds, and some were in the eight-pound category.

But Mexican bass lakes habitually come on the scene like a July 4th fireworks display, make bass-fishing history for a few years, and then fade away into oblivion. Lakes like Obregon, Hidalgo, Guerrero, and Dominguez are good examples. Each had its heyday. Most of them are only mediocre fishing holes now.

Ordaz could be the exception. For a number of reasons, this sprawling impoundment could remain the hemisphere's best bass-fishing lake for years to come.

For one thing, the lake is relatively isolated. It is tucked away in the Sierra Madre mountains seventy miles east of Los Mochis, and the only village nearby has a population of fewer than 300 persons.

Unlimited commercial fishing, which decimated other Mexican bass lakes, is not allowed here. Limited netting is permitted to control the population of tilapia, mojarra, and other rough fish, but bass are not taken in nets, nor may they be sold as a food fish. Because sportsfishing guides and commercial netters are one and the same here, this rule is well enforced.

Limits are generous, but not by Mexican standards. On Ordaz, a boat with two anglers is allowed twenty-four bass per outing, or a total of forty-eight fish per day. All fish retained must exceed two pounds in weight.

Diaz Ordaz, a new Mexican bass lake, is hot now, and it has the potential of remaining that way for years to come.

Fishing pressure is likewise limited by available guides and by the number of boats and motors provided by the lake's concessionaire, Bill Chapman. The last time I checked, Chapman had thirty fishing rigs available for visiting anglers and stated that he would maintain this number in order to limit angling pressure on the lake.

Mexican bass lakes have all been productive for a limited period of time, but none of them have been considered trophy-bass lakes. Ordaz should prove to be an exception, because Florida bass were stocked in these waters and are capable of growing to a large size. Couple this fact with a 365-day growing season and an unlimited food supply, and it appears that Ordaz could become the first south-of-the-border lake to qualify as a trophy-bass fishery. Ten-pound bass have been taken in these waters, and the number of fish in this category is certain to increase as the lake matures.

Bill Chapman, an American, has the operating concession for this lake and seems to be doing a good job with it. Bill, who has provided similar fishing services at other Mexican lakes over the years, is knowledgeable when it comes to providing the right services for visiting anglers and is determined to see that Ordaz remains a quality fishery for years to come. Chapman stocked the lake initially, is responsible for its regulations, and has a close working relationship with the Mexican government and the village of Bacubirito.

Chapman offers a fishing package that consists of the following: three days' fishing with a boat, motor, and guide for each two persons, three nights' accommodations in a new but rather rustic little lodge located in the village, three first-class meals daily, fishing license, boat coolers stocked with free beer and soft drinks, evening cocktails, daily transfers back and forth from the lake, and cleaning and freezing anglers' catches. Packaged for fishermen flying into Bacubirito by private plane, this all-inclusive package is priced at $675 per person.

Los Mochis, located ninety miles to the west, is the closest city with a commercial airport and might be considered the gateway to this region. Bacubirito is accessible by charter aircraft or by road from Los Mochis, the latter method taking three hours by car.

Visiting anglers are not required to purchase the Chapman package if they bring in their own boats, but they must hire a guide whether they use him or her or not. (The price for this guide is less than $20 per day.) Recreational-vehicle owners are welcome at Diaz Ordaz, but as of now there are no campgrounds offering water and electric hook-ups.

The best fishing on this lake occurs during the winter months, when the water is cool and the bass are in the shallows. Good fishing is also available during the spring and summer, with the best action occurring early in the morning and in late afternoon. At this time of year, visiting anglers can take a long midday siesta and still catch all the fish they want. The only poor fishing period might occur during September through October 15, when it rains on a daily basis and the fish appear to be off their feed. Chapman's fishing operation is closed during this period.

Submerged brush, trees, and cacti provide ideal cover for this lake's bass population, and this is where the fish are located. As a consequence, weedless lures and heavy lines are recommended. Bring some surface lures for morning and late action, but count on catching most of your fish with plastic worms and spinner baits.

Bill Chapman handles Diaz Ordaz reservations and can provide additional information. Reach him at P.O. Box 12163, El Paso, TX 79912. The telephone number here is (915) 581–3580. Information can also be otained from Associate Roberto Balderrama at Apartado 159, Los Mochis, Sinaloa, Mexico. The telephone number is 2–00–46. Balderrama owns several hotels in Mexico, including the first-class Santa Anita in Los Mochis.

COLORADO RIVER • Costa Rica

The Colorado River spills into the blue Caribbean near Costa Rica's northern border, and from January through May it is alive with tarpon and snook. Most of the fishing is done in the river and lagoons, but when the sea is calm it's possible to venture outside the river mouth where schools of tarpon are frequently bunched.

Tarpon average seventy-five pounds in the Colorado River, but some exceeding one hundred pounds are taken each year.

Tarpon average around seventy-five pounds in this river, but some exceeding one hundred pounds are taken each year. They make their move inside the rivers in January and gradually increase in number to peak during the latter part of March. In May they begin to move back out again; they cluster in schools at the mouth of the river or cruise up and down the surf line. Tarpon are frequently hooked in the surf, and when these fish weigh seventy or eighty pounds they present something of a challenge for an angler without a boat.

Snook are present in these waters, also, and are taken by casting lures into the shadows of the mangrove roots that line the rivers and lagoons. The larger snook become more numerous in April and increase in numbers through May. Fall is perhaps the best time for Colorado snook, though, but the action takes place on the beach. During September and October, surf casting regularly produces snook exceeding twenty pounds.

The lower Colorado contains other smaller species of gamefish, such as the machaca, guapote, and mojarra. All of these fish put up a good fight on light tackle and furnish sport for visiting anglers when they get tired of wrestling larger tarpon.

Accommodations and fishing facilities are provided by Casa Mar, a fishing camp that can accommodate up to twenty-four guests in six duplex cottages clustered around a main lodge. Each cottage has a private bath and is attractively furnished. The lodge is situated on seven landscaped acres near the mouth of the river. Meals are excellent, and most of them are served buffet style. Homegrown pineapple, breadfruit, bananas, papaya, and other fruits are served in season.

Fishing is done with wide-beamed sixteen-foot aluminum boats powered with new 25-horsepower engines. Guides are English speaking, skilled in boat handling, and knowledgeable concerning fishing.

The lodge is open January through May and September and October, with the winter season being the favored time for tarpon and the fall for large snook. Weekly packages operate on a Saturday-to-Saturday basis and include charter air fare from San Jose, seven days' fishing with a boat, motor, and guide for each two anglers, double occupancy accommodations, and meals. This package is priced at $1,275 per person in a party of two or more.

The charter flight from San Jose takes around thirty-five minutes, and because it is difficult to arrange flights in and out of San Jose on the same day, Casa Mar guests usually arrive on Friday and leave on Sunday. Two nights spent here in the capital of Costa Rica are not too much, because it is a hospitable, scenic city. A dollar goes a long way here, too.

If you're a fly fisherman and want to try your hand at taking a tarpon on a fly, this is the place to do it. Bill Barnes, owner and manager of the camp, is a fly fishing devotee, and he has developed techniques for taking these big fish on a fly with great consistency.

For details on fishing the Colorado, and a stay at Casa Mar, write to

PanAngling Travel Service, 180 North Michigan Ave., Chicago, IL 60601, Tel: (312) 263–0328.

PARISMINA RIVER ● Costa Rica

"Sabalo" is the cry. They roll in with the incoming tide, partially obscured by the dawn mist, huge mouths agape as they slash through schools of bait fish, silver sides flashing in the half light. An agile 40-pounder elbows a larger fish out of its way and sucks in a yellow streamer fly. Another silver king, burly-shouldered and fresh from the salt, clamps iron jaws on a magnum Rapala. Rods bend, and both fish come climbing out of the water in showers of spray, bodies writhing, heads shaking wildly to dislodge the hooks.

That's tarpon fishing. It's excitement, wall-to-wall action, gut-straining work, suspense that lasts until the brute breaks off or bellies up at the side of the boat. It doesn't matter. This great gamefish will go free in any case. Like climbing aboard a rodeo bronc, the ride is the thing.

The Parismina rises in the central Cordilleras and flows eastward to spill out into the Caribbean Sea. In its lower reaches, it's a typical jungle stream, draped with vines and overhanging tree branches bedecked with orchids, alive with scolding monkeys, colorful birds, and butterflies. The waters of its lagoons teem with machaca, guapote, and mojarra, but the sabalo is the fish the anglers seek, and to a lesser extent, the robalo (snook).

Most of the tarpon that enter the Parismina are in the fifty-five- to eighty-pound class, so medium to light tackle is used. Reels, both spinning and casting, will be loaded with twenty-pound test line. Rods will have enough backbone to set the hook but should have enough flex to cast a lure. Only artificials are used.

Most of the fishing is done in the river or in the freshwater lagoons near the river's mouth. But when conditions permit, and the Caribbean Sea is calm, boats can venture out into the ocean and reap a piscatorial harvest that is almost guaranteed.

How good is the tarpon fishing here? It's as good as there is available, but fishing for this gamefish is never a sure thing. I know some people who jumped an average of a dozen fish a day for an entire week. I know others who fished for an entire week and never had a strike. In tarpon fishing there are no guarantees. Sometimes rainfall or other weather variables make the difference. Sometimes the fish just won't take; at other times they will gulp down almost everything in sight. The season of the year doesn't seem to make much difference, either. There is just no way to predict when the action is going to be good or poor. On an average, though, an angler fishing these waters will jump twelve to fifteen tarpon a week and will boat three of these fish.

This is snook water, too. The Parismina holds the current IGFA record for

Big tarpon, burly-shouldered and fresh from the salt, provide the action here.

this species of fish with a burly 53-pounder taken in the fall of 1978. Each year a number of snook in the twenty-pound class are taken, with a sprinkling of fish topping the thirty-pound mark. When the conditions are right, these broad-shouldered snook are caught in the mouth of the river, but normally they're taken in the jungle lagoons.

Tarpon Rancho, located near the mouth of the river, provides accommodations for twenty angler guests. It's a first-class facility, consisting of a main lodge housing a lounge, dining room, and kitchen. There are also separate cottages with private baths. There are refrigeration and electricity—all the conveniences. Food service is excellent and includes lobster, steaks, and snooks.

Tarpon Rancho offers two seasons—January 15 to May 15, and late August to the middle of October. Tarpon and snook abound during both periods.

Week-long package tours are available, and they commence and end on Saturdays. Guests usually arrive in San Jose (Costa Rica's capital and major city) on Friday and fly out to the camp the following morning.

Price for a week's fishing here is $1,150 per person and includes charter air fare from San Jose, seven nights' accommodations, all meals, and fishing with a boat, motor, and guide for each two persons.

For details on fishing the Parismina River and Tarpon Rancho, write to PanAngling Travel Service, 180 N. Michigan Ave., Chicago IL 60601, Tel: (312) 263–0328.

REEF AND FLATS • Belize

Tucked away at the bottom of Mexico's Yucatan Peninsula, the little country of Belize (formerly British Honduras) has a number of things going for it. Its government is stable. It is the only English-speaking country in Latin America. Its waters are full of fish.

Belize's barrier reef, which lies a few miles off shore, is second in size only to Australia's Great Barrier reef and supports a myriad of reef fish, plus blue water predators hanging around looking for a meal. This coral breakwater also shelters the Belize inshore waters, making it easier to effectively fish them.

Belize flats are extensive expanses of crystalline water spread thin over a shimmering marl-and-sand landscape, dotted with sprigs of mangrove. Schools of torpedo-shaped bonefish ghost across these flats, sometimes skittish, sometimes brazen in their eagerness to suck in a fly or jig. These bones are on the small side, averaging two or four pounds, but they occasionally come in six-pound packages, and they certainly are plentiful. Anglers fishing these flats will occasionally see permit up to twenty pounds, but the average is under ten. Permit are difficult, of course, a good reason why most Belize anglers concentrate on bonefish, tarpon, and other species of fish.

Tarpon of every description are found in these waters. I once tied into a

Flats and tropical lagoons provide ideal habitat for tarpon, snook, and other gamefish.

100-pounder in the Belize River, but because I was fishing for twenty-pound fish with light tackle, I didn't have a prayer of landing the monster. They're available, though. Occasionally an angler is lucky enough to boat one. A number are sighted in these waters each season.

Much more common are tarpon in the twenty-five- to fifty-pound class, which roam Belize flats and channels in large schools and strike a wide variety of lures and streamer flies. These medium-sized silver kings leap high and often and are probably the main quarry of anglers fishing these waters.

The coast of Belize is a morass of vine-draped river channels, quiet lagoons, and mangrove-lined cays that provide prime habitat for smaller tarpon in the ten- to twenty-five-pound category. Using lighter tackle, either casting, spinning, or fly, you can get from these baby tarpon some of the best angling action that the tropics have to offer.

Snook fishing can be quite good in Belize waters, with most of the action occurring at the river mouths on a changing tide, or by fishing a surface lure back among the mangrove roots or overhanging trees. Belize snook average less than ten pounds but are occasionally taken in the twenty-pound category.

Belize has a couple of good fishing facilities that cater to visiting anglers. The first is KCS Lodge, located on the bank of the Belize River, at the edge of town. This is Vic Barothy's old place, and I am informed that the facilities, personnel, and fishing are just as good as they were in years past. The lodge offers modern accommodations for sixteen anglers in cottages surrounding a main lodge. The latter is air-conditioned. The cottages have overhead fans. Meals are good to excellent. Clarine and Bob Johnson are the camp managers. KCS Lodge is open year round. The price for five days' fishing is $890 per person in a party of two.

For guests who would like to avoid long boat rides back and forth from selected fishing destinations, KCS also offers package trips using a pair of sleek fifty-foot yachts. Each of these boats is air-conditioned, has a complete galley, and accommodates four angling guests in comfort. The crew includes the captain, guides and a cook. Fishing is done from outboard-powered skiffs that are taken along. The advantage of this type of arrangement is obvious. These yachts can cruise to offshore cays or up and down the coast to places beyond the reach of skiffs that fish out of the main lodge. As a result, excellent fishing usually results. A minimum of four anglers is required. The price for five days' fishing is $1,075 per person.

Ambergris Cay lies fifty miles up the coast and is one of the larger barrier reef islands lying off the coast of Belize. El Pescador is located here, and it's a superb little fishing camp with accommodations for twenty guests. The rooms have private baths, fans, and electricity. Meals are excellent, featuring such seafood delicacies as lobster and shrimp. The camp is owned and operated by Kathleen and Jurgen Krueger. Price for a seven-night/six-day package is $1,298, and it includes fishing with a boat, motor, and guide, accommodations, all meals, and round-trip charter air fare from Belize City. In comparing the two spots, it should be noted that the snook fishing is not as good here as it is in the Belize City area, but the tarpon and bonefishing are probably better. Weather is also more of a factor here than it is down the coast.

Belize is accessible by air from such U.S. gateways as Miami, New Orleans, and Houston.

For more information on fishing Belize and the two camps I've described, write to Jim Chapralis, PanAngling Travel Service, 180 North Michigan Ave., Chicago IL 60601, Tel: (312) 263–0328.

GATUN LAKE ● Panama

Sprawling Gatun Lake, located between Panama City and Colon in the central part of the Isthmus of Panama, has long been known for the part it plays in moving ships through the Panama Canal. More recently, it has been recognized for its fishing attributes. Both tarpon and snook found their way into this

Gatun pavon average three or four pounds and are hard fighters.

163-square-mile lake shortly after it was constructed, but more recently it has become a peacock-bass habitat.

They're abundant, too. Locally called the pavon, the peacock bass have literally taken over Gatun, regularly producing daily catches of one hundred or more fish per boat—and sometimes per angler.

The pavon is a beautiful fish. Its eye is as red as a tropical sun about to drop below the horizon at dusk. Its fins and gill covers are tipped with crimson. The back is usually dark green, and the sides a golden yellow or bronze, shading to a white or dusky yellow. On the tail is a bluish-black spot resembling the glowing eye of a peacock feather. In addition, this species of pavon has four black bars on each side.

This tropical bass is as game as it is colorful. The pavon strikes a lure with savage force, immediately comes out of the water with a spray-flinging leap, and may jump a half-dozen times before it can be led stubbornly to the boat. The fish is strong. I've hooked pavon that looked to weigh only three or four pounds, but I could not turn them as they raced for a nearby tangle of brush or a submerged log. They have powerful jaws that mangle lures and crush treble hooks into balls, but they do not have teeth. Beware, though. Their lips are rough and can strip all the skin off a thumb if care isn't taken in landing them.

There are several different species of peacock bass. The peacock pavon (with three stripes on its sides) goes to thirty pounds or better, and the speckled, royal, and butterfly pavon probably top out at five or ten pounds less. The Gatun pavon is a different species that averages between one and three pounds and possibly may go to ten pounds.

With light tackle, though, everything is relative. Gatun pavon are as large as and certainly more powerful than the average black bass we catch, and trout fishermen used to playing with twelve-inch brookies or rainbows will experience a new dimension in angling.

With the exception of the plastic worm, I've never seen a lure that a pavon wouldn't gobble up. Jigs are great lures because you can't crank a bait too fast for this fish. Spoons work well, and so do baits like Hellcats, Rapala minnows, and Rebels. But my favorite lure for peacock bass is a surface darter. When conditions are right on Gatun, break out a yellow darter and plan on having the time of your life.

Bob Griffin has an operation on Gatun that features top-quality boats and guides and offers several angling packages that include fishing, hotel accommodations in Panama City (I believe they use the Executive), a box lunch, soft drinks, ground transportation back and forth from the lake, and airport transfers. The current price for a four-night package, with three days' fishing, is $465 per person in a party of two.

The boats used are sixteen-foot aluminum John boats with convertible Bimini tops for sun protection. Guides speak a little English and are knowledgeable concerning fishing and boat handling.

This tour operates year round, but the driest months are from December through April, and this is the preferred period to fish Panama waters. Panama has a lot of rainfall, and plenty of humidity as a result. Regardless of the season, it's hot.

Spanish is the official language, but because of the long American presence in this country, many of the people also speak English. Language is not a problem.

There are also other things to do in this country. Coiba, which lies a few miles off the Pacific coast, offers excellent saltwater fishing and a quality fishing camp in Club Pacifico. Farther to the south are the Pearl Islands, and specifically Contadora. There's a beautiful resort hotel on this little tropical island, and excellent light-tackle fishing in the surrounding waters. Still farther down the coast, still on the Pacific side, is Pinas Bay and a place called Tropic Star Lodge. In this hemisphere, at least, this is the place to go for billfish. On the other side of the isthmus are the scenic San Blas islands, inhabited by the colorful Cuna Indians. Panama hotels are super, and there are lots of restaurants, casinos, and other night spots.

For additional facts on Panama, and specifically Gatun Lake fishing, write to Bob Griffin, Panama Tours, P.O. Box 2866, Hialeah, FL 33012. The toll-free telephone number is 1–800–327–5662.

ORINOCO RIVER • Colombia

The Orinoco River rises in the Parima Mountains of Brazil and flows in a northwesterly direction through dense Venezuelan jungle to Colombia, where it forms the border between these two countries. Although only 1,300 miles long, the Orinoco drains a 360,000-square mile region and is one of the mightiest rivers in the world. Most South American rivers are turbid, sluggish giants that wend their way through high mud banks carved out of dense rain forest. But, such is not the case with the upper Orinoco. For most of the year, this stretch of river runs blue and clear over and around clusters of granite boulders the size of houses. Where these black boulders are the thickest are areas of white-water rapids and swirling foam-flecked eddies. This is payara habitat, and that's what this angling adventure is all about.

Payara?

The name may not be familiar to you, but it's one to remember. Without a doubt, the payara is one of the classiest gamefish in the world.

It also is one of the most distinctive. The payara has a dental structure resembling that of an extinct saber-toothed tiger, as well as the muscular silver-scaled body of a tarpon. It strikes artificial lures savagely, stages a wild spray-flinging battle when hooked, and still has enough brute strength to strip all of the line from a conventional casting reel. In this stretch of the Orinoco, payara average around fifteen pounds, with fish twice this size always a possibility. Current record is a thirty-one-pound, eight-ounce fish taken within the last two years.

How large does the species get? I don't know for sure and I'm not sure anyone else does either. In this white-water environment, a twenty-pound payara is a formidable opponent, and a thirty-pounder is almost awesome. I've lost lots of big payara and I've compared notes with others who have had similar experiences. As a result, I believe that the species can go to forty-five or fifty pounds in this watershed.

Another exciting gamefish is the peacock bass, which abounds in streams flowing into the Orinoco, and in the numerous jungle lakes adjacent to them. In these waters, this colorful bass-like fish averages more than five pounds and is known to reach a weight of thirty pounds or more. Current rod-and-reel record is a twenty-six-and-one-half-pounder taken from these waters in 1982. The peacock bass is a handsome, multi-colored gamefish that willingly strikes artificial lures, jumps wildly and often, and puts up a powerful fight when hooked. From every standpoint, this beautiful fish is a superior gamester to our largemouth bass.

Dorado abound here, too. They don't grow as large as they do farther south in Argentina, and they lack the burnished golden hue of that species of dorado. But the Orinoco dorado is a wild and savage gamefish that mauls lures with its powerful toothed jaws, and leaps as high and often as the payara.

Woody Long landed this payara while fishing out of von Sneidern's Orinoco camp.

Dorado also prefer rocks and fast water, and average over ten pounds in this habitat.

Piranha grow large in these waters, too. I once caught a large black piranha which had enough heft to set a new world's record, but I filled out the application form with a felt-tip pen and got caught in a rain storm on the way home. The writing on the form became illegible, and so the old record still stands. Although not the fighter that the dorado, peacock bass, and payara are, this bluegill with teeth is still a fine gamefish.

Safari de Colombia is the operator of this fishing package, and is well recommended. This firm is owned and operated by Erland von Sneidern and his family, who have been in the safari business in Colombia for several decades. Erland von Sneidern pioneered sportsfishing on the Orinoco when he opened up a camp five years ago at the mouth of the Rio Mataveni. The present operation is located farther downstream, where guests can fish such tributaries as the Vichada, Tomo, Tuparro, and Sipapo rivers, and according to Erland is a superior location in every respect. Gateway to this new fishing grounds is Puerto Carreno, which is located several hours from camp by boat, and is an hour's jet flight from Bogotá. An eighty-five foot houseboat provides sleeping accommodations for twelve angler guests in double rooms. The houseboat also offers dining and lounge facilities. Fishing is done from outboard powered skiffs, accommodating two anglers and a guide. The latter are hard working native youths, knowledgable concerning fishing, and skilled boat handlers. These guides speak little or no English, but the average angler guest will not find this to be a problem.

Safari de Colombia offers a Saturday-to-Saturday package tour which operates during the December-through-March dry season. It is priced at around $1500, and includes transfers from Puerto Carreno, accommodations, three meals daily, and six full days fishing with a boat, motor, and guide for each two persons. Air fares are not included; neither are canned beverages, tips, and other expenses of a personal nature.

Recommended gear for these Orinoco gamefish is medium-to-heavy casting or spinning tackle. Revolving spool casting reels (Ambassadeur 6500 models, or larger) and open-face spinning reels are recommended, and should spooled with eighteen- to twenty-four pound test line. Make sure your rods have two-handed handles, because pistol-grip handles designed for our largemouth bass will be inadequate. Because there are no tackle stores in this part of the world, bring plenty of lures. Include a selection of magnum-sized Hellcats, Rebels, and Red Fins in both floating and sinking models, some large spoons, a selection of jigs, and some big surface lures. Short wire leaders are a good idea, so bring a batch. Make sure snap swivels are exceptionally strong. Bring extra line in case a large payara or peacock bass strips all the line from your reel.

You'll swat a few mosquitoes in this part of the bush, so bring plenty of insect repellent. Little jejens, similar to northwoods blackflies, can also be a problem. The tropical sun is even more of one. Include sunscreen or lotion (depending on your skin), sunglasses, a broad-brimmed hat, and long-sleeved shirts. Bring lightweight rain gear, a jacket for cool evenings, and a swim suit for an occasional dip in the river. Include a flashlight and batteries, and your own supply of liquor and cigarettes.

For details on fishing the Colombia side of the Orinoco, write Erland von

Sneidern at Apartado Aereo 777, Cali, Colombia, S.A. PanAngling is a representative of Sneiderns here in the United States, and can be reached as
follows: Jim Chapralis, PanAngling, 180 North Michigan Ave., Chicago IL
60601. Tel: 312 263-0328.

EL DORADO LAKES • Colombia

Miraflores is a little frontier outpost located on the Vaupes River in a remote
area of Colombia, and it consists of an unpaved air strip lined with a handful of
houses and small stores. Included in the collection are a couple of cafés,
several cantinas, a dealer in animal and reptile skins, a billiard parlor, an army
post, a hospital, and a radio communications center. Life moves rather slowly
in Miraflores, interrupted only by an occasional aircraft that lands and dis-
charges an assorted cargo of freight, animals, and people. This is the most
exciting thing that ever happens in Miraflores, so everyone turns out when a
plane lands.

Miraflores happens to be the gateway to the El Dorado Lakes, located an
hour's ride downstream by boat and accessible only by this means. This lake
system consists of six lakes, all of which were a part of the Vaupes River eons
ago. The river has since cut a new track through the jungle, leaving these
orchid- and vine-draped lakes on their own. Three of them are accessible by
boat in all but the driest periods. The others are landlocked most of the year
and are reached by a short hike through the jungle.

Peacock bass, locally called pavon, are the primary gamefish in these lakes,
and all four species are found here. Largest is the peacock pavon, which goes
to thirty pounds and is particularly abundant. Others are the royal, speckled,
and butterfly pavon, which average five pounds in size but grow considerably
larger. My largest peacock taken from this chain of lakes was an 18-pounder,
and the rod-and-reel record here weighed twenty-two pounds. Larger fish are
available, however. I have seen monstrous peacock bass in this clear water,
and I've been hooked up with fish that I guessed exceeded thirty pounds in
weight. In this connection, I think I should point out that unless a large
peacock bass is hooked in open water, the odds of your landing it are slim.
The species is extemely powerful, capable of breaking a line, straightening
out hooks, or breaking a rod. In my opinion, it is a much superior gamefish to
either of our black bass.

It also is one of the most beautiful fish found in fresh water. The body is
muscular and streamlined, devoid of the pot belly found on most trophy-sized
largemouth. Most are golden-hued, with a blazing red eye and a crimson-
tipped tail and fins. All have vivid black markings, which appear to differenti-
ate the species, and a blue rosette on the tail, which resembles the eye of a
peacock feather. Peacock bass are agile and aggressive. They charge a lure
like a barracuda and are so fast that they appear like a bolt of lightning in the

The author with a twelve-pound El Dorado peacock bass caught on a Rapala lure.

clear water. Most jump immediately when hooked and are accomplished aerial acrobats. From every standpoint, the peacock bass is a world-class gamefish.

Accommodations on the lake chain consist of a large main house with a half-dozen rooms on the second floor. Below is a spacious dining room that can seat twenty-four people, a kitchen, a bar, and storage facilities. Additional accommodations are provided in four nearby cottages, all with toilet and bath facilities. Other amenities include a swimming pool, light plant, running water, freezers, and refrigeration.

When I first fished here, El Dorado Lodge was the home of Miguel Navarro. Later, Miguel turned his place into a fishing camp that was patronized by a number of North American anglers each winter. Today, El Dorado is no longer a commercial operation, but I am of the opinion that it would welcome some angler guests and would take good care of them during their stay. The place is good enough to justify a little extra work in making arrangements to fish here, and because there has been no angling pressure for the past year or so, the fishing should be sensational.

Recommended tackle for these peacock bass is a sturdy casting rod with a standard (two-hand) handle. Use a revolving-spool casting reel loaded with eighteen-pound test line, and tie on a three-foot shock leader at the head of your line to absorb most of the wear that this part of the line receives.

Piranha, some up to eight pounds, are caught here with regularity, so some anglers use wire leaders. I have had better results with a monofilament shock leader, which is easier to cast and provides better line protection. There are no tackle stores in this part of the world, so bring plenty of spare rods and reels, extra line, and a variety of lures.

In the lure line, shallow running crank baits work well, as do surface lures, jigs, and some spoons. The spoons, in silver and blue, are piranha-proof and can be very effective. My favorite lure is a large yellow darter, worked on the surface near submerged cover. Leave your plastic worms at home. Peacock bass won't look at them, and piranha love to nip off their tails.

The season for this part of the country is December through March. Rain is rare at this time, the lakes are low and clear, and the fish are voracious. Strangely, there are no mosquitoes or other biting insects in this part of the jungle. Bring insect repellent as a matter of course, but you won't use much of it here.

Miraflores is accessible only by air, from either Bogotá or the city of Villavicencia, which lies on the edge of the llanos. Bogotá is the capital of the country and is a large city with fine hotels, restaurants, and varied sightseeing attractions. Daily flights are available to Bogotá from Miami and other U.S. and European gateways. See your travel agent for information of this nature.

For information on fishing at El Dorado, write to Señor Miguel Navarro, Lagos de El Dorado, Miraflores, Departmento Vaupes, Colombia, S.A. For information and perhaps travel arrangements to Miraflores, you may wish to solicit the aid of a seasoned Bogotá travel agency. A good one is the Lowrie Travel Agency, Calle 19 6–21, Piso 7, Bogotá, Colombia, S.A. Because this is not a package tour, accurate price information is difficult to provide. However, a dollar goes far in Colombia, so the cost of this trip will not be prohibitive.

ORINOCO RIVER ● Venezuela

If the Colombia side of the Orinoco is good fishing, then think what the Venezuela side must offer. First of all, this river flows for a distance of almost 500 miles before it reaches the Colombia border, and this area is wild, still largely unexplored. Except for the few tourists who fly in to take a look at the breathtaking Angel Falls, no one knows anything about this part of the world. Much of it has never been fished.

After the Orinoco leaves the Colombia border, it flows for another 700 miles before it empties into the Atlantic Ocean. This stretch of river is very large, and perhaps too turbid to provide the best fishing, but its clear-water tributaries have to be fantastic, and so do the thousands of lakes that sprawl alongside.

Unlike neighboring Colombia, which has an economy that is well balanced between manufacturing and agriculture, Venezuela more or less depends on the revenue from its rich Lake Maracaibo oil fields. This bonanza in black gold was discovered back in the early 1920s and has made Venezuela one of the most affluent nations in Latin America.

But all of this wealth has had a detrimental effect too. With no real incentive to do so, neither the government nor private industry has done much to develop some of the country's other natural resources. Steps are being taken, but there is much to do and a lot of lost time to be made up for.

For instance, I have been trying to get Caracas tour operators interested in opening up their back country to sportsfishermen for the past decade or so, to no avail. Some have expressed an interest, but nothing was ever done about the situation. This is despite the fact that Caracas is considerably closer to the United States than Bogotá is and is 400 kilometers closer to the Orinoco

The peacock bass is the principal gamefish of the Venezuela tropics and exceeds thirty pounds in these waters.

River, too. Fishing the Orinoco in Venezuela makes a lot more sense than approaching it from the Colombia side.

The largely uninhabited state of Bolivar is one example. Streams rising in the Parima foothills and La Gran Sabana flow clear over sand and rock bottoms, and during the dry season they are as beautiful as any river you'll ever fish. Examples are the Ventuari, Caura, and Erebato, and the Orinoco itself. On the silt-free Caroni River there is a one-hundred-mile-long lake with a huge dam that is being raised an additional 164 feet. This beautiful jungle lake is alive with gamefish now. When the project is finished, Guri Lake will be twice the size it is now, and possibly one of the world's most exciting fisheries.

Closer to Caracas and the civilized coast are a number of other llanos streams like the Arauca, Apure, and the Guanare. These rivers rise in the 16,000-foot Andes, and during the dry season they flow clear with glistening sand beaches at every bend. These rivers, and the lakes that adjoin them, are full of gamefish too.

Also on the Andes' eastern slope are a number of man-made impoundments averaging 10,000 to 35,000 acres in size. These are jungle lakes with standing timber, sawgrass, and other aquatic growth that make them ideal habitat for peacock bass.

Venezuela's principal gamefish is the peacock bass, which is known to exceed thirty pounds in the Orinoco watershed. This is a colorful fish that resembles our black bass in body conformity but strikes artificial lures more readily and fights considerably harder. The peacock bass, locally called the pavon, prefers a lake habitat and is commonly taken in and around shoreline cover, frequently in shallow water. In such an environment, the pavon will readily attack a surface lure, or almost anything you throw at this fish. There is one exception—peacock bass don't like plastic worms any better than I do. This gamefish grows rapidly, is delicious to eat, and is believed to spawn more than once each year.

In the rivers, particularly the white-water stretches, gamefish like the payara and dorado abound. Both fish are savage predators, are silver in color, and are talented leapers when hooked. In Orinoco waters the dorado probably doesn't often exceed fifteen pounds, but the payara may go to forty-five pounds or better. Other gamefish are also found in the Orinoco, and a few of them are the sardinata, the picuda, the piranha, the trahira, and the pacu. The pacu looks like a bluegill but frequently comes in twenty-five-pound packages.

The best time to fish these waters is during the dry season, which occurs from November through March.

At this writing, two Americans living in Venezuela are starting a fishing service and appear to be knowledgable on the subject. Clayton Lofgren and Glenn Webb initially will fish Lake Tamanaco, a 10,000-acre impoundment accessible by road. This lake is full of peacock bass in the eight- to ten-pound category and has yielded fish over nineteen pounds. Later on, the two will explore farther afield, opening up new angling waters as the demand requires. This pair offers a $995 weekly fishing package that includes six nights' hotel accommodations, all meals, ground transportation, and five days' fishing with a boat, motor, and guide provided for each two anglers. From a practical standpoint, everything is included except hotel and food costs in Caracas, liquor, and other items of a personal nature.

The gamefish I've described are hard on tackle, so bring two or more two-handed casting rods, with revolving-spool reels loaded with eighteen- to twenty-pound test line. Comparable spinning rigs (open face) will also suffice but are not quite as accurate for pinpoint casting as casting gear is. Bring a selection of large Hellcat, Rebel, and Red Fin lures. Add some big white and yellow jigs, spinnerbaits, and spoons. Don't forget your sunglasses, suntan lotion, and insect repellent. Because the sun is hot, bring cover-up clothing as well as tropical attire. Caracas is a festive place with lots of hotels, night spots, and good restaurants.

For more details on fishing in Venezuela, write to Clayton Lofgren, Edificio Don Julian, Piso 2, Avenida Principal de Chuao, Caracas, Venezuela, S.A. Another possibility is the Venezuelan Tourist Office, 450 Park Ave., New York, NY 10022.

AMAZON HEADWATERS ● Ecuador

Sam Hogan is one of a breed. A retired army colonel, Sam is a lanky ex-Texan with white hair and blue eyes who operates adventure safaris in the Amazon headwaters region. These are true wilderness experiences, conducted by an extremely capable outdoorsman, and Sam is one of the most pleasant companions I've ever shared a wilderness campsite with.

Sam's back yard is the Ecuador, Peru, and Colombia border country, which was formerly the territory of the fierce Auca and Jivaros. Oil was discovered in this region in the late 1960s, and these wild Indians were forced to retreat a little farther back into the bush. It's still jungle, though, as beautiful as there is in the entire Amazon watershed.

A typical Hogan safari starts in Quito, where guests are picked up at their hotel and are driven through mountains and jungle to the bank of the San Miguel River, where gear and people are transferred into dugout canoes for the trip downstream to Puerto Carmen. The night is spent in this little frontier town that is frequented by bush Indians, mestizos, and Texas oil men. There's a little hotel here, and although the food isn't fancy there's plenty of it.

The next day is spent traveling down the Putumayo to the Guepi, and then up this clear stream to a suitable campsite, arriving in time to set up camp and get in some fishing before dark.

The next three days are spent fishing, hunting, and exploring the Guepi, its

Sam Hogan (left) leads authentic adventure safaris into the Amazon headwaters region.

tributaries, and adjacent lakes. Available species of fish are peacock bass ranging up to fifteen pounds, the saber-toothed payara, dorado in the ten-pound category, piranha, varied species of catfish (which strike artificial lures), and the aruana. The aruana is a fascinating gamefish that is related to the barramundi of Australia, and it reaches a length of three feet and a weight of eight pounds. The aruana willingly takes on every artificial lure thrown at it, jumps high out of the water when hooked, and makes long runs. This gamester is also excellent to eat.

Another fish that may be encountered is the pirarucu, which grows to a length of fifteen feet and may weigh 400 pounds or more. This surface-feeding fish is usually taken by the Indians with spears or bow and arrows, but it will take a surface lure and is a formidable adversary when hooked. The flesh of this fish is very firm, tastes a great deal like veal or pork, and is highly prized as table fare.

Some hunting is also done on this jungle safari. Sam discourages his guests' bringing their own firearms into the country and provides a good selection of shotguns and rifles for their use. Game includes deer, two species of wild boar, tapir, paca, and capybara. The paca and capybara are rodents, with the capybara weighing as much as one hundred pounds. Caiman, a species of alligator, are hunted at night and are a real delicacy. Gamebirds include jungle fowl, waterfowl, and curassow. The curassow is a large bird that resembles a turkey but is a mite tougher.

Since no refrigeration is available, the members of this safari live off the land, eating the fish and game that they catch and kill. They dine in style, though. Loin of caiman, fried golden brown over the coals, is delicious. The same may be said for a succulent haunch of paca or capybara. I know of no wild game or product of a butcher shop that is the rival of either. On this jungle safari you can plan on eating well.

Living is primitive but comfortable. Depending on the circumstances, you will sleep on either cots or hammocks. The water you drink will be boiled or otherwise purified. Expect excellent service and camping gear and other equipment comparable to those of expensive African safaris. Mosquitoes and other biting insects are a possibility, but Sam knows how to pick an insect-free campsite, so don't expect a problem. The sun will be hot on the water, so bring along suntan lotion, a wide-brimmed hat, long-sleeved shirts, and other protection. Include a flashlight and extra batteries, rain gear, a bathing suit, sneakers, and no more than three changes of angling togs. One suit or sports coat and trousers will suffice for Quito.

In the fishing-tackle line, bring casting or spinning gear capable of handling fish fifteen pounds or larger. There are no tackle shops in this part of the world, so bring plenty of lures, extra line, and wire leaders. When you make your booking, Sam will send you a list of recommended tackle and clothing to bring along.

One more thing: The itinerary of these trips is not cast in concrete and can be changed to suit your desires. Want to catch a 500-pound catfish? Bring suitable tackle and tell Sam what you want to do. If you have an interest in tropical fish, Sam can show you millions of them. If wildlife is your thing, Sam knows more about the subject than anyone I know of.

Hogan's safaris aren't expensive, either. In a party of four, expect on paying $700 each for a seven-day/six-night package. For two people, the price is less than $900 each.

The best time to come is between October and March, when you'll encounter less rain than at other times of the year. Quito is the gateway, of course, and it is served by Eastern and Ecuatoriana Airlines.

For details on Hogan's safaris, write to Sam Hogan, Casilla A–122, Quito, Ecuador, S.A. For faster mail service, send your letter to Sam at USMLO/ Quito, APO Miami, FL 34039.

THE AMAZON • Brazil, Colombia, and Peru

The Amazon jungle still holds many surprises for the rest of the world, but one of the most intriguing is the one about man-eating catfish.

When I first heard this story I thought it was a myth perpetuated by a witch doctor who had been chewing coca (cocaine) leaves. Several poisonous South American snakes pose a threat to man in this part of the world. So do a twenty-five-foot anaconda, the jaguar, large crocodiles, and the piranha, of course. But a catfish? I simply didn't believe it.

Mike Tsalickis assured me the story was true, though. A resident of Leticia, Colombia, for the past twenty-five years, Tsalickis is a trained naturalist and one of the world's foremost authorities on Amazon wildlife. When he said that man-eating catfish actually existed, my disbelief was somewhat tempered. "How large do they get?" I asked him.

This dressed Amazon catfish without head and tail is still longer than the men carrying it. The species exceeds 500 pounds.

"Five hundred pounds," he replied.

"But Mike," I argued, "the world rod-and-reel record is only ninety-seven pounds."

He shrugged his shoulders. "Not my fault," he said.

Later, we visited a tired-looking clapboard structure on the Leticia waterfront. Up the ramp we went, past rolled-up jaguar skins and bales of wild boar hides. When we got to the door of a walk-in cooler, Mike opened the door and invited me in. "Take a look," he said.

The scene reminded me of a packing house storage room filled with sides of freshly killed beef. There was one exception, though: These carcasses did not have legs. Several dozen dressed catfish were hanging on the meathooks, and even without their heads and tails most of them were six feet or longer.

Later on I checked the proprietor's log book and found numerous entries of 250 kilos and more. One entry of 285 kilos caught my eye, and I whistled softly. That fish had dressed out at 570 pounds.

"And they're man-eaters," Mike insisted.

"You sure?" I asked.

"You bet," he replied. Then, as we sucked on bottles of Colombian beer, he related numerous instances of these big cats' (piraiba) gobbling up youngsters frolicking in the river shallows and attacking women washing their clothes and pulling them into the depths. The stories were hard to believe, but I had seen the evidence, and there was no denying that a 500-pound catfish was large enough to swallow a grown man.

Catching one of these giant Amazon catfish was my next ambition, and over the years I have tangled with a number of them. On the Araguaia, a Brazilian tributary of the Amazon, I have caught numerous cats that weighed sixty to one hundred pounds. I have fished for the species in Ecuador's Napo River, the Rio Negro in the vicinity of Manaus, llanos rivers like the Meta and Guaviare, and of course the Amazon itself. I have broken dozens of fifty- and eighty-five-pound test lines on these great fish, and on one occasion I landed a 9-footer that weighed 205 pounds but didn't raise an eyebrow on the Leticia waterfront.

Tackle for these Amazon giants should consist of a sturdy saltwater rod, a matching reel loaded with eighty-five-pound test line, a heavy wire leader affixed to a shark hook, and enough weight to get your bait down. Oh, yes—a belt harness will come in handy, too. Because there are no tackle stores in this part of the world, I recommend your bringing a spare rod and lots of extra line, leader, and hooks.

Always fish for these big fish from a boat. I made the mistake of doing otherwise on one occasion, I was fishing from the bank, and had to make a decision between losing a rod and reel or getting pulled into the water. Cutting the line would have been an option if I had been able to get my pocket knife out in time.

At any rate, the natives who catch these big fish with hand lines always wear their fish out by letting them tow their dugout canoes around for several hours. Then, when they can work the big cat up to the surface, they hit it over the head with a machete. This process is repeated until the fish is dead, and it may take an hour or more.

Piraiba are delicious to eat and taste a little like pork or veal. But because of its reputation as a man-eater, this fish is always marketed under a different name, usually valenton or bagre.

Catching a 250-pound Amazon cat is considerably more difficult than landing a marlin of comparable size in salt water. I say this because there are snags present in most Amazon rivers, and these giant fish are immensely strong. In most cases, the odds will be with the fish, and such is not the case when a properly equipped angler is hooked up to a large saltwater fish.

If you want to make angling history and catch a 500-pound catfish on rod and reel, the place to do it is in the Amazon basin. The Amazon River is probably a good bet, but so are most of the other rivers in the vast Amazon watershed. Manaus, Brazil, might be a good place to start, but Leticia, Colombia, and Iquitos, Peru, should also be good. Finding a boat and a knowledgable fishing guide in any of these spots should be relatively simple. All are served by jet aircraft. All have adequate hotels and restaurants to accommodate visiting anglers.

RIO NEGRO ● Brazil

Manaus is located on the Rio Negro, near its confluence with the Amazon River. At the turn of the century it was one of the most opulent and progressive cities in the world. Jenny Lind and Sarah Bernhardt performed here in a fabulous new opera house, and the city boasted electricity, trolley cars, a telephone system, and a customs house that was brought over, stone by stone, from England. This golden era didn't last very long, though; when the rubber boom collapsed, Manaus reverted back to a sleepy jungle outpost and remained that way until recent years. Now, the city is booming again—it is the center of the largest undeveloped region in the world, it is a thriving seaport, and it is rapidly becoming a popular international tourist destination.

There is much to see and do in Manaus, but one of the most interesting attractions is the outstanding sportsfishing potential of the surrounding area. Lakes lying along the Rio Negro and the Amazon abound with a variety of exotic gamefish, but there are no resorts or fishing camps in this wild region. Instead, large riverboats are used to reach these lakes, and they provide adequate facilities for visiting anglers. These diesel-powered boats feature a complete galley, dining facilities, separate staterooms, and lots of deck space for living and lounging. Outboard-powered skiffs are used for fishing, and guides are provided to operate them. The size of the crew will logically vary with the number of guests aboard, but in all cases the crew will include an experienced skipper and a chef capable of preparing quality meals.

A few of the species of gamefish native to these waters are: three members of the pavon family, including the thirty-pound peacock pavon; the saber-toothed payara, which is a highly acrobatic gamester that goes to forty pounds; the dorado, which reaches fifteen pounds in these waters and leaps like the payara when hooked; a savage predator called the trahira, which averages less than ten pounds; the high-jumping picuda, which reaches a length of six feet or more and is extremely difficult to hook and hold; the pacu, which resembles an overgrown bluegill; piranha; and a variety of catfish. One of these cats, a highly mobile fish called the surubim, strikes artificials, leaps high when hooked, and goes to sixty pounds or more.

All of these fish are outstanding gamesters. The colorful peacock bass are far superior to our North American black bass, in my opinion, and I feel that the payara and dorado are more powerful, harder-fighting fish than species like our steelhead or Atlantic salmon. I've hooked a dozen picuda, but I've never been lucky enought to land one. This situation makes Amazon fishing exciting, though. One of the most acrobatic fish I have ever caught was none of the above. It was a small-scaled, pinkish-colored fish, four feet long, and possibly weighing twenty pounds. It struck the topwater lure and jumped a dozen times before I could bring it in the boat. The guide had a name for it, but to date I have never been able to find out its scientific name. From a practical standpoint, an angler never knows what is going to strike a lure when it is cast out into these waters.

On one expedition up the Rio Negro from Manaus, we explored a half-dozen lakes that I'm certain had never been fished with sportsfishing tackle. Certainly the native guides had never seen a rod and reel before, and as of course they were in no position to make recommendations concerning which lures to use, we experimented. Using topwater plugs, weedless spoons, and spinner baits, we caught most of our fish in and around cover. In this respect, I found the fishing little different from that encountered on a Florida lake or a cypress-clogged bayou in Lousiana. The action was faster paced, of course, and instead of catching just largemouth bass, we hooked and landed a dozen or more species of fish.

Most of these Amazon gamefish are delicious to eat. The peacock bass, for instance, is one of the tastiest fish I have ever eaten, and Amazon residents tell me that the tambaqui is even better. This fish has a firm flesh that tastes something like pork, and it is difficult to land on a rod and reel. Larger fish like the pirarucu (up to 300 pounds), and some of the giant catfish, taste more like baby beef than they do fish. As might be expected, Amazon cuisine consists primarily of fish dishes.

The trip I am describing has not been neatly packaged for fishermen, but the people involved are experienced operators used to dealing with tourists. Most of their present business is from sightseers who want to see the con-

The picuda (small dorado) is one of a dozen fish that anglers will catch while fishing Amazon waters.

fluence of the Rio Negro and the Amazon, see someone tap a rubber tree, and buy trinkets from a small village of Indians who are possibly as wild as you and I are. They haven't seen enough fishermen to know what they require, but they are capable of providing it.

Since it will take one day of cruising to get really back in the bush, and a long half-day to return, I suggest that a seven-day package is ideal. This will give you five days of fishing, and that's not too much. From what I have been able to ascertain, the best season is from August through December, although I personally feel that Rio Negro lakes north of Manaus are probably fishable through March.

Bring casting outfits with large-capacity revolving spool reels, and rods with two-hand handles. Load reels with new twenty-pound test line, and bring spares of everything. Take along a variety of large-size lures, including spoons, surface lures, spinner baits, and others that regularly take large North American gamefish. Wire leaders are fine, but I prefer to use a longer shock leader made of forty-pound test monofilament. If you want to do some fishing for the giant cats that live in these waters, bring a saltwater rig capable of handling a fifty-pound or larger fish, as well as large hooks.

In the clothing line, be sure to include a wide-brimmed hat and long-sleeved shirts for sun protection. Bring a limited wardrobe consisting of three changes of clothing. A rain suit is recommended, and so is a jacket for cool evenings and when the boat is in operation. Sneakers are ideal footwear, particularly if they have nonskid soles. Include a swim suit and essentials like insect repellent, suntan lotion, and sunglasses. Mosquitoes should not be a problem because you'll probably anchor in the middle of a lake where a constant breeze will keep them away.

If you can arrange the time, plan to spend several days in Manaus, either before or after your trip. Manaus is an interesting city, both from a historical and present-day standpoint. There are several good hotels, including the posh Tropical, located outside the city, and the Amazonas and Lord, located in the heart of the city. Be sure to visit the market to see the great variety of fish available in the Rio Negro and Amazon waters. Other attractions include the opera house, Customs Building, the world's largest floating dock, and some of the old mansions. Manaus isn't Paris or Buenos Aires when it comes to dining, but there are a selection of interesting restaurants in the city, and a dozen night spots offering after-dark entertainment.

Manaus has a new bustling airport and is served by a number of airlines on a daily basis. Taxis provide economical and convenient transport to and from the city. See your travel agent.

Manaus is a boom town like Anchorage, Alaska, and as a result things are more expensive than they are elsewhere in the country. A dollar still goes a long way in Brazil, though, and I estimate that this fishing trip will cost no more than a comparable one in Canada.

A trip such as I've described is most feasible for a group of four to six persons, but when you book it, make certain that one outboard-motor and one skiff are included for each two anglers. You also should specify that the crew include a guide for each two anglers, in addition to the skipper, chef, and other necessary crew members. Other services will be provided as a matter of course by any of the following:

Amazon Explorers, Lord Hotel, Rua Marcilio Dias, 217/225, Manaus, Brazil, S.A. This firm can also be reached here in the United States as follows: Amazon Explorers, Professional Building, Rt. 9, Parlin, NJ 08859. Another possibility is Agencia Selvatur S/A Hotel Amazonas, Praca Adalberto Vale, Manaus, Brazil, S.A. Direct your inquiry to George Vasquez, who is a sports fisherman and will know what you're talking about. If you plan on staying at the Tropical Hotel in Manaus, you might also direct an inquiry to Tropical Tours Agencies, Ltda., Tropical Hotel, Manaus, Brazil, S.A.

ANGLING IN ARGENTINA

Argentina's trout country lies on the eastern slope of the southern Andes, which border Chile, and is a sprawling area made up of snow-capped mountains, spruce forests, deep blue lakes, and clear, swift-flowing streams. In these scenic surroundings, several species of salmonoids are plentiful and grow to record proportions. Rainbow trout, for example, average around three pounds and go to twenty or more. Brown trout average about the same size but get even larger. Even brook trout grow large in these waters, with the average being three pounds, and specimen fish frequently weighing up to ten pounds. Landlocked salmon, imported from Maine decades ago, have done better in Argentina than in their native habitat. The average catch is less than five pounds in the Traful River, and a trophy fish will average around twelve. In the Manso River, a species of hybrid salmon grows even larger.

In Tierra del Fuego, which is the jumping-off place for Antartica, huge sea trout abound. These are migratory brown trout that average ten pounds and have been landed in the thirty-eight-pound category.

The northern part of the country, which is too tropical to support trout and salmon, is dorado country. This great, golden-hued gamefish abounds in most of this region's rivers and is known to reach a size of seventy pounds or more. The dorado, in my opinion, is one of the première gamefish of the world.

The trout season in Argentina commences on November 15 each year and extends until April 15 of the following year. From a climatic standpont, this is the reverse of our Northern Hemisphere weather, where April corresponds to November and January is the middle of summer. In Tierra del Fuego the fishing period, for all practical purposes, is restricted to January and February

In Argentina's nutrient-rich lakes and streams, trout grow to huge sizes.

because of the earlier and later storms that plague that area. Fishing for dorado is even trickier from a seasonal standpoint but is most feasible in August and September.

Trout fishing in Argentina is a gentleman's game, as it is in Europe and in the eastern United States. The accent is on fishing with a fly, navigating a tough stretch of river to properly cover feeding trout, and the artistry involved in getting these fish to take our artificial offerings.

But here the resemblance ends. Argentina trout fishing is a gutsy game. Catches are measured in kilos instead of inches, and wispy-thin leaders are not suitable. Hooking a twelve-inch trout is pure accident here, because the quarry sought frequently exceeds five kilos (ten pounds) and has enough muscle to turn any encounter into a real brawl. This fact gives Argentina trout fishing a dimension that is difficult to duplicate elsewhere in the world.

Argentina is one of the least Latin of the South American countries, and neither does it bear much resemblance to countries like Italy and Spain. Buenos Aires, for example, reminds me of Vienna and Paris, the Argentine lake district reminds me of Switzerland, and the pampas recall the American west. Argentinians eat more beef than we do, and their steaks are flavorful and cut thick. Vineyards flourish throughout the country, and good wine is plentiful and cheap as a result. Dining is a delight in Argentina—and so is living, for that matter. Even the small hosterias located in rural areas always seem to offer first-class services and accommodations.

Argentine fishing guides have much in common with ghillies in Ireland or the British Isles, except that most of them are better educated and considerably more affluent. Most are excellent anglers, highly proficient with a flyrod, and extremely knowledgeable concerning their outdoor environment. The average lake-region guide will own his or her own car, and the better ones will be on a first-name basis with the large estancia owners in the region. The latter is important because most of the better fishing waters are on private land, and permission must be obtained to fish them.

Most of these guides are independent operators, providing week-long fishing packages that usually include the following: airport reception, vehicle for ground transportation, accommodations at local hotels or hosterias, three meals daily (with lunch usually an asado prepared in the field), table wines, fishing license, and other miscellaneous items.

Argentina is a big country, and the fishing areas are all located a considerable distance from Buenos Aires and San Carlos de Bariloche, and the Argentine lake region is located 850 miles to the southwest, on the eastern slope of the Andes. Tierra del Fuego is even farther away. Rio Grande is a five-hour jet flight from Buenos Aires. The dorado fishing is closer but still is several hundred miles to the north. As I mentioned, Argentina covers a big chunk of real estate.

Prices for Argentine fishing are difficult to predict because of the present state of the country's economy. This situation is to the visitor's advantage because a dollar goes a lot further in Argentina than it did a few years ago. Regardless, prices still vary all over the map. Jorge Donovan, a guide who is headquartered in Junin de los Andes, wants around $2,000 for a weekly package that includes six days of fishing. Turytravel, which is a Buenos Aires firm specializing in sportsmen's travel, charges $105 per day for similar services. Fishing International, a California-based sportsman's tour wholesaler, offers a two-week trip for less than $1,900. Laddie Buchanan, one of the outstanding guides in Argentina, offers quality services at a rate competitive with those of all of the above. PanAngling, a Chicago travel wholesaler, also offers Argentina angling packages, and so does Outdoor Safaris of Miami. Contacts for Argentina fishing are: Laddie Buchanan, Av. Pte., Roque Saenz Pena 825, 1363 Capital Federal, Buenos Aires, Argentina, S.A.; PanAngling, 180 N. Michigan Ave., Chicago, IL 60601, Tel: (312) 263–0328; Turytravel, Viamonte 524, Piso 3, Of. 11–(1053), Buenos Aires, Argentina, S.A.; and Fishing International, 4000 Montgomery Drive, P.O. Box 2132, Santa Rosa, CA 95405. Another excellent source of information is Hilda Lucia Bonfiglioli, Ministerio de Economia, Secretaria de Commercio, Buenos Aires, Argentina, S.A.

SAN MARTIN REGION ● Argentina

It was 5:30 A.M., and the summer mists of the Argentine dawn hovered low over the rushing water of the river. I had worked myself into a position to make the cast and was now ready. *Swish* went the back-cast, and the long line curled over the foam-flecked rapids to drop the pinkish fly in the eddy below the boulder. It drifted for a foot or so before a torpedo-shaped shadow rose from the depths to suck it in, and the time-honored battle betwen angler and trout began again.

The Rio Chimehuin is one of Argentina's première fishing streams. Its source is Lago Huetchulafquen, which is a large lake tucked away in the mountains a few miles from the Chilean border. Thereafter it flows in a southeasterly direction through the village of Junin De Los Andes to join the Collon Cura farther downstream. Throughout its fifty-mile length, the Chimehuin is a superb trout fishery but is primarily known for its large brown trout, which go over twenty pounds in this river. This species of trout is particularly favored by fly fishermen because it's an insect eater and rises to artificials more readily than other Argentine brooks and rainbows. The Collon Cura, after its confluence with the Chimehuin, is a broad, fast river filled with two- and three-pound rainbows but containing larger trout as well.

Another excellent trout stream in the vicinity is the Malleo, which flows out of Lake Tromen, located on the Chilean border, and joins the Alumine River north of Junin De Los Andes. Most of this classic trout stream is privately owned, so permission must be obtained to fish the better beats. This is no

Guide Laddie Buchanan hefts a fat brown trout taken on a fly.

problem for the better guides, who are usually well acquainted with the area land owners.

River outlets from source lakes, called "bocas" in this part of the world, are usually fishing hotspots. One such spot is the boca of the Chimehuin, where it flows out of Lake Heutchalafquen. This fishing hold annually produces trout of trophy proportions and has yielded browns in the twenty-four-pound category. Another excellent fishing spot is the confluence of the Malleo and Alumine Rivers upstream from Ignacio. This is a tremendous pool that also produces a lot of large fish. Still farther north are the Quillen and Alumine Rivers and lakes of the same name. The former seems to have more insect life than other streams in the San Martin area and is favored by dry-fly fishermen as a result.

Junin De Los Andes is located about forty kilometers north and east of San Martin and is the logical headquarters for anglers fishing this part of the Argentine lake region. In this village, the place to stay is the Hosteria Chimehuin, which is situated on the bank of the river by the same name. This little hotel is a watering hole for fly fishermen, and during the height of the season it attracts anglers from all around the world. Because accommodations are limited, every angler fishing the area cannot stay here, but the Hosteria Chimehuin is still worth a visit for lunch, dinner, or an hour spent in the bar talking fishing with other anglers. San Martin De Los Andes, a larger town, has a variety of hotel accommodations and is also a suitable headquarters for fishing this area. Both Junin and San Martin are reached by road from the Bariloche Airport, with San Martin being approximately 125 miles by road—a scenic three-hour drive.

Recommended fishing tackle should include an 8 System flyrod equipped with a reel loaded with a matching line and 150 yards of eighteen-pound test backing. Shooting heads will come in handy for fishing the larger rivers. Bring both floating and sinking lines and leaders testing ten pounds. To fish some of the smaller streams, bring a lighter outfit more suitable for smaller fish. In selecting flies for these waters, remember that the major diet of these trout is a small congrejo (crab), not insects. This shellfish accounts for the rapid growth and large size of Argentine trout, so it is considered beneficial. As a result, most of these streams are more suitable for wet flies and streamers than for dry flies. Muddlers, particularly in darker colors, are recommended. Other flies, tied locally, are also extremely effective. Popular sizes range from No. 4 to No. 8 with the No. 6 hook possibly the most effective. Larger 1/0 to 3/0 streamers are also frequently used for fishing for large brown trout in late evening.

Medium-weight spinning gear will suffice for most of the streams in this area. Reels should be loaded with eight- to twelve-pound test line. Bring a variety of spinners, but bear in mind that Argentina is one of the few countries in South America that offer fishing tackle for sale.

Chest-high waders are recommended for fishing these streams, but because long hikes are sometimes necessary, I prefer comfortable, light-weight stocking-foot waders. On most Argentine streams, felt soles can be a definite advantage. Weather in the lake region is a little like Canada's, with cool nights and warm, sunny days. Rain is infrequent, but I suggest carrying along a rain suit as a precaution. A warm jacket is a must, because some of the best brown-trout fishing will occur early and late when the temperature is on the cool side. Wind can be a factor, although not as much so as it is farther south in the states of Chubut and Santa Cruz.

Fishing packages in this region are available from a number of sources and usually will include the following: Reception at the Bariloche airport, auto-mobile transfer to either Junin De Los Andes or San Martin De Los Andes, hotel accommodations, breakfast and dinner, lunch in the field, daily fishing services with guide and ground transportation provided, and transfer back to Bariloche. Some angling packages will also include a fishing license and wine with meals.

For details on whom to get in touch with for services and price information, see the "Angling in Argentina" section.

BARILOCHE REGION • Argentina

San Carlos de Bariloche is located 850 miles southwest of Buenos Aires and is the center of the Nahuel Huapi Park and the sprawling Argentine lake region. Located on the eastern slope of the southern Andes, this scenic region is made up of snow-capped mountains, lush spruce forests, deep blue lakes, and swift, flowing rivers.

The town of Bariloche is located on the shore of beautiful Nahuel Huapi, the largest lake in the region, and resembles a Swiss alpine village. Bariloche has everything: fine resort hotels, charming little hostels and pensions, restaurants of every description, night spots, winter skiing facilities, and varied recreation attractions for the summer visitor.

Three species of trout and one species of salmon were stocked in these waters in the early 1900s, and all prospered. There are rainbow trout that frequently go to twenty pounds or more, brown trout up to thirty-two pounds, and brookies in the ten-pound category. Traful Lake and River, which lie north of Bariloche, were stocked with landlocked salmon around the same time and provide a fourth species of salmonoid for the angler.

Lake Nahuel Huapi is a beautiful lake some seventy kilometers long and five or six kilometers wide. It contains some extremely large brown and rainbow trout, but local angling pressure has reduced both the average size of the catch and perhaps the quantity of fish in the lake as well. I fished this huge lake twice, with some degree of luck on both occasions. The first time, I fished the boca of the Limay as the summer evening shadows began to lengthen and managed to come up with several trout in the five- to eight-pound range. More recently, Great Lakes fisherman Jack Parry and I plumbed Nahuel Huapi's depths with an electronic fish-locating device, and we put three fish in the boat, the largest being a rainbow that weighed eighteen pounds. Although Nahuel Huapi has good fishing by most lake standards, I suggest that visiting anglers appreciate the beauty of this body of water but do their fishing elsewhere.

The Limay River spills out of Nahuel Huapi and flows in a northeasterly direction to form the border between the provinces of Neuquen and Rio Negro. This is a fabled stream that has produced a lot of big trout, but because it is so accessible it receives a considerable amount of angling pressure. This is a big river, difficult to wade and to fish properly. As a result, most fishing occurs in a few spots along its watercourse, and the rest of it goes untouched. I have long felt that the best way to fish the Limay and other comparable Argentine streams would be by raft or float boat. This is the method used to fish a number of western American rivers and to fish similar streams in Chile. I have never been able to convince Bariloche guides that this was a good idea, so I have yet to explore the more inaccessible reaches of these streams.

The beautiful Rio Trafúl contains salmon as well as rainbow and brown trout.

The Correntoso area, which is located at the north end of Nahuel Huapi, is one of the best trout fisheries in the region. Lake Correntoso offers good fishing, and the boca of the Correntoso River is a renowned angling hotspot. Here, also, is Lago Espejo, which can on occasion be extremely productive.

Trafúl Lake and the river that spills out of it enjoy a reputation as the country's première salmon fishery, and this reputation is justified. The Trafúl is a beautiful stream that joins the Limay at a wide spot in the road called Confluencia, but the best fishing is located upstream, nearer the lake. On one trip to Argentina, I was fortunate enough to fish an inaccessible stretch of the Trafúl flowing through a large estancia and had outstanding success. The bag during two hours on the river on a rainy afternoon was a half-dozen rainbows and salmon, most weighing more than five pounds.

The Caleufu River, which flows through an uninhabited chunk of Argentine real estate twenty kilometers farther north, is an excellent fishing stream because it receives so little angling pressure. Big browns and rainbows abound in this river, and it would behoove the visiting angler to obtain permission to fish it.

South of Bariloche is the Manso River system, which flows through Lakes Martin and Steffen and crosses the Chilean border to empty into the Pacific. This is a beautiful river, wild in places, producing excellent fishing for trout and hybrid salmon.

The terrain in the immediate vicinity of Bariloche is alpine in nature, with thick forests, rumbling mountain brooks, and snow-capped mountain peaks. North and east, the terrain becomes more arid, and the landscape looks like the "big sky" country of Montana and Wyoming.

Although Bariloche is headquarters for this part of Argentina, serious anglers are advised to stay in the small hosterias in the immediate areas they'll be fishing. The Hotel Correntoso is popular with anglers, and so are little hosterias like the Villa Traful. There are also charming little Swiss-chalet hotels offering adequate accommodations, excellent meals, and a brand of hospitality that is certain to please. Bariloche guides are familiar with all of these places and will handle all of the booking arrangements.

The best way to fish the Bariloche region is to hire a good guide and put yourself in his or her hands. Depending on the season and the water conditions, your guide may choose to fish one or several locations in the vicinity. One day you may drive south to fish the Manso; on others you may fish rivers like the Correntoso or Traful to the north. On a one-week trip I fished a widespread region that included the Junin and San Martin areas as well as Correntoso, Traful, and streams south of Bariloche. It was an interesting experience, but it involved too much travel and not enough actual fishing. Your best bet, in my opinion, is to spend several days fishing an area like the Manso, Correntoso, or Traful. Plan on staying in a little hosteria in the immediate area, eating breakfast and dinner there, and having your guide fix a midday asado in the field. Fish two or three spots and allow one or two days to do some sightseeing in the Bariloche area.

Seeing Victoria Island is highly recommended. So are a cruise on the lake and seeing other local attractions. Have your guide take you to lunch at the local anglers' club, where you can admire the mounted fish on the walls and exchange views with other anglers, both local and visiting.

As might be expected, Bariloche is loaded with good hotels. You can stay in the middle of town at a variety of hotels and hosterias, or you can select a facility in more secluded surroundings. Highly popular is the sprawling Llao-Llao Hotel, located amidst landscaped surroundings some twenty kilometers from town. Halfway in between is a delightful little hosteria called the Del Viejo Molino. This small hotel is a delight and has as good a menu and wine list as there is in the area.

Most Bariloche fishing guides, except those who specialize in lake trolling, are expert fly fishermen and will tell you what to bring in the way of tackle and flies. Recommended will be 9 or 10 System rods, partially for the outsized fish you'll be trying to catch, but mostly to function in the strong winds that blow in this part of the country. In the forested mountain region, both north and south of Bariloche, wind won't be much of a factor. But when fishing the more open and barren country farther east, it definitely is. Your reel should be loaded with at least 150 yards of backing, and shooting heads and sinking tips are recommended. Most fishing will be with a wet fly, some tied to emulate the little congrejo, which is the major diet of Argentine trout.

But spinning can also be extremely effective. Early in the season, when the rivers are high and slightly off color, this fishing technique is more productive than fly fishing. Some of the big rivers, like the Limay and Collon Cura, are easier fished with spinning gear. If you are proficient with both types of equipment, I suggest that you bring them both along.

In the clothing line, dress as you would for Canada. Rain won't be much of a problem, but a light rain suit might still be handy to have along. Chest-high waders are a must, and they should have felt soles to help you keep your footing in some of the streams you'll be fishing. Consider the ultralight stocking-foot type, which are most comfortable for long hikes and won't necessitate excess luggage charges on the long flights required to get to this part of the world.

Most of Argentina's trout-fishing guides have their headquarters in Bariloche and are familiar with the surrounding fishing waters. These professionals offer angling packages in varied forms. Available are weekly trips that include reception, accommodations, meals, a fishing license, ground transportation—everything. Or, if you prefer, you can pay for your own accommodations, meals, and bar bills and hire a guide to provide fishing services and ground transportation. Do this by the day or by the week, whichever you prefer. For details concerning these services and those who provide them, see the "Angling in Argentina" section.

TIERRA DEL FUEGO • Argentina

Located at the tip of South America, 1,500 miles south of Buenos Aires, Tierra del Fuego is a long way from anywhere. It also is misnamed. As the story goes, Ferdinand Magellan saw the cooking fires of Indians when he first sailed through the strait that now bears his name, and he named the island Tierra del Fuego. That means "land of fire."

Tierra del Fuego is anything but. Located almost in sight of Antartica and the South Pole, this island is locked in the grip of ice and snow for nine months of the year and has a shorter summer than the northern extremes of Alaska.

Actually, the island is two different worlds. The northern part is flat prairie—barren, bleak, buffeted by almost continous gale-force winds. Millions of sheep, covered with thick wool coats to keep them alive during the harsh winters, share the lush pastures with two species of Magellan geese. The terrain is rain soaked, soggy, and dotted with small lakes and rivers that flow down from the highlands.

The southern half of the island is exactly the opposite. Here, snow-covered granite peaks tower high in the South Atlantic sky, lush spruce forests carpet the mountain slopes, blue lakes sparkle like jewels, and rushing mountain streams tumble down from the mountain heights. The place is scenic, with a picture-postcard quality that makes visitors reach for their cameras at every turn in the road.

The residents of Tierra del Fuego, which was settled by Scots, imported brown trout from Europe decades ago and stocked their streams. These imports adapted well to their new environment and grew larger than they did in their native Scotland. In these waters, sea-run browns average around five pounds, and sixteen- to twenty-pound fish are common. World-record brook trout possibly inhabit some of the Tierra del Fuego streams, and so do monstrous rainbows.

Each part of the island has something going for it from an angling standpoint. In the northern sector the rivers are large, and the sea-run trout that run up them each summer are of huge proportions. I've lost some giant fish in these streams, and on one occasion I watched my guide and fishing companion land an eighteen-pound brown on a flyrod. In two trips here, this was our largest fish, but all of us tangled with trout that we thought were larger.

The streams of the scenic half of the island are also jammed with trout, but they are smaller in size. An exception is the Rio Claro, which empties into Lake Fagnano from the north. On one trip here, I caught a pair of six-pound brook trout and had a brief encounter with another brookie that was of world-record proportions. The water of this stream was crystal clear, and I could see my fish plainly during most of the battle. In the end, however, the big brookie fouled the line on an underwater obstruction, and that was the end of the adventure.

This is one example of the type of fishing that is available in Tierra del Fuego. This river has virtually no fishing pressure, and there are dozens of others like it there. Most visiting anglers fish only the Rio Grande on the northern part of the island and some of the small mountain streams in the vicinity of Ushuaia in the south. The rest just aren't fished and could offer unbelievable fishing action.

Because Tierra del Fuego is so remote and difficult to get to, I suggest that a fishing trip here be of at least ten days' duration. Rio Grande should be the first stop, with the quarry being the sea-run browns that run up these large rivers. The Rio Grande is a logical choice, but so are a dozen other similar streams in the vicinity. These hard-fighting fish take a fly (wet) readily, but it should be noted that the high winds here frequently make fly fishing difficult. Your best bet is to start fishing extremely early in the morning (three or four o'clock) and to fish until the winds come up later in the day. At this time it might be advisable to switch to spinning gear, which also is a deadly way to

Lloyd Saulsbury with a brook trout taken from the Rio Clara. World-record brookies possibly inhabit this little-fished stream.

take these big trout. Flyrods should be long and strong enough to handle a good-sized fly in a strong wind. Use lines with shooting heads and plenty of eighteen-pound test backing. Leaders should test no less than ten pounds. Medium- to heavyweight spinning rods will suffice for these big fish. Open-face spinning reels are recommended, and they should be loaded with at least sixteen-pound test line.

All of the fishing is on private property in this part of the island, but visiting anglers should have no trouble getting permission to fish where they want.

A rental car can be obtained at the Rio Grande Airport and will be invaluable in providing ground transportation around this area. It also can be used to make the overland trek up to Lake Fagnano and over the mountains to Ushuaia. I suggest fishing both places. This huge lake contains lots of large fish, with the best action possibly occurring in the bocas of streams running into the lake. The streams on the north side of the lake see the least angling pressure and are recommended if the lake is calm enough to boat across and get to them.

The national park west of Ushuaia is worth a visit, because it is a thing of beauty. It also has a number of trout streams that can provide good fishing for small to medium-sized trout. It might be a better bet to try and gain access to the Mitre Peninsula area, which lies east of Ushuaia, and the road that connects it to Rio Grande. No paved roads traverse this region, but there are lots of big rivers here, and they must be accessible by some means.

The best hotel in Rio Grande is the Yaganes, which isn't much to brag about. The rooms are small, but the beds are adequate and so are the rest of the facilities. The hotel dining room has a menu featuring a lot of lamb and mutton dishes; seafood is also available. There is a delightful little hotel at the east end of Lake Fagnano that has adequate accommodations and fair to good food service. This is the place to stay when fishing this part of the island.

Ushuaia is a picturesque little coastal town that is visited by cruise ships and has seen a considerable number of tourists. As a results there are several good hotels, with the best possibly being the Albatros. Restaurants are plentiful, and the range of food is varied. The local speciality is king crab, and it is highly recommended.

The fishing season in Tierra del Fuego opens November 15 and closes the middle of March, but I suggest that the best time to fish these streams is from December 15 through February. Even then, expect lots of wind, some rainfall, and cold weather. Dress accordingly, bringing along a good rain suit and lots of warm clothing. Chest-high waders are a must. Felt soles are mandatory in order to fish the mountain streams, but they are not required for the rivers in the Rio Grande region.

Local guides are available in Ushuaia, and one of the best is Miguel Angel Vitola, who can be reached at Direccion de Turismo, Casa de Gobierno, Ushuaia, Tierra del Fuego, C.C. 9410, Argentina, S.A. Another way to go is to bring a seasoned guide down with you from Buenos Aires or Bariloche, and in this case I recommend Laddie Buchanan, Av. Pte. Roque Saenz Pena 825, 1363 Capital Federal, Buenos Aires, Argentina, S.A.

Depending on the widely fluctuating peso/dollar exchange rate, this trip could either be a bargain or relatively expensive. A dollar goes a long way in Argentina these days, but it should be noted that Tierra del Fuego is considerably farther from Buenos Aires than Anchorage is from Seattle. Alaska is expensive because of its remoteness and short operating season, and Tierra del Fuego is much the same.

PARANÁ RIVER • Argentina

Dorado.

I know of no other fish as savage, as powerful, and as beautiful. This South American gamester has a salmon-shaped body sheathed with golden scales and a mouth of razor-sharp teeth. In the Paraná, this fish averages ten to twenty pounds but is known to reach a size of sixty pounds or more. Current IGFA world record is a 48-pounder recorded in 1982, but much larger dorado have been taken by sports fishermen in previous years.

The utter ferocity of the dorado's strike is difficult to describe. A muskie, for instance, stalks a lure deliberately and then simply clamps it in his toothed jaws. A bass may strike a surface lure with explosive force, but prior to this sudden flurry of action, it moves within range slowly. Frankly, I can't think of a fish that attacks its quarry with such speed or fury as the dorado; if I compared its attack with the terrifying charge of a lion or leopard you might get the idea.

The dorado is difficult to hook because of its speed, but the toughness of its well-armed jaws has something to do with the situation too. For this reason, experienced dorado fishermen use only saltwater rods and spoons with a sharp single hook large enough to take a sailfish. No treble hook, they've informed me, is strong enough to hold a dorado.

In willingness to take to the air, only the tarpon compares with this golden-scaled acrobat; but again speed and agility make the difference. Both species can clear the water by six feet or more, and both shake their heads so violently that it's difficult to "freeze" the action with a camera. But here the resemblance ends. The tarpon's leap is performance in slow motion. The dorado's is a writhing sunburst that's almost too fast to see. This fact explains why a hooked dorado is far from being a trophy for a den wall. This fish is so adept at throwing lures that a good angler can expect to land fewer than half the fish he or she hooks.

Dorado country is not limited to the Paraná watershed. I've caught the species as far north as the Orinoco River and as far east as Peru, but these fish usually weighed less than ten pounds and were silver instead of gold in hue. In the Paraná, which flows from Iguazu Falls south to Buenos Aires, the species grows much larger and is sheathed in gold scales. It also is the pre-dominant species of fish in this large river, so common that dorado tourna-ments are held each August and attract thousands of participants and spectators.

Dorado fishing hot spots on the upper Paraná are Hernandarias, Esquina, Empedrado, Corrientes, Paso de la Patria, Posadas, and Monte Carlo. Apipe, a stretch of rapids just south of Posadas, was one of the best fishing holes on the river but is in the process of being transformed into a lake by a dam immediately below. I'm not certain just how far this lake is going to back up, but it is certain to destroy a stretch of dorado habitat. At that point, dorado

The principal gamefish of the Paraná River is the golden-sheathed dorado, one of the most savage predators that swim.

fishing on the Paraná will be concentrated in two stretches of river below and above this lake.

I have fished at a number of locations up and down the Paraná, but Esquina is my favorite. I say this because here is located a huge swamp that provides clear water and good dorado fishing even when the Paraná is muddy and in full flood. Incidentally, this happens frequently. This mighty river rises in the jungles of Brazil, which are subject to heavy rainfall for a considerable period of the year. As a consequence, river levels are difficult to predict, and this makes planning a dorado fishing trip complicated.

For example, I once participated in a dorado tournament in Posadas, and flood conditions virtually negated any possibility of angling success. We moved downstream to Apipe with only fair results and ended up in Esquina, where the fishing was excellent.

All of this fishing lies north of Buenos Aires, a distance of 510 kilometers to

Esquina. These areas are reached from the downtown airport, and most of the flights leave early in the morning. It's therefore necessary to fly into Buenos Aires the day before, stay overnight there, and then continue back north to the dorado fishing grounds the next day. Buenos Aires isn't unpleasant duty, though. It's a large city, with 12 million or more people, but it has a charm all of its own and is a delightful place for sightseeing, shopping, and dining. Buenos Aires is loaded with great restaurants; one that you don't want to overlook is La Cabana. This is the best steak house I've ever eaten at, bar none.

August to September is the prime dorado fishing period, with good fishing also a possibility in April and May. Book your trip well in advance with a good guide, but I strongly recommend that both of you remain flexible concerning the actual departure date. High water can make a difference between a successful fishing trip and a disaster, and plans should be made accordingly. Be prepared, therefore, to head south on a moment's notice or to cancel the trip on equally short notice.

Dorado fishing is done from boats, with trolling being the favored method of taking this gamefish. I prefer, however, to work a river bank, casting into cover that holds baitfish and dorado that are stalking them. The fast stretches of river are usually the most productive, because dorado habitat is usually associated with white water, rocks, and strong currents. Other good spots are the bocas of smaller tributaries, rock reefs, or rocky points off small islands.

The dorado has tough, toothy jaws and is difficult to hook. Use saltwater lures or those suitable for muskellunge or striped bass. Single hooks are preferable to trebles and should be kept razor sharp. If you troll you can use light saltwater tackle as Argentine anglers do, but if you like to cast I recommend a large-capacity bait-casting reel loaded with twenty-pound test line. Your rod should have a stiff action and a long handle that you can get both hands on. Comparable spinning outfits will also suffice.

Although it is possible to hire a local guide in a town like Posadas or Esquina, I think it makes more sense to retain a guide like Laddie Buchanan, who is equipped to fish any spot on the river, depending on local water conditions. As mentioned before, flexibility and mobility are important factors in fishing for dorado. Financial arrangements with a guide like Laddie can include accommodations, meals, and fishing services, or only his fishing services. Either plan is feasible in this part of Argentina because accommodations and meals will be provided in small, modern hotels and in restaurants, respectively. Plan on paying from $100 to $200 per day, depending on services provided and the Argentine peso and the U.S. dollar exchange rate at the time you go.

For more information on Argentine dorado fishing, write Laddie Buchanan, Av. Pte. Roque Saenz Pena 825, 1363 Capital Federal, Buenos Aires, Argentina, S.A. Another good information source is Hilda Lucia Bonfiglioli, Ministerio de Economica, Secretaria de Commercio, Buenos Aires, Argentina, S.A.

Chilean float boats are rocker-bottom skiffs designed to hold a botero and one fisherman.

ANGLING IN CHILE

Chile stretches for a distance of 2,600 miles from the Peruvian border to the tip of the South American continent. The upper part is arid and of little interest to the visitor, but the region south of Santiago is made up of snow-capped peaks towering above forested mountain slopes and pastoral valleys, sprawling deep blue lakes, and hundreds of rivers and streams tumbling down from Andes heights to spill into the Pacific Ocean. All of these waters, both rivers and lakes, are teeming with trout.

From the angler's standpoint, perhaps the most important part of Chile is known as the "Chilean Lake Region," which extends from Temuco south to Puerto Montt. This region lies just across the border from Argentina's lake region but perhaps has even more lakes and rivers to fish. Angling centers of note are Villarica, Pucon, Chan-Chan, Llifen, and Petrohue. Some of the better-known lakes are Villarrica, Gualletue, Panguipulli, Rinihue, Ranco, and Maihue. Noteworthy rivers in the area are the Tolten, the Liucura, the Enco, the San Pedro, the Calcurrupe, the Petrohue, and the Cumilahue.

South of Puerto Montt is an area that little is known about but that is reputed to offer some fantastic trout fishing. Here are a number of rivers, like the Manso, that originate in Argentina, Puelo, Simpson, and Serrano. Serrano is close to Punta Arenas, which is located on the Strait of Magellan, across from Tierra del Fuego. Punta Arenas, despite its remote location, is a sizable town and has good air connections with the rest of the country.

Trout were stocked in Chilean streams about the same time they were in Argentina, and they prospered equally well. Most are browns and rainbows, but a few streams contain brook trout too. Most Chilean trout average several pounds, and a number of specimens in the eight- to twelve-pound category

are caught each year. Twenty-pound trout have been taken in Chile, and some of the country's lakes must still contain fish of this size.

From what I have been able to observe, Chilean waters receive less angling use than those in Argentina. Visitors have been fishing these lakes and streams for years, but the locals don't appear to do as much fishing as they do across the border. Volcanic eruptions have created some stream deterioration, though, and law enforcement, in some areas, is not as good as it could be. Compared with what it is in other parts of the world, though, the trout fishing in Chile is fabulous.

Santiago is the capital of the country, a beautiful city with fine hotels and restaurants, wide boulevards, attractive parks and plazas, shops, night spots, and a variety of other attractions. Many residents speak English, and a surprising number of them are the blond descendants of Swiss, German, English and Scottish ancestors. With the bounty of the south Pacific so close, one (correctly) expects a great variety of seafood to be available in shops and restaurants. Lamb is also plentiful and cheap and, to a lesser degree, so is beef. Chile, of course, is wine country, one of the most productive in the world.

The Chilean Lake Region is located 500 miles south of Santiago and is reached by jet flights that take an hour or so, or by a train that takes twelve to fifteen hours. If you have the time, the latter method of travel is highly recommended. The route is scenic, the people are friendly and hospitable, and the sights along the way are extremely interesting. It is an excellent way to see more of this fascinating country, and you'll find the trip a rewarding experience.

Remember, the seasons are reversed in this part of the world. The fishing season opens the middle of October and closes the following April. Spring occurs in our fall, summer during January and February in the Northern Hemisphere, and autumn when our Easter lilies are beginning to push out of the ground. The best fishing, in my opinion, occurs early and late, but be aware of the fact that the spring run-off (October and November) can create high-water conditions. This is not the season for dry-fly fishing, but it can produce some large fish. Anticipate some rain, because the cool Humboldt Current hugs the Chilean coast and frequently nudges rain-bearing clouds inland. Nights are usually cool in the lake region. Days can be delightfully warm or cool, depending on the amount of sunshine.

PUCON AREA ● Chile

Floating is the best way to fish some rivers, and this fishing method has been developed into a fine science in Chile.

Guides in this part of the world are called boteros, and they perform their craft in shorter rocker-bottom skiffs designed for only two persons. The angler sits in the bow of the boat to conveniently work the best fishing water when it comes within casting range. The botero is positioned farther astern with a pair of oars. Downstream the boat goes, racing through white-water rapids, skirting swirling eddies, drifting lazily through still pools. Maneuvered by skilled hands, the boat is always under control, and the angler is always able to fish the best water. On occasion, the boat is beached so that the angler can fish a certain piece of water more thoroughly.

The day begins with a pre-dawn drive along a narrow mountain road, following a flatbed truck carrying the boats. When the put-in place is reached, the stubby little boats are unloaded and skidded down the bank into the water. Muscle is required to do this, but not as much as will be needed to load them back at the end of the day.

It's scenic country. Snow-draped volcanos, now silent, stand like sentinels on the horizon. Mountain slopes are covered with thick stands of spruce, and the lush valleys with green grass and wild flowers. An eagle swings overhead, its graceful body silhouetted against puffy white clouds. The air is clean. The river runs strong and clear, ruffled with waves as it hurries down boulder-strewn chutes, turning as blue as the sky when it pauses to catch its breath.

At mid-day there is a pause for lunch. A fire is built immediately, and the wine is put into the river to chill. A brace of trout are split open for the skillet, and tender strips of beef and lamb are skewered on long green sticks. The cooking process begins, and the fragrance of cooking meat heightens waiting appetites. The guides—clad in floppy hats and bulky wool sweaters—chat in low tones as the meat is turned one final time. Finally, the wine is uncorked and the food is served. It's a feast accompanied by a salad, loaves of freshly baked bread, and foil-wrapped ears of corn baked in the coals. After lunch, there is a brief siesta before the boats are launched again for the remaining float downstream.

Many Chilean rivers are excellent float streams, but a pair I'm familiar with is the Trancura and Liucura, located east of Lake Villarrica in the Pucon area. Both are challenging streams, offering a variety of fishing water for both the fly and spin fisherman. Another popular float stream in the area is the Tolten, which flows out of the opposite end of Lake Villarrica and always holds large trout.

There are two places to stay in the area, the Gran Hotel and the Hotel Antumalal. The former is located at the foot of the Villarrica volcano, on the shore of the lake. It offers 122 modern rooms, a private beach, boating facilities, a dining room, a bar, and a nightclub. It's a highly popular tourist destination.

Smaller, and more exclusive, is the Antumalal, located on a hill overlooking the lake. This facility offers fourteen spacious rooms with private baths, as well as an excellent bar and dining room.

A double room at the Antumalal is priced at around $100 during the high season and is somewhat less at the Gran. A day's fishing includes ground

The author with an average-size trout taken while floating the Trancura River.

transportation, guide, boat, and lunch and will cost in the neighborhood of $30 per day. Good guides are available in the area and are known by the managers of both hotels.

For more information on fishing in this part of Chile, write to Turismo Cocha S.A., Agustinas 1173, Casilla 1001, Santiago, Chile, S.A. Another qualified Santiago operator is Sportstour, P.O. Box 3300, Santiago, Chile, S.A. For travel details, get in touch with your travel agent or Eastern Airlines. If you encounter any communications problems with Chilean operators, contact Corporate Communications (Latin America), Eastern Airlines, Miami International Airport, Miami FL 33148.

LLIFEN REGION ● Chile

Located southeast of Valdivia, between Lago Ranco and the Argentine border, are some of Chile's most beautiful trout streams. The Cumilahue is one such stream. Others are the Cahunaahue, the Furaleliu, the Nilahue, the Carran, and the Hueinahue. A slightly larger river, in the same area, is the Calcurrupe, which is suitable for both wading and floating.

These are classic fly fishing streams. In addition to the pancora, which is that little crab which Chilean trout thrive on, these rivers are also rich in insect life. Hatches occur with regularity, and these trout feed heavily when they're in process. Wet flies and streamers work best from the season opening until the middle of November, and thereafter dry flies and nymphs are most productive. Wet flies, fished on top, also produce good results throughout the season.

These rivers contain both rainbow and brown trout, both averaging approximately three pounds. Accurate catch records kept on the Cumilahue indicate that an angler fishing this river will land an average of thirty fish per day. Some of these trout will be small ones, and some will be larger than the average. Good fish in the five- to seven-pound category are a possibility each fishing day, and even larger trout are available. Record for the Cumilahue is a twenty-two-pound brown taken in 1975. These trout rivers are restricted to fly fishing and are subject to a kill limit of two trout per day. Actually, anglers are encouraged to release all the trout they catch except those desired for food, mounting, or photo purposes.

The place to stay in the Llifen area is Cumilahue Lodge, which is located right on the bank of the river it is named after. Built in 1965 specifically as a fishing lodge, this facility has five bedrooms (all with private baths), a large living room with a fireplace, a spacious dining room, a tackle room, bar facilities, landscaped grounds, a private air strip, boats, and ghillies. Cumilahue is owned and operated by Adrian Dufflocq, an angler with international acclaim and certainly one of Chile's best fly fishermen.

Week-long fishing packages here include reception at the Valdivia Airport

Fly fishermen fishing the Cumilahue River will land an average of thirty trout per day.

or the closer Paillaco train station, and ground transportation to the lodge. This is a two-and-a-half-hour drive through some of Chile's most scenic countryside. The week's angling itinerary includes fishing the Cumilahue, particularly the late-evening hatches for which this stream is famous. Also included are daily excursions to such streams as the Cuhanahue, the Furalelfu, and others in the area, depending on which is the most productive at the time. Usually, the Calcurrupe is included in the itinerary, and when fishing this stream anglers have the option of wading selected stretches or spending the day floating. Provided are all meals, including either picnic or asados prepared on the river bank. In either case, complimentary wine will be provided. On the seventh day, transportation is provided back to either the airport or the railway station in time to make connections north to Santiago.

Another transportation option is to go to Rinihue, which is about the same distance as Valdivia, and take a series of three lake cruises across the Argentine border to San Martin De Los Andes. From here, you can go south to Bariloche, where you can catch a flight to Buenos Aires and return home via a different route. I have made this trip, and if you have time I heartily recommend it.

The bottoms of these streams are strewn with moss-covered boulders, so felt-soled waders are a must. In the tackle line, bring a pair of flyrods. One should be a relatively heavy outfit capable of casting a #8 weight forward line and large-sized wet flies designed to emulate the pancora. Include a lighter #5 or #6 outfit to fish smaller streams and for dry-fly and nymph fishing. A double taper line is recommended for this rod. Reels should be backed up with eighty yards of eighteen-pound test line for the larger one, and at least fifty yards for the smaller outfit. Bring a variety of leaders tapered down to different breaking strengths. Popular flies are as follows: Platinum, Blonde, Grey Ghost, and Mickey Finn streamers; Muddler Minnow and an assortment of woolly worms in wet flies; nymphs such as the Hares Ear and Montana Nymph; and dry flies in patterns like the Royal Wulf, Adams, Irresistible, and Olive Dun. If you prefer, plan on picking up most of your flies in Chile. They're available, well tied, and reasonably priced.

The price for an all-inclusive week of fishing here is around $1,000. The overnight train fare from Santiago for a sleeping compartment is $35 each way. This is an interesting and extremely scenic trip and is highly recommended.

Remember, the seasons here are the opposite of ours. Our winter is their summer—and is a delightful time of the year in the Chilean Lake Region. For fishing, however, perhaps the best period is during the month of March. This is the equivalent of September in this hemisphere and usually means cool nights, warm, sunny days, and actively feeding trout.

The weather this far south in the Andes is similar to that of Canada in midsummer. Bring warm clothing including rain gear. Unlike Canada or Alaska, however, biting insects are not a problem.

For more information on fishing at Cumilahue Lodge, write to Adrian Dufflocq, P.O. Box 14138, Santiago, Chile, S.A. For reception in Santiago, sightseeing, hotel accommodations, and travel arrangements within the country, get in touch with either of the following: Sportstour, P.O. Box 3300, Santiago, Chile, S.A., or Turismo Cocha S.A., Angustinas 1173, Santiago, Chile, S.A. For travel details, ask your travel agent or Eastern Airlines.

The Tamar River is considered one of England's best fishing streams.

Europe 5

TAMAR RIVER • England

Born in the boulder-strewn highland moors of England's west country, the Tamar River, which divides Devon from Cornwall, is considered one of the country's best fishing streams. Four tributaries flow into the Tamar at this point and contribute to this sports fishery. They are the Wolf, the Lyd, the Carey, and the Thrushel, and they also have their origin in the wild moorlands.

Atlantic salmon begin to run up the Tamar and Lyd in mid-April and become more plentiful as the season progresses. In these streams, fishing is rated as good throughout the summer and even better in September and the first two weeks of October. These salmon average around ten pounds, but larger fish in the twenty-pound category are always present and offer an added incentive for the trophy-seeking angler.

Fishing for sea-run brown trout, called peal locally, begins to get hot the last week in June and continues that way until the end of September. These migratory fish average a little less than two pounds, but 6-pounders are taken every season. The staple fish of this Devon fishery is the native brown trout, which provides action for fly fishermen from May through September. These are wild fish, on the smallish side, but they rise readily to artificials and put up a spirited fight when hooked on light tackle.

Headquarters for angling in this area is the Arundell Arms, located in the quaint little village of Lifton. This quality country inn owns twenty miles of fishing water on the Tamar and its tributaries and has been one of England's première fishing hotels for more than half a century. Most of the hotel's twenty-three spacious bedrooms have private baths, and an adjoining annex provides equally comfortable accommodations. The dining room overlooking the terraced gardens serves gourmet-class meals and is lauded for its choice wine selection. The famed "Long Bar" is also the village pub and is the favorite watering hole for guests and locals at the end of the day.

To say that the Arundell Arms caters to fishermen is an understatement. Box lunches are packed for anglers as a matter of course, and if guests want to fish past the dinner hour, a tasty cold supper will be waiting for them on their return. In the garden, an ancient cock-fighting arena has been turned into a rod room. Two angling professionals, one a Welsh open-fly casting champion, supervise this facility, assign daily fishing beats, pass out stream maps, and offer advice on fishing techniques and equipment. Salmon and trout flies are offered for sale here, and numerous items of fishing tackle and apparel are available for rent. Also available to guests is private instruction in fly fishing techniques, as well as several day courses for both beginners and anglers who want to improve their skills.

Angling guests are assigned beats on a daily basis, according to the species of fish they are interested in. Each of these stretches of river is usually composed of both fast and still water, with several holding pools for the migratory salmon and peal. These streams are fished in the classic English manner, upstream with a dry fly or wet if a guest prefers. Salmon and trout are caught during the day, but the wary sea-run browns are taken mostly after dark.

Prices are reasonable. A seven-day/six-night package, for example, is priced at less than $500 per person and includes six nights' accommodations, all meals, five days' fishing on private beats, and care of your catch. The price for a ghillie (angling guide) is around $10 per hour. A three-day course on fly fishing techniques is also available. All of these prices will vary, depending to the dollar/pound exchange rate at the time.

English weather is unpredictable, but you can expect some cool days and perhaps some rain. Dress accordingly, and be sure to take a rain suit. Hip boots or chest waders are also required, but these can be rented if you desire. Angling attire is slightly more formal here than elsewhere in the world. A jacket and tie are recommended for evening dining. Bring your fishing vest and selection of flies, but expect to pick up a few of the local patterns preferred by these well-bred fish. If your old fishing hat is too shopworn for this environment, you might consider picking up one of the soft English tweed hats that work so well for this purpose.

To reach Lifton from London, proceed to nearby Exeter by either train or commercial air. Rental cars are available there, or the hotel can arrange ground transportation if requested.

For information on this fine British hotel and the Tamar River, write to Ann Voss-Bark, The Arundell Arms, Lifton, Devon, England P116 0AA. The telephone number is Lifton 056 684 244. For additional information on fishing in Great Britain, write to Catherine Althaus, British Tourist Authority, Queens House, 64 St. James Street, London, England SW1A 1NF.

FISHING SCOTTISH WATERS

Fishing is not free in Scotland, but it's reasonable.

In this country, every inch of fishing water is privately owned and used as a resource by land owners. Here, you pay for the privilege of casting over a school of salmon or trout, but in the process you're assured that no one else is going to wade in beside you and spook your fish.

As a result, the lakes and streams in this country are not jammed with fishermen, as some of ours are. Sections of these waters are divided into "beats" and are assigned a limited number of anglers for a specified period of time. If you lease a two-rod beat on the River Spey, for instance, only one other angler will be allowed to fish that stretch of river with you. The system is a good one. It works in the British Isles, and I sometimes think that it might be the way to maintain quality fishing on some of our lakes and streams too.

Although you pay for fishing rights, the fees are not exorbitant. They range for a dollar or so on trout streams to up to $100 per day on the best salmon rivers. The letting of fishing rights is a source of income in Scotland, and as a result land owners usually do a good job of maintaining their fisheries.

The Atlantic salmon is Scotland's première gamefish and reaches a good size in some of the country's streams. The Tay is one example. Tay salmon run large, averaging eighteen to twenty pounds, and big fish in the forty-pound category are caught each season. Other streams, like the classic Tweed, produce fish averaging less than ten pounds. In addition to the Tay and Tweed, other renowned salmon rivers are the Spey, the Dee, the Don, and The Deveron. Despite offshore netting near their North Sea mouths, these rivers continue to produce nice catches of salmon. But because these popular streams are usually reserved far in advance, the visiting angler would do better to fish more remote rivers that aren't as well known. Two examples are the Kirkaig and the Oykel. A few of Scotland's streams, like the Tweed and Don, have good runs of spring salmon, but the majority fish best in late summer and early autumn. Each stream is different, though. Before reserving a beat on a Scottish stream, ask to review week-by-week catch records for the past several years.

Scotland's rivers also contain sea trout, and they run up to ten pounds in some of these rivers. The best fishing for this species occurs in the north of Scotland and in the Orkney and Shetland islands. Fishing with a fly produces most of the action in the streams, but spinning is perhaps more effective in tidal pools. The latter waters offer truly outstanding fishing during the long, partially lit nights of summer in this latitude. Loch Maree is excellent sea trout habitat, too. These fish commence running in this western highland lake in July, and the fishing continues throughout the summer until the season's end on October 15. The average weight for the species is slightly more than two pounds, but fish in the eight- to ten-pound category are taken each year.

There are a multitude of lakes and streams in Scotland.

Loch Maree holds the British sea-trout record with a 21-pounder taken in 1948. As in other Scottish waters, fishing is uncrowded on this lake. It is divided into eight beats, and a single boat is assigned to each beat.

The brown trout, the most prevalent species of fish in Scotland, is found in virtually every loch, burn, and river in the country. Brownies share some of these waters with salmon and sea trout (sea-run brown trout), but they are also the only inhabitants of others. A good example is some of the highland lochs in the northern part of Scotland. Brownies grow to a large size in these fertile waters, and because they're wild fish they are highly prized for their fighting ability.

Pike fishing is good in Scotland, also. Scotland holds the British pike record with a 47-pound, 11-ounce fish taken a number of years ago, and I personally know that a number of pike exceeding thirty pounds are taken from Scottish waters each year. So common are salmonoid species that the average Irish angler looks no further. Pike are almost completely ignored as a gamefish, nor are they sought for table fare either.

No national license is required for fishing in Scotland, but anyone intending to fish for salmon or sea trout must first obtain the written permission of the authority owning the fishing rights to that body of water. This permit may or may not include the payment of a fee, but in most cases it does. For brown-trout fishing, the laws are not as stringent, but there is a closed season from early in October until the middle of March. Salmon and sea-trout seasons vary from stream to stream, and sometimes from year to year as well. No fishing is permitted in Scotland on Sunday.

Scotland has a cool climate. The western coast usually has a mild, wet winter with temperatures ranging from 40 to 45 degrees Fahrenheit during January, with the east coast being slightly colder and drier. Spring and early summer are also cool, with average midsummer temperatures usually no higher than 60 degrees. This is ideal fishing weather, incidentally. A few years ago I was fishing the North Esk River when the weather got warm enough for farmers to work in the fields without their shirts. Temperatures that high meant that fishing was poor. As a rule of thumb, bring rain gear and warm clothes for fishing in Scotland.

ANGLING HOTELS • Scotland

Angling has been a tradition in the British Isles ever since the days of Dame Juliana Berners and Izaak Walton, and this tradition lives on in the hallowed halls of a handful of angling hotels. These hostelries are run for fishermen by fishermen and offer a pleasant blend of comfort, good food, and hospitality in the process. These establishments own or rent fishing beats for the use of their guests, maintain these fisheries in top-notch condition, and provide quality fishing in uncrowded conditions. Most of them have fishing pros in residence who can provide instruction for both the novice or expert angler.

Brown-trout fishing is good in Scotland's hill lochs.

Ghillies are usually available for those who desire their services, and advice from management and other guests is always freely given in these surroundings. Rod rooms are a standard feature of most of these hotels. So are conveniences like drying facilities, fly-tying benches, flies for sale, and equipment for hire. Crackling fires are usually available to warm an angler's backside after a day afield, and both guests and hotel employees will listen to your angling exploits.

In a way, Scotland's angling hotels have a lot in common with some of Canada's better fly-in fishing camps. They're also different, though. If you haven't tried one, you're in for a treat.

Coul House Hotel

The small Coul House Hotel is located in the northern highlands amidst scenic surroundings, approximately twenty miles northwest of Inverness. The one-time stately home of the Mackenzies of Coul, this attractive hotel features comfortable bedrooms, a dining room that serves outstanding meals, a TV room and lounge, and two cocktail lounges where anglers exchange stories at the end of a day's fishing and the villagers gather to socialize. It's a friendly place, an ideal headquarters for a Scottish angling vacation.

Coul House controls a stretch of the Alness River, which is a developing and well-maintained salmon and sea-trout river. Anglers fishing this river will fish a different beat each day and will share it with no more than two other rods. Each beat has from two to seven holding pools and from five to fifteen runs and resting pools. Salmon average between five and ten pounds; sea trout are in the one- and two-pound range. The Alness also offers excellent fishing for brown trout. The hotel can also offer, if it is desired, fishing on other nearby streams, such as the Blackwater, the Glass, and the Conon, and on a number of nearby trout lakes.

Proprietor Martyn Hill offers a Sunday-to-Sunday angling package that includes six days of fishing, accommodations, and breakfast and dinner daily. Not included in this package price are box lunches, the services of a ghillie, and a rental car. The car is recommended for local transportation and can be rented in Inverness. Ghillies are available and might be useful during salmon fishing. According to Hill, they're not necessary for trout fishing. This weekly package operates from April 1 to the end of October and is priced at less than $300.

For details, write to Martyn A. Hill, Coul House Hotel, Contin, By Strathpeffer, Ross-Shire, Scotland.

Scourie Hotel

The Scourie, a nineteenth-century hotel, overlooks the Bay of Scourie on Scotland's north coast, 115 miles north of Inverness. All twenty-two bedrooms have hot and cold running water, fireplaces, and electric outlets, and some have private baths as well. The hotel kitchen has a good reputation and specializes in serving Scottish cuisine in a pleasant dining room. For evening relaxation, there is a cocktail lounge also frequented by residents of the village.

The hotel offers brown-trout fishing in more than fifty hill lochs spread over an area of 6,000 acres. Some of these lakes hold trout up to ten pounds in weight, and others have fish averaging more than a pound. Salmon and sea-trout fishing is available on an eighteen-mile stretch of the Dionard River and on a shorter stretch of the Duartmore. Good fishing is also provided with private beats on a number of coastal lochs in the area. Boats and ghillies are available to fish these beats, and there are modest daily charges for these services. In both lakes and rivers, fishing is restricted to a fly rod and artificials. The best salmon-fishing months are July and September, with the most action for sea trout occurring in July, August, and September. The best trout fishing is during May, June, and July.

Because this is a very remote part of Scotland, no public transportation is available. Rental of a car is therefore recommended at the airport in Inverness.

Daily rates, including accommodations and three meals, average less than $30 per person and include brown-trout fishing on all the hotel's beats. Modest charges are made for fishing waters shared by other proprietors.

For more information on fishing in this area, write to Ian Hay, Scourie Hotel, Scourie, Sutherland, Scotland.

Kenmore Hotel

Established in 1572 when Colin Campbell granted a lease to Hugh Hay to start a hostelrie, the Kenmore Hotel is Scotland's oldest. It's located on the bank of the River Tay in a small village and offers its guests a combination of old-world charm, elegance, and comfort. Accommodations are provided for eighty guests in thirty-nine bedrooms, all with private baths. The Kenmore's dining room is renowned for its cuisine and wine selection, and its cocktail lounge is the favorite gathering place of both residents and villagers.

The hotel owns four miles of the Tay River and has the right to fish sprawling Loch Tay as well. The Tay, renowned as a salmon fishery, also produces excellent trout fishing for the Kenmore's guests. The trout fishing is free, but modest charges are made for salmon fishing. Beats are allocated on a half-day basis and are rotated so that each angler gets a chance at the most productive pools. Both fly fishing and spinning are allowed on this big river, with the latter being perhaps the more productive. On Loch Tay, trolling is the way most of the salmon and trout are taken. The salmon fishing on this river commences January 15 and closes in mid-October. Trout fishing opens in March and closes a week earlier than salmon fishing does. Salmon run large on the Tay, and the best fishing occurs in March and April.

Modified American Plan accommodations go for an average of $40 per day, salmon fishing fees an extra $6 per half-day. Fishing on Loch Tay with a boat and ghillie costs more.

Because Kenmore is located only forty miles north of Edinburgh, it is easily accessible by road. From Glasgow to the southwest, the hotel is only a two-hour drive. A rental car is recommended.

For more information on fishing this stream, write to Ian Mackenzie, Manager, Kenmore Hotel, Kenmore, Perthshire, Scotland.

Tulchan Lodge

Tulchan Lodge was built in 1907 as a fishing and shooting lodge on the 23,000-acre Tulchan Estate and was frequented by famous sportsmen wanting to catch salmon and shoot grouse. Recently the lodge has been refurbished to new standards of comfort and luxury, and it still caters to discriminating sportsmen.

The concept of Tulchan is that of a lodge and not a hotel. Blazing log fires and oak paneling are complemented by exquisitely decorated rooms to create a warm and friendly atmosphere of exclusive luxury. The lodge boasts a fine wine cellar, a dining room serving delightful cuisine, a cocktail lounge, rod and gun rooms, and a variety of other facilities for its sporting guests.

Tulchan Lodge is located on the Spey River and controls eight miles of this famous salmon stream. This stretch of river is fast flowing, with pools ideally suited to fly fishermen. The river is divided into four beats, each two miles long, on both banks of the river. They are easily accessible and are equipped with huts and boats. An experienced ghillie is assigned to each beat to provide guidance and instruction. Normally four to six rods fish each beat, and the salmon average around twelve pounds. The season is from the middle of February through September, with the best fishing occurring from the middle of April to the end of June. During the peak of the season, the odds of catching fish here are excellent.

Compared with other angling hotels in Scotland, Tulchan is expensive. The European Plan rate, including breakfast and tea, is around $80 per person per night. Breakfast and dinner vary from $12 to $30. The fishing tariff for a week of fishing is in excess of $400 during the better fishing period.

During the fall and winter, the estate offers excellent shooting for grouse, pheasant, and a variety of other gamebirds. Reservations and price information on these shoots are available on request.

Tulchan Lodge is located a short distance from Inverness and is best reached by automotile. Pick up a rental car at the Inverness Airport.

For more information on this facility and the fishing it offers, write to Tulchan Lodge, Grantown-on-Spey, Moray, Scotland.

LOCH LOMOND • Scotland

Our ghillie turned the wooden skiff into a secluded bay and switched off the small British outboard. "Let's try here," he suggested. "There's some big bloody pike in this hole."

The bay was shallow and clogged with huge granite boulders and shiny green aquatic growth, so my companion and I both tied on weedless lures. He chose a black-and-yellow spinner bait, and I decided on a red-and-white Dardevle. "Will this do?" I asked our ghillie.

Bryan McClean's rugged face was tanned from exposure to the harsh Scottish climate, and a hint of a frown furrowed his forehead. "It may take the odd one," he finally admitted. "Ye wouldn't by chance have a silver spoon, would ye?"

I stuck with the lure that takes most of the pike in North America, and my decision turned out to be a good one. Within a few hours we had caught and released eight good fish, with the largest scaling almost seventeen pounds on my DeLiar. I've had faster pike-fishing action before, but not with a cen-

Pike grow faster in Scotland than they do in North American waters.

turies-old castle looming in the background or a flock of sheep grazing contentedly on the shore.

Loch Lomond is a large and scenic lake that lies less than an hour's drive from Glasgow and is a renowned big-pike fishery. It held the Scottish record for many years with a 46-pound, 8-ounce fish taken by Tommy Morgan in 1948, but for some reason this record was thrown out and replaced by a 34-pound, 12-ounce catch made in 1980. By the spring of the following year, this record was bettered by a thirty-six-pound Lomond catch, and this bonny loch was well on the way to making angling history again.

Big pike are nothing new to Lomond, though. Jim Pairman has been operating the Balmaha Marina for the past seventeen years, and he informed me that anglers had been catching twenty-five- and thirty-pound pike in Lomond for as long as he could remember. According to Pairman, anything less than a record wouldn't raise an eyebrow in his part of the country.

I still had reservations, though. Although Loch Lomond is an extremely large lake and appears to be ideal pike habitat, I couldn't see how it could have this reputation. Fishing pressure tends to strip a lake of trophy-sized pike because of their aggressive nature, and Lomond was located too close to civilization not to see plenty of fishing pressure. I told the marina operator this and pointed to the handful of boats trolling in a nearby bay.

Pairman stuck a battered pipe in between his teeth and sucked on it for a moment before answering. "They're not fishing for pike, though," he said.

"They're not?"

"No," he told me. "Those lads are trolling for either salmon or trout."

Additional research indicated that he was correct. Most of the anglers fishing this big lake are trying to catch salmon, sea trout, or brown trout, and they always kill their catch, for either sale or home consumption. On the other hand, the average Scot doesn't eat pike, so most of them are released when caught. The few anglers who seriously fish for pike make it a point to release their fish after they are weighed and measured. They don't eat pike either.

There are no statistics on this subject, but I'm of the belief that the pike in Scotland probably grow twice as fast as they do in U.S. and Canadian waters. In this land of kilts and bagpipes, pike grow 365 days per year, and I'm guessing that it takes less than fifteen years to produce a specimen of fish weighing thirty pounds. In Canada, the average growth rate is less than a pound per year.

From what I have been able to ascertain, there are no restrictions on pike fishing in Loch Lomond, but a permit is required to fish the lake from February 1 to November 10, and it costs around $3 per day or $9 for a week. Boats are available for hire from Thistle Cottage in Luss, the Inverbeg Hotel, or either the Balloch or Balmaha marinas.

Fishing-tackle requirements for Loch Lomond pike are no different from what they are for our northwoods or Canadian waters. I prefer a moderate- to stiff-action casting rod rigged with a revolving spool reel. Recommended is a rod handle that you can get two hands on, not a pistol-grip handle. Load your reel with sixteen- to twenty-pound test line, which will cut through aquatic vegetation without breaking. A pair of outfits like this should suffice, because if you break a rod here a replacement is easy to pick up at a local tackle shop. Take along a variety of pike lures, including wobbling spoons, Big Mepps spinners, Magnum Rapalas, and a few spinnerbaits. Be sure to bring a supply of short wire leaders.

Anticipate cool and rainy weather in Scotland, regardless of when you go. Be sure to bring along a good rain suit, warm clothing, a wide-brimmed hat, and waterproof boots or shoes. Actually, the same type of clothing suitable for Canada or Alaska is appropriate for this part of the world.

Pike fishing in Loch Lomond is fair to good throughout most of the season, but from what I have been able to find out it is at its peak in April and May. I fished this lake in June and was told that I should have been there earlier. The next year I came in April and encountered a snowstorm and the record cold snap of the century. Things like this happen occasionally, but on a year-in, year-out basis I suggest that spring is the best time for pike action on Loch Lomond. The fish are in the shallows then. They're easy to locate. And they should be aggressive.

There are several hotels in the vicinity, but my favorite is the Buchanan Arms in nearby Dryman. This fine country inn has twenty-four modern guest rooms, a dining room that serves outstanding wine and cuisine, a hospitable bar and lounge, and a charm that is certain to delight the most discriminating traveler. The bed-and-breakfast rate varied from $25 to $35 per night when I was there, and it is probably slightly more now. The manager, Andrew Lane, is an extremely accommodating fellow and will be happy to help you put together a quality Loch Lomond fishing package.

As mentioned previously, Loch Lomond and the village of Dryman are located less than an hour's drive from Glasgow and are accessible by both rental car and bus. The former is recommended because there are numerous things to do and see in the area, and a vehicle will come in handy.

For more information on fishing Loch Lomond, write to any of the following: Buchanan Arms Hotel, Drymen, Stirlingshire G63 0BQ, Scotland; Hamish Cathie, Travel Scotland Ltd., 10 Rutland Square, Edinburgh EH1 2AE, Scotland; or Sports Travel International, 10A Rutland Square, Edinburgh EH1 2AS, Scotland.

ANGLING IN IRELAND

Most of Ireland's lakes and streams contain fish. Many of these waters are privately owned and are inaccessible to the visiting angler, but others are available on a fee basis or are completely free. As a general rule of thumb, the more productive fishing waters are subject to the stiffest fees and the most restrictions.

The Atlantic salmon is the most sought-after of Ireland's species of gamefish because it is an excellent fighter and highly prized as a food fish. Irish salmon that have been at sea for several years can go to thirty pounds or more, but most are younger fish, called grilse or peal, averaging around six pounds. Once they enter fresh water, salmon stop feeding and strike lures by reflex action, not as a result of hunger. Atlantic salmon do not die after spawning, as Pacific species do, but their ranks are still being seriously depleted by commercial netting, poaching and, to a lesser degree, sportsfishing.

The Moy River is one example. Anglers fishing this river during 1984 caught fewer than 1500 salmon, but commercial netters fishing off the mouth of this river took around 30,000 fish legally. How many more salmon were

The brown trout is one of the most common and most widely distributed of Irish gamefish.

taken illegally is anybody's guess. The upper Caragh River is a beautiful salmon stream that used to produce 400 or 500 nice-sized salmon each spring. Today, between 150 and 250 fish is considered an average season's catch, because this river is also heavily netted at the mouth. Salmon fishing in Ireland isn't what it used to be.

Migratory brown trout, known in Ireland as sea trout, represent a substantial fishery in the rivers and lakes along the country's west and south coasts. In these acid waters, this species averages less than one pound, but two- and four-pound fish are always possibilities. Unlike salmon, sea trout do not quit feeding altogether in fresh water, but they can occasionally be difficult to catch. The best sea-trout fishing can occur when the river is on the rise, at which time these hard-fighting little gamefish will readily take a spinner or fly. When the water is low and clear, the best trout fishing occurs at dusk and after dark. Larger sea trout enter the streams as early as April, but generally speaking the best sea-trout fishing occurs from June to September.

The brown trout is one of the most common and most widely distributed of all Irish gamefish. The species is found in virtually every river and lake in the country and is Ireland's most popular gamefish. Large limestone lakes like Sheelin, Corrib, and Derg produce large browns in the five- to ten-pound category, while smaller lakes and streams with a similar pH factor yield fish only slightly smaller. Brown trout inhabiting acid lakes and streams will usually average less than a pound, but what they lack in size they make up in aggressive fighting ability. Streams having access to the sea will also be populated with sea trout.

"Dapping" for trout is practiced in Ireland during the mayfly season, which begins the second week in May and lasts through June. Required equipment is a long light rod (up to thirteen feet), twenty yards of flossed silk blow line attached to monofilament, and either a natural or artificial mayfly. Other requirements include a lake full of trout, a skiff, and a stiff breeze. When fishing the dap, you keep your rod tip high and let the breeze skip your fly across the waves. The process is akin to trolling, and it's an effective way to take large trout, and plenty of them. As far as I know, "dapping" is unique to Ireland.

Pike are called "coarse" fish in Ireland and are not particularly popular with locals, who historically are oriented toward salmon and trout. This species of fish is widespread, however, and grows to a large size. The pike record is thirty-eight pounds, although in years past the record was listed at fifty-three pounds. In reply to my query on this subject, I was informed that the fifty-three-pound record was suspect, so it was scrapped in favor of the later catch. Several thirty-pound pike are caught in Irish waters each year, though, and twenty-pound fish are relatively common too. European anglers have discovered Irish pike fishing, and now this country enjoys a certain amount of angling traffic from France and West Germany. Regardless of this attention, however, angling pressure for the species is relatively sparse.

A license is required to fish for salmon and sea trout, and it varies in cost from $3 for a week to less than $15 for the season. No license is required to fish for brown trout or pike. In addition, private land owners usually charge fees to fish their waters, and these may range from $3 to $25 per rod, per day.

Heard about how beautiful and green Ireland is? Well, it got that way because the weather is cool and the rainfall abundant. Prepare for rain whenever you go, and bring along quality rain gear and footwear to keep you dry.

Fishing for Atlantic salmon in Ireland is not like fishing for silver salmon in Alaska, nor does the Irish brand of pike fishing have much in common with angling for pike in Saskatchewan. The surroundings are much more civilized, and the action will not be as fast paced as you may have grown used to. But, it is still a delightful experience. Irish hospitality is legion, and you'll find the food and lodgings first class. The price is also right, a real bargain when compared with prices in other parts of the world. Expect your Irish fishing trip to be a different and extremely pleasant experience.

RIVER SHANNON ● Ireland

Ireland is famous for its pike fishing.

I remember lunching at Glaslough Castle a number of years ago and seeing a mounted pike that was supposed to have weighed fifty-two pounds when it was caught.

The River Shannon is one of the première pike fisheries in Ireland.

"Where did it come from?" I asked.

My host, Desmond Leslie, pointed through the window at the lake outside the castle. "There," he said, "in our lake."

I had tackle in the trunk of the car, so when the opportunity presented itself I asked Leslie if I could spend an hour or so fishing. He agreed and sent for one of his employees to act as a guide, and before long I was fishing this beautiful lake.

Reasoning that Irish pike probably had much in common with Canadian pike, I tied on a red-and-white Dardevle and started casting into the lily pads that lined the lake shore. As we moved slowly along the bank, I continued to fish the weeds, thinking about the giant mounted pike I had just seen. "Big pike in this lake?" I asked him.

My ghillie leaned on his oars for a moment and tugged a battered pipe out of the pocket of his tweed jacket. "What do you mean by big?" he asked.

"Twenty pounds," I replied.

Michael Flanigan smiled as he lit his pipe. "That's not a big pike," he said.

"What's a big one, then?"

"Thirty pounds, maybe."

"Are there still fish that big in this lake?" I asked.

Before he could reply, my wobbling spoon disappeared in a swirl of water and something tried to wrench my rod from my hands. I set the hook instinctively, gripped the rod handle in both hands, and watched the line peel off the revolving spool. "Have a net in this boat?" I asked.

"Yes," he replied. "But we're not going to need it for a long time."

He was right. I never saw that pike. I fought the fish for more than half an hour before it finally got entangled in the weeds and snapped my twelve-pound test line.

"That was a big pike." Flanigan said.

That was my introduction to pike fishing in Ireland, but since that time I've learned that my experience was not unusual. Irish pike grow to a large size, and they abound in most of the island's numerous lakes and streams. The present Irish record, for example, is forty-two pounds and there are a number of thirty-pound fish taken every year.

The River Shannon is one of the première pike fisheries in Ireland. It's the country's longest river, rising in the north and flowing in a southerly direction for more than 200 miles. With its tributaries, like the Suck and Brosna, the Shannon drains almost a fifth of the island. Some of the lakes in the system are Allen, Ree, and Derg. Derg Lake, 30,000 acres in size, is approximately fifteen miles long and two to five miles in width. Accommodations and fishing centers on the Shannon are Carrick On Shannon, Athlone, Ballinasloe, Portumna, Broadford, and Ennis.

Most of the Shannon is ideal pike water. It is a placid, slow-flowing stream, wild in some places, much of it underfished. Islands abound along this watercourse, and the Shannon's network of large and small lakes provides ideal pike habitat. Aquatic weed growth is plentiful, and the supply of food fish is almost unlimited. Because the Shannon and its tributaries flow through chalk and limestone country, these waters produce larger fish than those having a more acid base. Growth rate is another factor, too. Ireland's mild, open winters allow these pike to grow much faster than they do in Canada, and this factor and others contribute to the large size of Irish pike.

There is no closed season in Ireland, nor is there a period of the year when fishing is not productive. The best action of the year, however, occurs during spring and fall, with April and May producing most of the trophy fish. Fishing pressure is slight for several reasons. Ireland, particularly in this area, has a sparse population. Irish sports fishermen historically concentrate on trout and salmon, whereas meat fishermen spend most of their time fishing for species like perch, rudd, roach, and tench. As a result, visiting anglers have the pike fishing almost to themselves.

Tackle for Irish pike differs little from that used in our country or in Canada. Recommended is a bait-casting outfit with a medium- to stiff-action rod, a reel loaded with twenty-four-pound test line, and wire leaders. The same lures that work for pike in Canada also produce strikes in Ireland. Spoons are good, and so are spinner baits worked in the weeds, surface lures, and shallow to medium running crank baits. Fishing with live bait is not legal in Ireland and is not particularly effective for pike anyway.

Guides, called ghillies locally, are highly recommended and provide services at very reasonable prices. Prepare to be surprised, though—the Irish ghillies I fished with were impeccably dressed in a cap, necktie, knickers, and tweed sports coat. All were highly professional, excellent fishing guides, and pleasant companions.

Facilities abound along the Shannon watercourse, and one of them is the Bush Hotel, located in Carrick on Shannon. This fine little hotel has twenty-five centrally heated guest rooms, most with private baths. Modern and progressive, the Bush has been around for 200 years and has been owned by the same family for six generations. Modified American Plan accommodations are available here for around $25 per day in a party of two, and fishing on Lough Allen or the upper Shannon can be arranged for an additional $15 per day, per person. River pike, according to the local Angling Club secretary, average ten to twelve pounds in size and go up to twenty pounds. In Allen and other surrounding lakes, pike average two pounds heavier, with an occasional 25-pounder being caught.

Situated on the shore of Lough Derg (Lake Derg) farther downstream, is an early-nineteenth-century hotel called Gurthalougha House that offers the following package for around $40 per day: bed and breakfast, packed lunch, evening meal, use of a boat, and services of a ghillie. This little hotel is set among one hundred acres of landscaped ground and forest about three miles from the quaint little village of Terryglass. Portumna, which has fewer than 2,000 residents, is the largest nearby town of any consequence. Lough Derg, largest lake on the Shannon watercourse, offers good pike fishing at most seasons of the year, with April and May being the favored period. According to reports, pike in the ten- to sixteen-pound category are caught here with regularity.

Farther down the lake at Scarriff is the Clare Lakelands Hotel, which is a family-operated hotel with twenty-four modern guest rooms, a popular bar and lounge, and a highly rated dining room. The Modified American Plan rate at this hotel is $20 per day and is based on two people sharing the same room. Fishing with a boat, motor, and guide is available on a daily basis for an additional $20 per day, which figures out to a reasonable $30 per day per person, including fishing, accommodations, and meals. Padraic Cahill, secretary of the local angling club, informed me that anglers fishing this part of Lough Derg could expect to boat ten to twelve pike each day, each averaging eight to eighteen pounds.

Dromoland Castle, former residence of Ireland's ancient kings, is also located in County Clare and is just eight miles east of Shannon Airport. Now a luxurious resort hotel, Dromoland offers sixty-five beautifully furnished guest rooms, all with private bath, stately halls, a handsome bar and lounge, and an elegant dining room that serves sumptuous meals. Prices at this hotel start at $75 per day, double occupancy, and do not include meals. Fishing with a boat, motor, and guide is priced at an additional $25 per day. Including Lough Derg, there are forty good pike lakes within a radius of twenty miles of Dromoland that have produced pike ranging up to thirty pounds.

Shannon Airport is the gateway to the River Shannon fishery and is served on a daily basis by a number of U.S. and other foreign carriers. All of these facilities can arrange ground transportation from this airport, but you might consider renting a car, as your ghillie possibly may not own a vehicle, and there may be some merit in fishing several different spots during your stay. I mention this because the fishing craft used here will likely be a skiff powered with a small outboard. Consequently, you won't fish as much territory as you would in Canada or on a large lake here at home.

For more information on fishing at these spots, write to the following: Tom Maher, The Bush Hotel, Carrick On Shannon, Co. Leitrim, Ireland; Michael Wilkinson, Gurthalougha House, Ballinderry, Nenagh, Co. Tipperary, Ireland; Clare Lakelands Hotel, Scarriff, Co. Clare, Ireland; or Dromoland Castle, Newmarket-on-Fergus, Co. Clare, Ireland. A few other sources of information are: Sean O'Rourke, Carrick On Shannon Angling Club, Mullaghmore, Carrick On Shannon, Co. Roscommon, Ireland; Hugh Gough, Coarse Angling Officer, Central Fisheries Board, Balnagowna, Mobhi Boreen, Glasnevin, Dublin 9, Ireland; and Padraic Cahill, Scarriff, Mountshannon & Whitegate Angling Club, Scarriff, Co. Clare, Ireland.

MOY RIVER ● Ireland

The Moy rises in the Ox Mountains of County Mayo, flows southward in the direction of Swinford, then west and north again through Foxford and Ballina. Swift and rocky for the most part, the Moy is a fair-sized stream north of Swinford and a big river by the time it reaches Foxford. It also is one of Ireland's best salmon streams. According to the Department of Fisheries, the Moy gets the greatest salmon return of any river in Ireland.

One of the best sections of the river is a five-and-a-half-mile stretch between Ballina and Foxford that is controlled by Mount Falcon Castle. This piece of water contains a number of good lies and annually produces around 1,500 salmon for its anglers. According to Robert Gloag, director of angling and shooting for the castle, the average guest who fishes this water for a week goes home with at least four salmon. Five boats and ghillies are available to fish certain of these stretches, while the rest of the beats are fished from the bank.

Although the Moy gets a few spring-run salmon, it is most noted as a summer fishery. This run, which occurs from June through September, sees a fair number of salmon weighing ten to fifteen pounds, but the majority of

Some of the Moy beats may be effectively fished with a fly, but spinning is usually more productive.

these fish are grilse (locally called peal). These fish are taken in a variety of methods, because unlike some other Irish streams the Moy is not restricted to fly fishing. Some of the beats may be fished effectively with a fly; others are more productive when fished with spinning equipment. Of the 1,700 salmon yielded by this fishery in 1983, it should be noted that 85 percent of them were taken by the latter method.

Mount Falcon is a sprawling castle-like mansion situated on a one-hundred-acre estate beside the Moy. This hotel features attractively furnished bedrooms with private baths, a dining room that turns out superb meals, a library, lounges, tennis facilities, and other amenities. The hotel serves wine but does not have a liquor license. As an indication of the quality of Mount Falcon's facilities and services, it has been awarded a prestigious "A" rating by the Irish Tourist Board.

Accommodations, with three meals daily, are priced at $40 per person. The hotel's River Moy salmon beats are let at $5 per rod for bank fishing, and the rate is $20 per person, in a party of two, for a boat and ghillie.

Moy salmon, mostly grilse, will average around only six pounds, so heavy tackle is not required. An 8 System fly outfit should suffice for salmon, but a lighter outfit is recommended for sea and brown trout. Recommended salmon flies for the Moy, in 5 to 8 sizes, are Hairy Mary, Blue Charm, Badger, Shrimp, and Black Doctor. As mentioned previously, spinning is permitted on this stretch of the Moy and is the favored way of taking fish on most of the beats. Recommended is a light- to medium-action rod and an open-face reel loaded with six-pound test line. In the lure line, Mepps spinners work admirably, but bring along a selection of other small spoons and lures too. Also plan on purchasing a few favored flies and lures locally.

County Mayo is in the west of Ireland and is slightly closer to Shannon than Dublin. Hotel management can arrange transportation, if desired, but a better alternative might be to rent a car.

For more information on Mount Falcon Castle and the River Moy, write to Robert Gloag, Mount Falcon Castle, Ballina, Co. Mayo, Ireland. Another source of information is Brian Geraghty, Angling Advisor, Irish Tourist Board, Baggot St. Bridge, Dublin 2, Ireland.

BALLYNAHINCH RIVER ● Ireland

The Ballynahinch River, sometimes called the Owenmore, was once considered the finest salmon river in Ireland, and it still is a salmon and sea-trout fishery worthy of note.

Located in the county of Galway, in the west of Ireland, the Ballynahinch is a short river less than three miles in length. It is a dream stream for fly fishermen because it was extensively developed for this purpose by one of its former owners. The river is divided into seven beats, each accommodating a total of two rods (fishermen) at a time. There are also two beats on Ballynahinch Lake that offer a different kind of fishing for four additional anglers. These beats are let for the whole day, from 10 A.M. to 7 P.M. So that everyone gets a fair chance at the most productive sections of river, the beats are rotated on a daily basis.

Although it is not known as a spring-run river, enough early salmon enter the Ballynahinch to offer anglers a chance to catch fish during the March-through-May period. The peak fishing period for salmon is June through September, though. Ballynahinch salmon average around ten pounds, but 25-pounders are not uncommon. Records kept over the past decade reveal that this fishery produces an average of 236 salmon each season, with actual catches fluctuating from year to year. Unlike, those of some other privately owned waters in Ireland, salmon taken from this river belong to the angler and not the property owner.

The Ballynahinch is possibly a better sea-trout stream than it is a salmon fishery. Angling for these migratory trout commences February 1 and

Records indicate that the Ballynahinch River produces an average catch of 3,500 sea trout per season.

remains good through October. According to available records, the Ballynahinch produces an average catch of 3,500 sea trout per season.

Fishing rights on Ballynahinch Lake and the entire stretch of river belong to Ballynahinch Castle. Constructed as the ancestral home of the O'Flahertys, chieftans of Connemara, it eventually became the possession of the Maharajah Jam Sahib, also known as Ranjitsinhji. This Indian prince and renowned cricketeer was an avid angler and is largely responsible for the development of the Ballynahinch River into a quality salmon and sea-trout fishery. Today, the castle is a first-class resort hotel, catering specifically to sportsmen and their families.

The castle is situated amidst landscaped grounds and gardens at the base of one of the Twelve Bens mountains. It is surrounded by lush forest, overlooks the river, and is less than a five-minute hike from the equally scenic Ballynahinch Lake. The castle has twenty lavishly furnished guest rooms, all with private baths. There are a dining room serving tasteful meals, a popular bar and lounge, tennis courts, cheerful open fireplaces, and an angling headquarters offering tackle for rent.

Ballynahinch water, both river and lake, is reserved exclusively for fly fishing, so limit your equipment accordingly. European anglers historically use ten- to fourteen-foot rods for salmon, but I think that a 9½ foot, 10 weight graphite or fiberglass rod will be adequate for the size fish you'll be seeking.

Atlantic salmon are formidible adversaries, so make certain that your reel has sufficient backing and a sturdy drag system. For sea trout and the occasional brown that will rise to your fly, a number 6 System outfit should be sufficient. Popular salmon flies, in 5 to 8 sizes, are Jock Scott, Silver Doctor, Blue Charm, Hairy Mary, and Galway Thunder. Recommended trout flies, in 9 to 11 sizes, are Black Pennel, Watson's Invicta, Blue Zulu, and Connemara Black. Flies are available for purchase, and if you want to rent equipment, it is available at the hotel. Fishing the Ballynahinch is probably more civilized than what you may be used to. Chest waders aren't necessary, for example, because casting platforms allow anglers to work the best lies with dry feet. In this respect, knee-high boots are sufficient. European anglers dress a little more formally than we do, so if you want to blend into the Connemara fishing scene you might take this fact into consideration. Your ghillie will probably wear a necktie, but it isn't necessary that you do so. Just pay a little more attention to your dress than when fishing the Canadian wilds or our waters. Plan on dressing each night for dinner, however.

Bed-and-breakfast rates at the Ballynahinch Castle during the high season are $25 per day. For full American Plan accommodations the tab is $44 per day, per person. The charge for fishing is $25 per day, per beat, with each beat limited to two rods.

Ballynahinch also offers excellent shooting for woodcock and pigeon, for guests present during the fall hunting season. Rates are reasonable and are all inclusive. Write to the management for details.

Ballynahinch Castle is 174 miles from Dublin and only eighty-nine miles from Shannon. The Shannon Airport, therefore, is the logical gateway to this Galway destination. Management will make arrangements for ground transportation on request, but I suggest a rental car as an advisable alternative. Having "wheels" while visiting this area is a good idea because there is much to see and do here.

For details concerning Ballynahinch and what it has to offer, write to John O'Connor, Manager, Ballynahinch Castle Hotel, Co. Galway, Ireland. Another source of information is Bord Failte, Baggot Street Bridge, Dublin 2, Ireland.

LAERDAL AND GAULA ● Norway

When it comes to Atlantic salmon fishing, Norway is considered the place to go. This Scandinavian country has more than a hundred quality streams, and many of them are big, brawling rivers that produce salmon of outstanding size. The Tana is one of these. This far-north river currently holds the Atlantic salmon record with a 79-pounder taken more than fifty years ago. This catch was no fluke, however. Since then, the Tana has produced fish in the sixty- and seventy-pound category and regularly yields salmon yielding fifty pounds. Other comparable rivers, many of which enjoy even greater popularity, are the Alta, the Namsen, the Nide, the Laerdal, the Surna, and the Passvik.

Most of these larger streams are located in the northern part of Norway and are fed by huge glaciers located 4,000 feet or more above sea level. This constant source of water keeps these rivers running full and strong and gives them an advantage over other streams that must depend on melting snow or precipitation during the spring and summer months. With these streams, if the amount of snow or rainfall is below average, the water becomes low and the salmon cannot ascend them. A continual source of water is, therefore, a big advantage.

The size of Norway's salmon attracts anglers from all over Europe, and for the past century the best beats on the more productive rivers have been extremely valuable. Most of them are booked years in advance and fetch fees of many thousands of dollars. Other factors have contributed to this situation. Acid rain has had a negative effect and is believed to have ruined the lakes and small streams in a 13,000-square-kilometer territory. Excessive drift netting has taken its toll on Norway's salmon population, as has commercial fishing far out at sea. As salmon become more scarce, the rental fees for the better beats skyrocket. The Alta River is one example. The last time I checked, it was possible to pay up to $6,000 for an opportunity to fish the Alta for a week, but unfortunately there were no openings available. To a lesser degree, a similar situation exists on a number of Norway's most popular salmon streams.

With certain exceptions, the salmon season in Norway opens June 1 and closes September 1. Usually, fishing conditions are reliable from June 20 to the end of August, but there are always variables caused by weather, water flow, stream location, and the stream type. Generally, after a winter of heavy snowfall, the salmon tend to run later. After a mild winter or early spring they run correspondingly earlier. Heavy fish, for the most part, tend to be among the early arrivals.

Anyone fishing Norway must buy a federal fishing license. This is no big deal. It can be purchased in any post office and doesn't cost very much. In addition, however, it is necessary to obtain a permit from the person or organization controlling the stretch of river you intend to fish. If you buy a fishing package, both of these fees will be included in the overall price. Norway also has a law decreeing that all fishing tackle, including waders, must be disinfected before it can be used in Norwegian waters. This regulation does not constitute a problem, though, because disinfection stations are scattered throughout the fishing area.

It never gets dark in that land of the midnight sun, and the salmon historically are more active during the long twilight period than they are during the day. As a result, most anglers do their fishing at night and sleep during the day.

Most Norwegian rivers also have runs of sea-run browns, and particularly in

Salmon fishing beats on rivers like the Laerdal and Gaula should be booked as far in advance as possible.

the western rivers these fish grow to a large size. In rivers like the Aurland and Laerdal, the species runs from ten to twenty pounds and provides sport comparable to that of the larger salmon.

Heavier tackle is recommended for Norwegian rivers than for other salmon streams in Europe. These rivers are usually larger, with strong current and small holding pools. As a result, rods must be rugged enough to handle a forty-pound fish in turbulent water. For this task, the average European angler uses a twelve- or fourteen-foot two-handed rod, but Americans are more inclined to use a 10 weight rod nine-and-half or ten feet long. Reels should be backed with at least one hundred yards of twenty-pound test Dacron. Shooting head and weight-forward lines are used. Leaders may test ten or twenty-pounds, depending on the water being fished and the size fish anticipated. Other gear should include felt-soled waders, a fishing vest, sunglasses, a warm jacket, and a rain coat. Plan on using big flies with a few of the most popular patterns being as follows: Silver Doctor, Grey Doctor, Dusty Miller, Jock Scott, and Blue Charm. When you are fishing snow-melt water with a greenish tinge, an orange-colored fly is frequently most productive. Excellent flies, incidentally, may be obtained locally.

One of Norway's most popular salmon rivers is the Laerdal, which has about sixteen miles of salmon water below an impassable waterfall. Salmon average sixteen pounds on this stream, with heavier fish a possibility. Sea trout average better than five pounds. No boats are used on this stream. Fishing is from the bank (from specially constructed platforms) or by wading. A package trip that includes seven days of fishing, lodging, meals, local ground transportation, and transfers to and from Oslo is available from Fishing International for a price of $3,500.

PanAngling offers a similar package on the Gaula River, located near Trondheim, which is now considered one of the five best salmon streams in the country. This package features fishing on a twenty-mile stretch of private water that is purported to have ten of this river's best pools. The Gaula is a wading stream with salmon averaging twenty pounds, and occasional heavy fish weighing twice that much. This weekly package includes transfers from Trondheim, seven nights' accommodations at a small country inn, all meals, ground transportation, and six days' fishing with an experienced guide. The price is $3,300.

Cavalier Consultants offers a fishing package in the North Cape region that features fishing on the Lakselv, Borselv, and Komag Rivers. These are smaller wadable streams that offer fair-sized salmon, an opportunity to catch heavy fish, and good sea-trout fishing. Fishing beats are also available on the Neiden and Tana Rivers, which are also in this far north region. The package price is $1,700 and includes seven nights' accommodations, all meals, ground transportation, angling fees, and seven days' fishing with a professional ghillie.

For information on fishing the Gaula River, write to PanAngling Travel Service, 180 N. Michigan Avenue, Chicago, IL 60601. For details on the

Laerdal package, write to Fishing International, 400 Montgomery Drive, Santa Rosa, CA 95405. For information on fishing the North Cape region, write to Cavalier Consultants, 115 E. 86th St., New York, NY 10028.

Fly-Spesialisten has beats on a half-dozen Norwegian rivers and can be reached at Kronprinsesse Marthas pl. 1, Postboks 1641 Vika, Oslo, Norway.

THE ALANDS ● Finland

Sandwiched in between the Soviet Union and Sweden, Finland occupies a 130,000-square-mile territory that includes some 60,000 lakes, and untold miles of streams and shoreline.

The Atlantic salmon used to be Finland's première gamefish, but shortly after World War II most of the country's best salmon rivers were dammed up to provide hydroelectric power. Today, about the only salmon fishing left in the country is in three far-north border rivers: the Teno, the Naatamo, and the Torino. Of these, the Teno (called Tana on the Norwegian side) is perhaps the best. This is a big river, usually fished with a boat, and it regularly produces fish in the ten-to thirty-pound category. Like other Scandinavian salmon rivers, however, the best beats are usually booked well in advance and are relatively expensive.

Sea trout (anadromous brown trout) have been stocked in streams throughout the country and now constitute a sizable fishery. Unlike the sea trout found in Ireland or the British Isles, these sea-run browns grow to a large size. Fish in the four-pound category are common, and the species goes to twenty pounds or more. Finland's record, caught in the Gulf of Finland, weighed twice that much.

Walleye pike, called pike perch, occur in abundance in central and southern Finland and are considered quite a table delicacy. The Finnish record is 16.5 kg., or thirty-six pounds.

The most popular gamefish in the country is the northern pike, however, which is found throughout the country, in both fresh and salt water.

Pike in salt water? I didn't believe this when I first heard it, but after a considerable amount of research I discovered that the Gulf of Bothnia, which separates Finland from Sweden, has a very low salt content. As a result, northern pike live at sea and grow to large proportions on a rich diet of Baltic herring.

One of the best pike fisheries, as a result, appears to be in the Aland Islands, an archipelago lying more than seventy-five miles out in the Gulf. The Alands comprise 6,500 islands divided into sixteen municipalities and are populated by slightly more than 20,000 people. This Nordic archipelago is an autonomous province within the republic of Finland. It has its own government, its own flag, and an interesting history that dates back many centuries. During the Viking Age, for instance, Aland was the most densely populated part of Scandinavia.

Pike grow to a large size in the Gulf of Bothnia, which separates Finland from Sweden.

Most of the population and tourist action occurs on the so-called Aland mainland with its two communities of Mariehamn and Godby. The rest live on a handful of the larger islands scattered out in the gulf, connected to the mainland by a ferry system that provides daily transportation back and forth between the out-islands. These islands are sparsely populated, but a number of them have tourist facilities called Holiday Villages, which are comparable to some of our Northwoods resorts. These facilities usually consist of a cluster of housekeeping cabins, a camp store, and a large sauna. Most offer boats and motors for rent, and some have such amenities as a restaurant, a bar, and a swimming pool.

The prices of these vacation facilities are quite reasonable. At a place called Ekers Vacation Cottages you can rent a two-bedroom log cottage with a fireplace for $150 per week. A fishing skiff, including life preservers, costs $12 more. On the remote island of Kumlinge, there is a delightful little hotel called the Remmaren Inn with rooms priced at $32 per day and meals averaging around $5 each. This little hotel has nineteen guest rooms and a marina with various sizes of fishing boats for rent. Throughout the islands, a half-dozen other small hotels offer similar facilities.

Most Aland visitors are not serious anglers. Remmaren Inn guests, for instance, are let out on the shore of a remote island and walk the bank casting blindly. Most are successful, though. Pike caught this way average less than ten pounds, but 20-pounders are not uncommon.

Aland pike are called "herring pike" because they have an abundant food source in the schools of Baltic herring that thrive in these waters. As a result, these pike have an unusually fast rate of growth and reach a large size. In this connection, Erkki Norell of Rapala suggested that pike exceeding twenty kilograms (forty-four pounds) were available in this saltwater habitat. Matti Hook, of the Finnish Tourist Board, told me that Finland's rod-and-reel pike record was forty-eight pounds and that he had personally landed a pike that weighed thirty-five pounds. As a further illustration that Finnish pike grow large, it should be noted that a 25.5-kilogram pike (fifty-six pounds) was taken a number of years ago. This fish was shot with a rifle, so its taking does not constitute a rod-and-reel record.

These pike go for the same lures that our North American pike do, because a wobbling spoon is the favored lure in these waters. But, because this fish's primary food source is the herring, I believe that a large Rapala minnow might be even more productive. Make sure that your lure selection includes some large weedless spoons and spinnerbaits to work the weedbeds. Load large-capacity reels with line testing a minimum of twenty-four pounds, and make sure that your rods have enough backbone to effectively cast the large lures you should be using. Short wire leaders are also recommended.

Fishing for pike is legal at any season in the Alands, but note that no fishing from the shore is allowed between April 15 and June 15. This is the nesting season for sea birds in the area. A fishing license is required and is available from post offices and most country stores. The price is $3.

The Alands are a popular Scandinavian tourist destination, but happily the best fishing does not occur at the same time as the tourist season. As might be expected, the vacationing families and sightseers are out in force during June, July, and August, but the best pike fishing occurs in September and October and to a lesser extent in the spring.

Mariehamn is the principal city of the Alands and has a population of around 10,000. It is accessible by cruise ship from Turku, Finland, and from Stockholm and two smaller Swedish cities. Year-round air connections are available from both Stockholm and Helsinki.

For general information on fishing in the Alands, write to the Aland Tourist Board, Box 60, SF–22101, Mariehamn, Finland, For details on fishing the waters surrounding the remote island of Kumlinge, write to Ray Soderholm, AB Trivselhotell, Hamngatan, 7, SF–22101, Mariehamn, Finland. Two travel agencies are reported to offer package fishing tours and can be reached as follows: Ab Sand–Strands Tourist Office, Torggatan 15, P.O. Box 9, SF–22101, Mariehamn, Finland; and Viking Tours, Storagatan 2, 22100, Mariehamn, Finland. Organized fishing trips are available in the vincinity of Kustavi Island, and details on relevant services and facilities can be obtained from General Manager, Kustavin Merimotelli, 233360 Kustavi, Finland. For additional information on Finnish pike fishing, write to the Finnish Tourist Board, 75 Rockefeller Plaza, New York, NY 10019.

I am informed by two reliable sources of information that comparable pike fishing is also available in the Swedish archipelago, which lies immediately to the west of the Alands. Pike in this saltwater habitat average close to ten pounds, and 20- and 30-pounders are possible. The weekly rate for this fishing is $1,960 per person, and this package includes accommodations, meals, and complete fishing services. For details, write to PanAngling Travel Service, 180 N. Michigan Ave., Chicago, IL 60601.

Gamefish Index

AMAZON CATFISH: Rio Negro, Amazon headwaters, Orinoco River, upper Paraná River.

ATLANTIC SALMON: George River, Laerdal River, Gaula River, Moy River, Lake Michigan, Tamar River, Tierra del Fuego.

BONEFISH: Bahamas, Belize flats, Florida Keys.

BROOK TROUT: Tierra del Fuego, Bariloche district, San Martin region, Minipi lakes, selected Chilean rivers, Gods River and other Canadian waters.

BROWN TROUT: Rio Grande and other Tierra del Fuego streams, rivers in the Argentine and Chilean "lake districts," Laerdal and Gaula Rivers, San Juan River, Bighorn River, Niagara River, Great Lakes and most of their tributaries, streams and lakes in Ireland, Scotland, and England.

CHAR: Tree River, Chantrey Inlet, George River, Kobuk River, Kuskowim Bay rivers, Painter Creek, Unalakleet River.

CHINOOK SALMON: Kenai River, Bristol Bay streams, Hakai Pass, Iliamna streams, Kuskowim Bay rivers, Painter Creek, Alaska panhandle waters, Great Lakes, Niagara River.

CHUM SALMON: Most Alaskan streams and coastal waters.

COHO SALMON: Unalakleet River, Kuskowim Bay streams, Painter Creek, Bristol Bay, Iliamna streams, Lake Michigan, Alaska panhandle waters, Hakai Pass, and other British Columbia waters.

CUTTHROAT TROUT: Flathead River, coastal rivers in British Columbia, most of the streams in the Alaska panhandle.

DOLLY VARDEN: Flathead River, Bristol Bay streams, Iliamna streams, Katmai streams, Painter Creek, southeast Alaska rivers, Unalakleet River.

DORADO: Paraná River and tributaries.

GRAYLING: Kazan River and other Northwest Territory streams, most Alaskan streams with exception of those in southeast region.

LAKE TROUT: Great Bear Lake, Great Slave, Kasba, Nueltin, Chantrey Inlet, Black Lake, the Great Lakes, some Alaskan and British Columbia lakes.

LARGEMOUTH BASS: Ocala lakes, Lake Diaz Ordaz, Lake Seminole, Lake Okeechobee, Toledo Bend.

MUSKELLUNGE: Eagle Lake, Lake of the Woods.

NORTHERN PIKE: Sickle Lake, Mackenzie River, Aland Islands, Churchill River, Waskiowaka Lake, Loch Lomond, Shannon River, Kasba Lake, Hatchet Lake, and most other lakes in northern Saskatchewan, Manitoba, and Ontario.

PACU: Amazon River and its tributaries, Orinoco River.

PAYARA: Orinoco River, Columbia llanos streams, Amazon and most of its tributaries.

PEACOCK BASS: Orinoco River, El Dorado lakes, Rio Negro, Amazon headwaters, Gatun lake.

PERMIT: Belize, Bahamas, Florida Keys.

PICUDA (smaller species of dorado): Orinoco River, Rio Negro, Amazon and its tributaries.

PINK SALMON: Most Alaskan streams and coastal waters.

PIRANHA: Amazon headwaters, Rio Negro, most of the lakes and smaller streams in the Amazon basin.

RAINBOW TROUT: Lakes and streams in the Argentine "lake district," Iliamna streams, Katmai, and Bristol Bay regions of Alaska, Tierra del Fuego rivers, Great Lakes, New Zealand, western streams like the San Juan. Bighorn, and Big Hole, Lake Tanycomo, Niagara River.

SEA TROUT (sea-run brown trout): Gaula and Laerdal Rivers, coastal rivers in Scotland, Ireland, England, and the Scandinavian countries, Tierra del Fuego.

SHEEFISH: Alaska's Kobuk, Kuskowim, and Yukon Rivers.

SMALLMOUTH BASS: Beauchene lakes, Lake of the Woods, Quetico.

SNOOK: Parismina and Colorado Rivers in Costa Rica, certain rivers and lagoons in Belize, Bahamas, Florida Keys.

SOCKEYE SALMON: Katmai and Iliamna regions, most other Alaskan rivers.

STEELHEAD: Coastal rivers in Alaska and British Columbia, Great Lakes, especially those waters stocked with the Skamania species, Niagara River.

STRIPED BASS: Toledo Bend, Lake Seminole.

TARPON: Parismina and Colorado rivers in Costa Rica, the Caribbean coast of Belize, Florida Keys, the Bahamas.

WALLEYE: Gunisao, Churchill River, and other waters in Saskatchewan, Manitoba, and Ontario, Lake of the Woods, Quetico Wilderness, Lake Erie.

Fishing Holes Index

ALAND ISLANDS (FINLAND): Northern pike.
AMAZON HEADWATERS (ECUADOR): Peacock bass, picuda, payara, catfish.
ANGLING HOTELS (SCOTLAND): Brown trout, sea trout, Atlantic salmon.
BALLYNAHINCH RIVER (IRELAND): Sea trout, Atlantic salmon, brown trout.
BARILOCHE (ARGENTINA): Rainbow trout, brown trout. brook trout, landlocked
   salmon.
BEAUCHENE LAKES (QUEBEC): Smallmouth bass, northern pike.
BIGHORN RIVER (MONTANA): Rainbow trout, brown trout.
BONEFISH FLATS (BAHAMAS): Bonefish, permit, tarpon, snook.
BOW RIVER (ALBERTA): Rainbow trout.
BRISTOL BAY (ALASKA): Five species of salmon, rainbow trout, steelhead, cutthroat,
   Dolly Varden, lake trout.
CANYON CREEK (MONTANA): Brown trout, rainbow trout, cutthroat.
CHANTREY INLET (CANADA): Arctic char, lake trout.
CHURCHILL RIVER (SASKATCHEWAN): Walleye, northern pike.
COLORADO RIVER (COSTA RICA): Tarpon, snook.
DIAZ ORDAZ (MEXICO): Largemouth bass.
EAGLE LAKE (ONTARIO): Muskellunge, walleye, lake trout, northern pike.
EL DORADO LAKES (COLOMBIA): Peacock bass, piranha.
FLATHEAD FLOAT (MONTANA): Cutthroat trout, Dolly Varden.
FLY FISHING SCHOOL (SCOTLAND): Brown trout, Atlantic salmon, sea trout.
GATUN LAKE (PANAMA): Peacock bass.
GAULA RIVER (NORWAY): Atlantic salmon, sea trout.
GEORGE RIVER (QUEBEC): Atlantic salmon, brook trout, lake trout, Arctic char.
GREAT BEAR LAKE (CANADA): Lake trout, Arctic grayling.
GREAT SLAVE LAKE (CANADA): Lake trout, Arctic grayling.
GUNISAO LAKE (MANITOBA): Walleye.
HAKAI PASS (BRITISH COLUMBIA): Chinook salmon, coho salmon.
HATCHET LAKE (SASKATCHEWAN): Northern pike, lake trout, walleye.
ILIAMNA LAKE (ALASKA): Rainbow trout, five species of salmon, steelhead, cut-
   throat, Dolly Varden, grayling, lake trout.
KASBA LAKE (CANADA): Lake trout, northern pike, Arctic grayling.
KATMAI WILDERNESS (ALASKA): Rainbow trout, five species of salmon, grayling,
   Dolly Varden, lake trout.

Index

Credits

p. 140	Photo by Safari Outfitters
p. 142	Photo by the author
p. 151	Photo by the author
p. 153	Photo by PanAngling
p. 156	Photo by PanAngling
p. 158	Photo by the author
p. 160	Photo by Mark Sosin
p. 163	Photo by the author
p. 166	Photo by Robert C. Smith
p. 168	Photo by Homer Circle
p. 173	Photo by the author
p. 177	Photo by Chuck Cadieux
p. 182	Photo by Lloyd Saulbury
p. 185	Photo by Bud Toomey
p. 189	Photo by the author
p. 192	Photo by the author
p. 195	Photo by the author
p. 199	Photo by Adrian Dufflocq
p. 205	Photo by British Tourist Authority
p. 212	Photo by the author
p. 215	Photo by Irish Tourist Board
p. 217	Photo by Irish Tourist Board
p. 223	Photo by Irish Tourist Board
p. 230	Photo by Finnish Tourist Board